EXPAND, GROW, THRIVE

5 Proven Steps to Turn Good Brands into Global Brands through the LASSO Method

Are you looking for a way to better manage and grow your brands' equity? Then you need to read *Expand, Grow, Thrive*! Its proprietary LASSO framework provides fresh strategic insights for managing your brand equity through licensing globally.

— Christine Cool, Licensing Manager for PMV Group, makers of Chupa Chups.

Expand, Grow, Thrive is the first of its kind to finally tell the story of how brands expand through licensing.

The book not only shares wonderful examples of how our most loved brands such as Coca-Cola, the NFL, and Star Wars make their way into our homes and into our lives, it also offers a powerful methodology for how to ensure they keep doing so. This book is perfect for anyone interested in knowing how brands expand and grow or simply wanting to know how the brand licensing industry works.

— Jamie Stevens, EVP, Worldwide Consumer Products, Sony Pictures Entertainment

Study it carefully if you want to succeed.

Pete Canalichio's book provides a definitive framework which unlocks the riddle of profitable growth, brands, and licensing, with clear prescriptions and vivid examples.

— Jeff Lotman, CEO and Founder of the premiere brand licensing agency Global Icons

I've heard it said that when the student is ready, the teacher appears. After a reading of Pete Canalichio's *Expand, Grow, Thrive*, I now know that nothing could be more true. As founder of a grassroots start-up brand, I think that Canalichio's methodology of brand building fundamentals is likely not only a must-read for the big-guy, household brand names, but also an essential educational guide for the small guys with big ideas. If you need to put some guard rails up on your road to licensing success, I highly recommend this book.

— Warren G. Tracy, President and CEO of The Busted Knuckle Garage

The information in *Expand, Grow, Thrive* is incredibly useful. When I oversaw Coke's brand licensing operations in the late 1990s there was no external resource to explain how the industry worked or how we could use licensing to delight our consumers and grow our brands. This book finally unlocks the mystery and offers a powerful LASSO framework to guide brand owners and their licensees.

— Tom McGuire, Founder and Managing Partner,
Talent Growth Advisors and former Vice President,
The Coca-Cola Company

Pete's sagacity and organizational leadership throughout these pages will not only engage and inspire leaders to a visionary level, but provide a host of pragmatic expansion and growth strategies to implement, to thrive, and drive with, for years to come. Leaders committed to their own development as well as the success of their organizations must read and share this inspiring leadership book.

— Peter Weedfald, SVP Sales & Marketing,
Sharp Electronics Marketing Company of America

In *Expand, Grow, Thrive,* brand building professionals from the associate brand manager to the senior marketing executive will find valuable insights for building more dynamic and sustainable brand growth. Through many entertaining, real-world examples faced by brand developers around the world, this book provides not only the lessons learned but the systems and approaches to enable others to benefit from them in their own work. In the LASSO method, the reader has a tool that serves as a powerful and proven structure for evaluating brand development choices whether you are a global brand or simply aspiring to become one.

— Nat Milburn, Managing Director,
Sionic Mobile Corporation and former Global Vice President,
External Business Development,
Newell Rubbermaid

This is an excellent book chock full of practical advice and information for professionals wanting to expand their knowledge of the brand licensing industry. *Expand, Grow, Thrive* provides a solid basis of brand licensing coupled with deep insights and real life "how to" examples. Fun anecdotes as well made for an enjoyable read. I must say I found myself taking notes throughout the book to reference later.

— Maura Regan, Executive Vice President,
Licensing Industry Merchandisers' Association (LIMA)
and former SVP and General Manager,
International Media Business, Sesame Workshop

EXPAND, GROW, THRIVE

5 Proven Steps to Turn Good Brands into Global Brands through the LASSO Method

BY

PETE CANALICHIO

United Kingdom – North America – Japan
India – Malaysia – China

Emerald Publishing Limited
Howard House, Wagon Lane, Bingley BD16 1WA, UK

First edition 2018

British Library Cataloguing in Publication Data
A catalogue record for this book is available from the British Library

ISBN: 978-1-78743-782-1 (Print)
ISBN: 978-1-78743-781-4 (Online)
ISBN: 978-1-78743-975-7 (Epub)

ISOQAR certified
Management System,
awarded to Emerald
for adherence to
Environmental
standard
ISO 14001:2004.

Certificate Number 1985
ISO 14001

INVESTOR IN PEOPLE

To my dear friend, greatest contributor, and LASSO Model co-creator,

Mark Di Somma

We started this collaboration almost three years ago in Miami. We had a dream of sharing with the world the story of how great brands build equity, reach, and revenue by partnering with great organizations. We also dreamed of creating a tool that brand owners could use to measure their brands' expansion optimality.

Well, we did it. Together.

Thank you for your insights, encouragement, and support. I couldn't have done it without you. For this, I'll forever be grateful.

Contents

Acknowledgments

No significant personal achievement ever comes to fruition without the support of many. This book is no exception. For me it started when I attended a book writing workshop nine years ago in New York City that was hosted by Elizabeth Marshall and Janet Goldstein, co-founders of Book Breakthrough. Their workshop was so exceptional and inspirational that I went back the following year. Armed with a plan, a belief, and a working title, LASSO The World's Greatest Brands, I wrote the first draft of my book proposal.

I knew the more stories I could incorporate into the book, the richer and more engaging it would be. With this goal in mind, I reached out to a host of industry leaders, some of whom were friends and colleagues, and others who simply believed this story should be told. They graciously gave up their time and willingly shared their brand and business secrets and, in turn, brought my concepts to life. I will forever be beholden to each of you: Kenneth Beaupre, Brand Advocacy and Licensing Manager at Caterpillar; Clayton Burrous, President and Owner at Sunbelt Marketing Group; Elise Contarsy, Vice President Brand Licensing at Meredith; Christine Cool, Licensing Manager at Perfetti Van Melle; Will DePippo, Assistant Director, International Licensing at Sesame Workshop; Jennifer Dorian, General Manager at Turner Classic Movies; Mike Dunn, President, Chief Brand Officer, Octane5; John Friend, Head of Consumer Products, International Expansion — 343 Industries; Darran Garnham, CEO, MTW Toys; Michelle Grech, award winning Brand Builder and former

President of MELT Sports; Bryce Jones, President at CollectorDASH; Bill Jones, Founder and Chairman at CollectorDASH; Tim Kilpin, President & CEO of Activision Blizzard Consumer Products Group; Charles Klein, Leading Fashion, Licensing and Hospitality Lawyer, Davidoff Hutcher & Citron; Kelly Knock, Licensing Expert and LIMA Board of Director; Ted Larkins, SVP/General Manager at CPLG North America; Jeff Lotman, CEO at Global Icons; Heather Margolis, Sr. Manager at Turner Classic Movies; Mark Matheny, Founder, Licensing Matters Global; Tom McGuire, Founder & Managing Partner, Talent Growth Advisors; Nat Milburn, Managing Director Enterprise Development Sionic Corporation; Teri Niadna, Managing Director at Brandgenuity Europe; John Parham, President, Director of Branding, Parham Santana; Marc Pevers, former Director of Business Affairs, 20th Century Fox; Steve Scebelo, Vice President, Licensing & Business Development at NFL Players, Inc.; Anthony Shaut, Director of Royalty Audits at Spielman Koenigsberg & Parker; Bill Shaw, President at Entrepreneur Media; Holly Stein Shulman, President, HJS Associates; Danny Simon, Owner, The Licensing Group; Jamie Sykes Stevens, Executive Vice President, Worldwide Consumer Products and Licensing at Sony Pictures; Vince Thompson, Founder, Chairman and CEO of MELT Sports; Tony Toland, President at Credit & Financial Services; Warren Tracy, Owner, The Busted Knuckle Garage; Simon Waters, General Manager & Senior Vice President, Entertainment & Licensing, Hasbro; Peter Weedfald, Senior Vice President Sales & Marketing SHARP Home Appliances — SEMCA; Rick White, President at Atlantic League of Professional Baseball; and Pete Yoder, Vice President Cartoon Network Enterprises. Your contributions were immeasurable.

Along the way, I made a friendship with one of the Licensing Industry's biggest advocates and most passionate members, Goran Kernyak, President at *BEL, Brand Extensions and Licensing*. Goran became one of my biggest advocates. His immense contributions cannot be fully captured here. He took his valuable time to read assorted drafts and offered critical input. Moreover, he brought his publishing expertise, which was invaluable. Words are powerless to express my gratitude, Goran!

To Karla Wintersteiger, Associate R&D Manager at *BEL, Brand Extensions and Licensing* magazine, your selfless and painstaking efforts in transposing my Brand Licensing Dynasty training platform not only provided the key information I needed, but were also incredibly inspirational. Thank you for everything.

A special thanks goes to Jennifer Dorsey, Editorial Director, Books, and Charles Muselli, Vice President of Business Development at Entrepreneur Media who each offered critical advice and encouragement when I was looking for a publisher. You made all the difference.

Thanks to my agent, Bill Gladstone, Owner, Waterside Productions, who believed in me and in the book I wanted to write. Your expertise and experience along the way have been incredibly helpful.

A critical step in writing this book was the development of an algorithm that could power the LASSO Model. A tremendous thanks goes to Gautam Naishadham, Research Scientist, who worked with me and brought his genius to bear to build exactly what was needed. I truly appreciate you.

There is no book if no one knows about it. For this, I want to express my utmost thanks and appreciation to Karnika Yashwant, CEO of Key Difference Media, who built my website, petecanalichio.com and has been instrumental in the marketing of *Expand, Grow, Thrive*.

To my past and present colleagues at Licensing Brands including Priyanka Khare, Caterina Carter, Bill Jachthuber, Kari Lywood, Rashad Cain, Justice Freedom, Omer Latif, Nicole Love, and Vijaya Subrahmanyam, who gave so much to make this project successful, please accept my deepest thanks.

To Durga Ramachandhiramani, Robyn Cooper, and Lauren Godshall, how can I ever possibly thank you for the tremendous hours of research, editing, advice, perspective, and encouragement you gave? You were the greatest team anyone could ever want.

To my wife, Emily, and to my children, Andy, Tim, Ellie, and Maddi who encouraged me to never give up on my dream to write this book and kept up my spirits through all the many revisions and challenges I encountered along the way, I am eternally grateful. You are my greatest joy.

Finally, I want to thank my Creator who through his Son makes all things possible. To you be the glory.

Introduction

Prelude: Addressing the Expansion Riddle

The pressure to grow is unrelenting. Decision-makers seek it. Investors insist on it. Customers are buoyed by it. A growing company exudes confidence, prestige, and acceptance. People want to work for companies that they feel are going places, literally and figuratively. In part, that's psychological. But, as McKinsey's research shows,[1] it's also because there seems to be no alternative. Companies that are not growing are declining.

Companies pursue growth strategies for all sorts of reasons. They expand to incorporate new strengths; add new activities; explore new territories; become more competitive; explore potential; escape convergence, saturation, stagnation, or commoditization; and much more ... Too often though, as Lawrence Capron observes,[2] the motivation for growth is being able to claim growth, or at the very least evolution. Perhaps this is because managers feel they have little choice in the matter. "Companies must continually evolve to stay relevant, innovative, and competitive."

Welcome to the *expansion riddle*. Companies are under pressure to grow, but every action, and therefore every option, comes with risk. Standing still is dangerous, especially in dynamic sectors, but so is staying in one market, and so is diversifying into other

---

1. http://www.mckinsey.com/Insights/Growth/Why_its_still_a_world_of_grow_or_go?cid=other-soc-lkn-mkq-mck-oth-1510&kui=UnIpO0F3xWinuF8SDBwOnQ
2. http://insights.som.yale.edu/insights/how-should-companies-evolve

markets. And size does nothing to lessen the riddle. As Marc Emmer says,[3] "The larger the core business the harder it is to diversify, because a new business must grow at many multiples of the existing business to contribute enough margin to reduce [concentration] risk."

For all its popularity, growth is far from a sure thing. Bain asserts that in recent times 90% of companies worldwide have failed to achieve sustained, profitable growth.[4] They cite three common reasons for this: companies fail to even come close to realizing the full potential in their core business; they diversify too far in pursuit of fast growth; or they fail to successfully redefine their core, meaning they quietly rot.

Even if you have been growing, there's little to guarantee that the momentum you've worked so hard to build will continue to impel you forward. When McKinsey examined the top performers on the S&P Index, "less than half of the S&P companies that increased their revenues faster than GDP from 1983 to 1993 managed to do so from 1993 to 2003. Fewer than 25% of the outperformers of 1983 to 1993 remained in that group through 2013."[5] In other words, the predisposition to decline, even over a period of just three decades, is high. Companies that are not planning for sustained growth over longer time frames, rather than quarter by quarter, are likely to find themselves under increasing downward pressure.

Here's another important finding from McKinsey's work. As little as 25% of a company's growth can be attributed to market share acquisition from competitors; so, for all the talk about competing head to head and brand to brand, the returns on such toe-to-toe fights amount to little more than jostling in the wider scheme of things. The vast majority of growth springs from competing in the right markets and from making acquisitions that provide scale and increased market presence.

---

3. http://www.vistage.com/blog/growth-strategy/growth-strategy-entrepreneurs-dilemma/
4. http://www.bain.com/consulting-services/strategy/fundamentals-of-growth.aspx
5. http://www.mckinsey.com/global-themes/employment-and-growth/why-its-still-a-world-of-grow-or-go

But identifying where that growth will come from is less straightforward than it sounds. McKinsey's own research found that 75% of managers believed the company would realize growth, at least through an increase in share prices, if they looked at opportunities beyond their core business in the next five years. However, over half of those polled also said growth would come from refining what they currently focus on, and a similar number thought that divestment of a currently held activity that they now judged to be noncore would generate increases in share prices over the next five years.

Of the 1435 companies Jim Collins evaluated in his landmark book, *Good to Great*, only 11 companies emerged as great: Abbott Laboratories; Circuit City; Fannie Mae; Gillette Co.; Kimberly-Clark Corp.; the Kroger Co.; Nucor Corp.; Philip Morris Cos. Inc.; Pitney Bowes Inc.; Walgreens; and Wells Fargo. Each had demonstrated a pattern of good performance, punctuated by a transition point, after which it shifted to great performance (defined as a cumulative total stock return of at least three times the general market for the period from the transition point through 15 years). In fact, the 11 companies that Collins identified averaged returns 6.9 times greater than the market — more than twice the performance rate of General Electric under the legendary Jack Welch.[6] Even so, several of those companies would later fail — a sign that even greatness is no guarantee of future success.

Investing for growth is another dilemma. Emmer's view is that "If the total industry revenue has strong momentum, the argument can be made to spend 80 percent or more (in terms of sales, marketing product development, etc.) on growing its core business. If a market is in decline, then the company should invest 40 percent or more in growing new businesses."[7]

Some conclusions from these findings seem obvious; others less so. Obviously, no company grows by doing nothing. Those companies that take an active part in capitalizing on fast-growing

---

6. http://www.jimcollins.com/article_topics/articles/good-to-great.html
7. http://www.vistage.com/blog/growth-strategy/growth-strategy-entrepreneurs-dilemma/

sectors are more likely to reap greater rewards than those that try only to reap organic benefits. Secondly, many companies are not recognizing their own latent potential, either because they can't see it or they don't want to act on it. These companies probably have work to do in terms of defining and refocusing their operations around their core strengths. Thirdly, while diversification is seen by many as an effective growth strategy, the search for growth must not be at the expense of focus or relevance, because a lack of either is potentially disastrous. The judgment calls around when to shift and when to focus are critical. Companies that have diversified too far and find themselves spread too thin need to rein in their borders. Finally, historic greatness and growth is no guarantor of future prosperity.

Growth itself will peter out over time unless there is an effective and competitive long-term growth plan in place. Finally, the majority of growth is likely to come from riding inherent growth in prosperous sectors and/or acquiring influential scale, and corresponding efficiencies through merger and acquisition and/or another expansion strategy.

By contrast, a brand can also try and change too much. In the 1990s, LEGO's sales were declining. Convinced that their core audience wanted toys that offered instant gratification, LEGO began moving away from its core product, iconic building blocks, into theme parks, children's clothing, video games, books, magazines, television programs, and retail stores, all in the name of growth. By 2003 the brand was in serious trouble. Turnover was down 30% year-on-year. The following year, sales fell another 10%. Still the research told them they were doing the right thing. Further swayed by this data, "LEGO was [even] considering dumbing down its toys, making the kits simpler and even perhaps increasing the size of its iconic brick."[8] It wasn't until the company stopped following the data, and started talking to LEGO players that they realized their mistake. Young users wanted LEGO kits to test and stimulate themselves. Thanks to some keen and timely

---

8. Quoted in Lindstrom, M. (2016). *Small data* (pp. 1–2). New York, NY: St Martin's Press.

insights by Martin Lindstrom,[9] senior management rethought its growth strategy and LEGO returned to prosperity.

So, what have we learned so far?

1. Do what you're good at — which means really know yourself as a company and as a value proposition.

2. Have a plan to grow — not just for now, but for the long term as well.

3. Expand where it makes sense but only as far as it makes sense — diversify, but don't dilute. Expand into areas that are growing already, and know when to stop.

4. Be part of something bigger; preferably, much bigger.

When you frame growth in these terms rather than just the numbers, companies have five ways to hit their precious growth targets.

1. They can stay in the markets they know and build out new products and services to win market share.

2. They can merge or acquire (or be merged or acquired by) another company, meaning they can take over someone else and pay, in cash, shares, or both, to gain a bigger footprint and a higher profile, provided that they can then gain the efficiencies to make the investment work.

3. They can franchise their operations, meaning they can replicate what was working into a bigger and bigger footprint using third parties.

4. They can license, meaning they can work with others to capitalize on the successes they already have both in markets they know and in less familiar sectors.

5. They can use combinations of these strategies.

---

9. https://www.martinlindstrom.com/

In an interview on how companies should evolve,[10] *Laurence Capron, co-author of* Build, Borrow, Buy[11] *and Professor of Strategy at INSEAD says,* "Choosing the right approach to adaptation and growth is difficult; as a result, many companies find a model and stick with it, even in contexts where it might not be effective." Too often, companies choose to grow in the way they feel comfortable, rather than in the manner that is strategically right. "They become good at executing a specific mode and so they repeat and repeat and repeat even in contexts and under conditions which might not be suitable," says Capron.

Background, it seems, can play a huge role in the decisions that leaders take around how to pursue growth. Engineers love products, so leaders with this training tend to focus on internal innovation. Bankers or financiers will pursue deals. Those that have experience in M&A will focus on that. But the companies that succeed in growing bring flexibility as well as experience to their growth strategies. They understand, contrary to what instinct might tell them, that there is no single way to move forward.

They also understand that growth is not always generated from within the company walls. Often managers overestimate how competitive their internal resources are, says Capron, and therefore they underestimate what it takes to get where they want to go. The hardest decisions are around internal and external mix: what do you grow through your own R&D; what do you buy and build; what do you partially invest in through what she refers to as "sequential engagement." A company like Cisco, for example, will use investment mechanisms like a minority stake to get a seat on the board. From there, they can decide which company to buy to create a better fit. "Sequential engagement can be very useful because you can really structure it in such a way that closes the gaps with early steps. Then, as you become more comfortable, you can then go for full control. Or not. The options remain open."

---

10. http://insights.som.yale.edu/insights/how-should-companies-evolve
11. https://www.amazon.com/Build-Borrow-Buy-Solving-Dilemma/dp/1422143716

Brand licensing can work in a similar way: enabling a company to engage with others and to work in other sectors without making a full-blown commitment. Often, when we talk to people about brand licensing, they are surprised to think of it as a way to achieve serious long-term growth. Sadly, the term is both loaded and misunderstood. Brand licensing is frequently portrayed as a series of deals intended to exploit an organization's intellectual property. Some see it as a gimmick for brands past their "use-by date" who wish to trade on their nostalgia. Others think of it as the cause of the very thing that Bain warned against: how a brand overextends into places that confuse customers and appear more opportunistic than thought-through.[12] While brand licensing, when practiced poorly, can manifest itself in any of these ways, those shortfalls should not be attributed to brand licensing per se.

Many assume brand licensing and promotional merchandising are the same. Again, this is a mistake. While both are marketing initiatives, and both often involve objects, there are important differences between merchandising items and licensed items. Merchandising is the stuff you give away to try and get exposure. It's an eyeballs strategy based on raising awareness of a logo. Brand licensing, on the other hand, assumes there is a customer relationship in place already, that the relationship has intrinsic value, and that fans will pay for opportunities to access the brand in ways that they haven't been able to do previously. They may pay in cash, or time, or both — but how they pay is less important than why they want to pay. They invest because the brand has value for them, and they are looking for ways to access additional value.

About 25 years ago, brand doyen David Aaker wrote an evergreen piece on the good, bad, and ugly of brand extensions.[13] These principles still ring true as we look at the foundations for brand expansion going forward. Every year, he observed, hundreds of companies introduce new brands and new products onto

---

12. http://www.bain.com/consulting-services/strategy/fundamentals-of-growth.aspx
13. http://sloanreview.mit.edu/article/brand-extensions-the-good-the-bad-and-the-ugly/

shelves bulging with choice. The bring-to-market cost of doing so frequently runs into the millions of dollars, and yet only a tiny percentage of these new options will succeed in meaningful ways. Brand licensing shortcuts the process by providing a new product or service with powerful ready-made associations that have already been cultivated by the brand, often over many years. As Aaker observed, for consumers the Weight Watchers brand means weight control, Jeep means adventure, and Hershey has a taste all its own. This is no coincidence. These brands have invested huge amounts to prompt consumers to think of their names in these terms. A brand is an engine — powerful not just for what it is, but also for its ability to generate value literally out of thin air.

A powerful brand with a proven legacy, through licensing its brand name to a product, or opting to partner or joint venture in a direction that feels natural (like it belongs with the brand or brands involved), will provide recognition, and thus awareness, for that product almost out of nowhere. The association itself is critical. Work by Aaker and Keller found that the perceived quality of the brand in its original context was a significant predictor of how the extension would be evaluated *as long as there was a fit* between the two product classes.[14] That association will then encourage consumers to trial the product because they see the presence of the brand as a reassurance of quality. Equally, the brand benefits by introducing products to market that fit with its image, but also extend that image into new areas.

The story of Vidal Sassoon hair dryers illustrates this perfectly.[15] In the late 1970s, Gerry Rubin was running a company called Helen of Troy selling hair dryers and styling tools to the trade. Rubin had a good share of the professional hairstyling trade and was making a living but basically the market was stalled. As he pondered his options, his father alerted him to the fact that hairdresser to the stars, Vidal Sassoon, was licensing his name. Throwing everything he had at the opportunity, Rubin won the

---

14. Quoted in Aaker, D. A. (1991). *Managing brand equity*. Jossey-Bass Inc.
15. http://www.inc.com/magazine/19881201/6322.html

brand license. The decision paid off handsomely. His Sassoon-labeled products did $10 million in sales in their first year alone, outstripping sales of all his other products, and then continued to climb year-on-year.

So you see, licensing has the potential to deliver on many of the growth demands for global brands, but the result is far from automatic. It takes significant judgment and sensitivity to make the wider offer feel natural and delightful for consumers. Too often, the link between idea/product and brand is not thought-through carefully enough. Ideas and brands are thrown together in what feels, to consumers, like marriages of convenience or greed.

The challenge for all brands looking to grow their presence revolves around adding new dimensions to something in which people are already in love. Franchising, for example, is all about skillfully replicating a recipe for success and adapting it carefully for local conditions. But reinterpretation can also be a critical part of how an idea evolves. As we say, it all depends on how consumers see the brand and connect it with where it is going. For example, *MasterChef* started out in 1990 as a competitive cooking show in the United Kingdom with a format devised by Franc Roddam. Revived and updated in 2005 by the BBC, the show was reworked in Australia to make it more suited to that antipodean audience. Ironically, that focus helped the show take off globally. Today it is a licensed format, owned and run by Shine Group that bills itself as "the most successful cooking format on earth."[16]

The success of *MasterChef Australia* lies in the fact that it is indefatigably Australian. That's why Australian audiences are drawn to it season after season. But what *MasterChef Australia*'s interpretation has done is to add value by changing the format and introducing new and interesting experiences that audiences outside of Australia also enjoy. The choices of judges, dishes, and ingredients add local relevance. Guest judges from within Australia and beyond bring authority and credibility. The stories of the amateur

---

16. http://deadline.com/2014/10/masterchef-joe-bastianich-shine-international-mipcom-851783/

contestants, or "characters," whose personalities and back stories bring drama and emotion, remind everyone, as Andrea Toniolo so crisply put it, that "food is life."[17] There's drama, pain, heartbreak, triumph, tension, personality ... everything that an audience is looking for ... over plates of amazing food that people literally sweated over. Does it bear any resemblance to life in a commercial cooking environment? Absolutely not! Does anyone care? Clearly not. It's real enough that people relate to it. And unreal enough that they are not tuning out.

We've never had so many brands — and because of that, brands now matter more and less than ever.

Let's start with the bad news. Having a brand is good, but that alone will not be enough. John Gerzema and Ed Lebar argue that brands across the board have suffered key drops in awareness, trust, regard, and admiration over the past 25 years.[18] Their research revealed that this was true not just for a few brands, but for thousands of brands encompassing the entire range of consumer goods and services, from airlines, automobiles, and beverages to insurance companies, hoteliers, and retailers. They found that most brands were not adding to the intangible value of their enterprises the way they used to do. They ascribed this to three things:

1. Excess capacity — The world is overflowing with brands and consumers are having a hard time assessing the differences between them.

2. Lack of creativity — Consumers expect more big ideas from brands and they expect them faster. That's not happening quickly enough.

3. Loss of trust — Brand trustworthiness has declined markedly.

---

17. http://www.andreatoniolo.com/the-success-of-masterchef/
18. http://www.strategy-business.com/article/09205?gko=8a197

Therefore, brand presence alone will not generate growth the way companies might once have hoped. Instead, the brands that will thrive are those with a clear vision of their future in terms of direction and point of view. They must be inventive in the sense that they continue to redefine what they mean to people. And they must be dynamic because they penetrate popular culture, creating excitement, and giving people ideas to discuss. Brands, like growth, are dependent on movement.

Here's the good news: Whether they admit it or not, consumers are now brand-dependent. To understand why, we need to quickly explore two things: the changing presence of brands and the changing meaning of brands. Let's start with presence. After World War II, as countries like the United States entered a new era of consumerism, a brand was very much about a product and its name. In the restricted marketing environment of mainstream broadcasting channels, companies pushed their monikers to millions of people through a very small number of channels, knowing that simply by raising awareness, they had a good chance of lifting sales. Fast-forward to today and that style of marketing has long since departed. Brands are now about far more than just names, and the channels available to publicize them have increased out of all proportion. Consumers are also time-pressed and looking for mechanisms that shortcut their decision-making. Brands provide recognition, familiarity, and personality. These are the reasons why the presence of brands has exploded.

At the same time, in this high channel, high-media-consumption environment, the very meaning of a brand has changed. Today, a brand is not just a product or service, it can also be an event, a celebrity, a film, a TV series, or a political party. Brand has come to mean anything that is recognized as an entity in its own right and is treated as such by both mainstream and social media. We also talk about brand as a style, type, or interpretation — as in "her brand of ..." These changes have normalized the term beyond marketing. Brand is now a description for elements that many of us view as modern-day life, and that have a specific character that is indigenous to them.

When a company looks to grow by expanding its brands, it does so by taking the brand beyond its current confines — into areas where it hasn't been before. So when companies talk about brand growth, what they are really talking about is expanding an idea/thing/celebrity and/or object further into the lives of consumers. The mechanisms may vary but it is not just the brand itself, or its intellectual property (IP), that is being leveraged. It is the relationships that people have with the brand because of how it appears, what it means to them, and a desire to lift their involvement.

In 2011, at a TEDx talk in Salt Lake City, Amy Lukas talked about the challenge of getting ideas to scale.[19] Her thoughts mirror our own in terms of the expansion riddle. "Scalability of an idea," she observed, "is the change of an idea in size and complexity." It's such a beautiful thought, because it reminds all of us that no idea can remain static. It must morph to survive, and as it does so, it takes on a life of its own, changing shape and density, involving more people, becoming more relationship based, and needing to address new challenges.

The irony of growing an idea is that you can expand an idea, but you often can't expand it while it is just an idea. It's too raw. It's too broad. There's nothing for people to identify and hold onto. There's not a *thing* for them to talk about with others. Concepts are exciting for entrepreneurs, artists, and other creators, but they're like air to most recipients. Real, but not so real that people can appreciate their value. In our busy world, people don't have time for conceptual explanations. They want an idea to be packaged in a form they recognize. They want to be able to call it something. They need it to be crisp, simple, and likeable. And they need it to deliver a story and experience through emotions, language, and design. *If ideas are to take hold and then change in size and complexity, they need a brand.*

---

19. https://www.youtube.com/watch?v=890wEm3ZvWA

I met Mark Di Somma, one of the core contributors of this book, by chance. All right, not quite by chance. I met him at a conference where we were both speaking. I was there as a brand licensing expert; Mark was there as a creative strategist. Two guys of Italian heritage. I'm from Atlanta, Georgia, and Mark is from Wellington, New Zealand, but we both share a passion for brands and how they work. Mark was fascinated by the same question as me, what will succeed, and then how do you build on that? There was no way of knowing, we agreed. But, as we talked further, drawing on what each of us had seen thrive and fail over the years, a couple of things became very clear.

When we looked around at all the literature, there were shelves of books on growing your company presence, plenty on how to buy, sell, and negotiate for existing brands and businesses, quite a few on franchising, some on licensing. There was also plenty of publicity around the kinds of deals that were being struck. But what was missing, it seemed to us, was a framework that people in charge of growing brands could use to expand their marque methodically and responsibly into a broader phenomenon. What was also missing were the strategic criteria for knowing when to do that in order to meet growth targets.

New formats, new partnering arrangements, and new corporate extensions are breathing new vitality into how and where ideas are seen through brands, and the environments in which they are experienced. While these changes are innovating brand growth frameworks in new and exciting ways, they are also making it more complex and more fraught. How should a brand look to grow? When is the right time to do so? How and when can it best capitalize on opportunities to hit the daunting growth targets that are increasingly expected?

As I said, Mark and I wanted to find a framework and test that framework across various areas in order to compare and contrast the success factors. Does a licensed celebrity brand, for example, succeed for different reasons than a well-known not-for-profit brand? Does a corporate brand operate under different dynamics than the one in the entertainment sector? Just as importantly, what might each learn from the other? To find out, we sat down with people who are working for, or who have worked for, brands that we thought had done a great job. We asked them about their approaches, their beliefs, their experiences, and their disappointments.

Having analyzed dozens of examples, we narrowed the critical elements of successful brand empire-building down to five key factors: the five first letters of which form the acronym LASSO. I will explore the implications of these in coming chapters.

Lateral

Owners of powerful brands expand their brands into new territories while staying true to the idea for which they are renowned. By doing this, these brands are able to continue to connect with people who know and trust them, and at the same time, to take the relationship into new spaces. This is particularly important at a time when more and more brands are looking to connect with customers across a broader front. Expanding a brand beyond its operating sector into wider life categories encourages customers to think of "their" brand in new ways. Bulgari has expanded into resorts selectively scattered across the globe over the past 10 years; *Better Homes and Gardens* has extended into a home textiles and decor program that is exclusive to Walmart; Pantone, a color chart service, now can be found on mugs and tabletop products and in books, taking advantage of the brand's color equity to shift the brand into entirely new channels of distribution.[20] The real challenge is to strike the right balance between surprise, whereby the brand appears where it was not expected, and alignment, whereby the appearance of the brand in this sector makes sense because it mirrors what the brand already means. If the association is too lateral, or if the brand isn't strong enough, the whole arrangement simply looks fetching, like a bridge too far for consumers to believe and be interested in. There are many examples of brand expansions that have gone terribly wrong: Bic's 1998 venture into

---

20. http://www.brandchannel.com/2016/12/05/brandspeak-licensing-michael-stone-120516/

perfume in the United States[21] or disposable pantyhose in Greece, Austria, and Ireland.[22] Consumers didn't *get it* and the extensions ultimately failed.

In a nutshell, this means there needs to be clear line of sight between what the brand says and stands for, and everywhere that it is seen. These associations can be literal or emotive, but they need to be well thought out. They must stem from something you will notice that I talk about a lot in this book — a brand's *expansion point*. The expansion point is the common reference point for every place that the brand moves into, and also is the singular idea that relates consumers to the brand. Two questions are pertinent here. Firstly, how does the addition expand on what people know about the brand already? Secondly, where can that expansion take the brand next? Each addition is like a station on a rail network, carrying the traveler further from the point they started from, and yet linked back to that starting point intuitively and effortlessly.

Addictive

If a brand is to grow into other categories, it must generate curiosity. It must encourage consumers to seek it out wherever they find it — and not just that, but to return time and time again to experience that brand again. As they do so, the brand needs to find ways to make each experience interesting and cumulative. Perhaps no brand extension release to date exemplifies this concept better than *Pokémon Go*. The concept for the game was conceived in 2014 by Satoru Iwata of Nintendo and Tsunekazu Ishihara of the Pokémon Company as an April Fools' Day collaboration with Google. In fact, it was originally called the Google Maps: Pokémon Challenge.[23]

---

21. http://perfumeshrine.blogspot.com/2012/12/bic-fragrances-perfume-history-of-les.html
22. http://brandfailures.blogspot.com/2006/11/brand-extension-failures-bic-underwear.html
23. https://en.wikipedia.org/wiki/Pok%C3%A9mon_Go#cite_note-22

"Through a partnership between Nintendo and Pokémon, Niantic's mapped a fantasy world brimming with Charmanders, Squirtles, Weedles and more onto real-world streets, parks and buildings by employing a miracle of algorithmic wizardry and real-time location data."[24] From the moment it was released in July 2016, the game had players competing for virtual turf mapped onto real-world landmarks such as churches, sculptures, or museums.

In order for a brand to be addictive, each point of contact must be surprising and delightful in its own right. At the same time, that point of contact must motivate the buyer to come back for more, knowing that the experience they have next time will build on what they already know. When this is working well, customers are presented with more and more ways to interact with the brand, across a range of media and sectors, and each time that they do, it strengthens their loyalty to the brand and increases their interest in seeking out further encounters. From a business point of view, this ensures not only that the brand has bankability but also that the relationships themselves can be proactively managed to keep customers on the lookout for new opportunities. Such reliance significantly decreases the risk of introducing new product into market.

Storied

History makes a brand interesting. It adds heritage to what is happening. It helps people feel like they are part of something that stretches back way before their time. Story also brings familiarity. Every human being understands the format of narrative: it is hardwired into us as a way of sharing. Brands that can expand what they offer within the context of expanding a familiar story are able to take customers on a journey that feels both familiar and new. Stories are involving and collective, but they are also personal.

---

24. http://time.com/4401279/pokemon-go-review/

Rogue One: A Star Wars Story was released in late 2016, but is set just prior to the first *Star Wars* movie, *A New Hope*, which came out in 1977. Peter Debruge of Variety shares:

> Not only does *Rogue One* overlap ever so slightly with *A New Hope*, but it takes that blockbuster's biggest weakness, that a small one-man fighter can blow up a battle station the size of a class-four moon, and actually turns this egregious design flaw into an asset. Now we know *why* the Death Star has an Achilles' heel and *how* that information fell into Princess Leia's hands.[25]

It's this level of story that has made the *Star Wars* series (with the release of *Rogue One*), the highest-grossing film series on record with over $4 billion in total revenue predicted. As a point of reference, *Gone with the Wind* at $3.4 billion, was a distant second.[26] *Rogue One* could also help keep "the Force strong" with Disney's *Star Wars* merchandise sales. In 2015 the franchise pulled in $700 million in merchandise sales with *The Force Awakens*, and the latest haul is expected to be even larger.[27]

Storied brands compel people to collect memories that link them back. They are wonderfully intriguing because they have had so much human involvement already. There is a powerful sense that "adding on" makes the past more special, and the present seem so much more potent. If you can build a brand with legacy, and at the same time add new timeless and universal ideas from that legacy, all the elements to draw a crowd are at your command. This is also an excellent way to grow a brand from its core strengths and explore ways to keep a historic brand current.

25. http://variety.com/2016/film/reviews/rogue-one-a-star-wars-story-review-1201939299/
26. *Guinness World Records* (Vol. 60, 2015 ed.). 2014. pp. 160–161. ISBN 9781908843708.
27. http://fortune.com/2016/12/13/disney-star-wars-rogue-one-box-office/

Scalable

Increasingly, brands operate across bigger and bigger vistas, but achieving scale is complicated. There is always a delicate balance to be drawn. On the one hand, an idea must expand to fill the bigger arena where it wishes to be seen. That in turn adds all sorts of complications in logistics, culture, language, and so much more. On the other, the brand must remain true to what people first fell in love with. The hardest point of scalability is knowing which parts to make even bigger and which to adapt or omit. The other critical decision is resolving the expansion riddle — expanding the brand purposefully into sectors that fit with the brand, but are also growing at rates that will add critical momentum. Brand licensing should be viewed, from a scalability point of view, as a form of merger and acquisition. You are merging the brand of one sector with the momentum of another sector in order to achieve new levels of growth and scale to create a hybrid presence, which is more powerful and effective than either expansion would have been alone.

One extraordinary example is Coca-Cola Shoes sold in Brazil. The program, which started in the 2000s, boasts dozens of different styles today. With sales over $100 million, Coca-Cola Shoes are now the second most popular brand in the Brazilian market behind Nike. In fact, with the success of shoes, apparel, and accessories, the Brazilian market accounts for more than 30% of Coke's global licensing business.[28] Coca-Cola Shoes even has its own website which boasts, "With a differentiated line of sneakers, high boots and sandals, we help spread all the vibrancy and optimism of Coca-Cola through our actions and our products."[29]

Scalability is a combination of brand equity, footprint, presence, and growth. More brands should judge their licensing decisions in

---

28. http://www.coca-colacompany.com/stories/on-the-track-coke-designs-exclusive-apparel-collection-for-rio

29. http://www.cocacolashoes.com.br/#sobreAcocacola

this way when it comes to market penetration. You're not just looking to enter into a new market through a licensing program, you're looking to link the brand to the levels of growth in that market as well. Do this carefully. Expanding your brand into a market with stalled growth may meet the scalability criteria in terms of footprint and even presence, but it almost certainly won't enable the brand to hit its growth targets.

Own-able

Finally, and perhaps most importantly, the brand must know what it owns. This is a complex and involved area; aspects of which are beyond my core expertise. For example, every brand today fights a major battle protecting its IP against fast followers and copycats. Brand protection strategy has never been more important for large brands that also face knockoffs and the illegal use of their trademarks, nor has the monitoring of income streams to ensure that payments such as royalties are accurate and timely. There is a company called Credit and Financial Services, founded by Tony Toland, Sr. whose primary purpose is to ensure licensees follow through on the obligations of their contracts. According to Oliver Hoeltje, Assistant Finance Director, Global Business Development for P&G, Credit and Financial Services runs the back office for their Licensing and M&A departments. "[C&FS' work] gives me peace of mind. I don't need to worry about it." They are very good about what they do, which ensures that P&G not only receives the royalties earned on all officially licensed products sold, but ensures the licensee is not selling any unapproved product. Coupled with products like Brand Comply offered by Octane5 that use holograms to ensure branded products sold are officially licensed and not contraband, Credit and Financial Services protects for brands what is truly own-able.

While companies must have their intellectual property protected through copyrights, patents, trademarks, and trade secrets to ensure long-term profitability and maintain market relevance, "ownership" of the brand often lies with consumers. Martin

Lindstrom opines that "products are produced in the factory; brands are produced in our minds." As such, consumers often lay claim to the ownership of a brand and treat companies as simply the guardian of those brands. That is why when a "guardian" does something they disapprove of, consumers quickly make their displeasure known. Perhaps the most famous example of this was when Coca-Cola launched New Coke on April 23, 1985, eliminating Coca-Cola's 100+ year-old formula on which the company was founded for something that taste-tested better than Pepsi. There was such public uproar that the company reversed course and by July the original formula was back.[30]

More broadly though, when a brand chooses to expand beyond its current borders either geographically, reputationally, or in terms of offering, it must know what aspects of the brand it will carry across to the new sectors, and where it will adapt its core DNA in order to be competitive within that sector. The brand additions must not only feel like they belong to the brand, the brand itself must seem bigger, deeper, and broader because of the activities that now take place under its name. In other words, the expanded brand needs to connect its own dots in ways that consumers recognize and enjoy. Key to that is the brand having very clear ideas on what it considers proprietary and therefore sacrosanct. At the same time, it must judge carefully when and how to incorporate the thinking and inputs of others, through mechanisms like codevelopment, joint innovation, and open source, in order to continue changing and growing what it represents at the speed that consumers demand.

Not everyone is convinced that growth is the best agenda today.[31] Some argue that expanded consumerism is now an outdated economic driver, and that I would be better off to pursue agendas that focused on disciplined use of local resources or

---

30. http://www.cbsnews.com/news/30-years-ago-today-coca-cola-new-coke-failure/
31. http://www.brandingstrategyinsider.com/2013/09/brand-marketing-and-the-anti-growth-strategy.html#.WCBARSS5rm4

strategies that encourage people to consume less. Others have told me that globalization is dying as an economic force — that the pushback with Brexit, Trump, and less free trade is a return to a more parochial and bipartisan market. This book makes no attempt to refute any of these arguments. I can certainly see a case for companies choosing to take a more contained approach. I agree that there is also pressure on companies to do more within their own regions. But I am neither an economist nor a politician. From a brand perspective, Mark and I would argue that the LASSO framework is still applicable, and that companies may choose to pursue it with different levels of intensity or scope. They may choose to pull back on their scale, for example. They may choose to pursue a less addictive path in the interests of preserving resources. Brands will go where consumers dictate.

But in terms of the framework itself, how should companies be using LASSO to pursue their growth agenda? I'll delve into this in more detail soon. But for now — the LASSO framework points to a way of growth that addresses the concerns I discussed at the beginning of this introduction. By using the brands they have as the basis for growth, companies can make more of the assets that represent their brand portfolio. By carefully strategizing their expansion plan, they can ensure that they don't stray too far from the powerful associations that they have built with consumers. And by continuing to refine and update their brands, and the performance of their brands, they have a market-sensitive mechanism for continuing to strengthen their core business. Just as interesting, by tying their brands to dynamic parts of the economy, companies can look to lift overall performance at the same time as they broaden market presence.

There is a huge untapped potential here. But before I go any further, let me share a real-life riveting tale with you.

Pinning Their Hopes

A great brand licensing program isn't simply looking to extend a brand into new places, it's looking to work with what people know and love in order to change the emotional scale at which the brand operates.

A Tale of One Pin, Two Brands, and 3,000 People Waiting in the Cold

Scott Pitts felt like he had just placed his head on the pillow when the phone rang in his small Olympic apartment one-half mile from the Outdoor Medal Ceremony in Honshu, the main island of Japan. It was 12:56 a.m.

> "Who could be calling me at this hour?" thought Scott. It was the final day of the Nagano Olympic Games, and Coca-Cola's Nagano Olympic merchandise manager was beyond exhausted. He had been in bed barely two hours. A pause … then the phone rang again.
>
> "Hello. This is Scott Pitts," he mumbled, trying to shake himself awake.
>
> A Japanese voice responded, "Pitts-san, this is the Nagano Police. Your presence is required at the station immediately."

"My presence is required at the station? Why? What's wrong?" Scott implored, collecting his bearings.

"You must have a business permit," stated the police officer.

"I don't understand. Why do I need a permit?" Scott asked. "What the heck is going on?"

"There is a line forming outside the Coca-Cola Olympic Pin Trading Center. This is not authorized without a permit."

Scott scratched his head, thinking, "Why would there be a line forming outside the Coke Pin Trading Center at this hour?" While Coke's Olympic licensing program had many facets, the most important was the Coca-Cola Pin Trading Center located in downtown Nagano. Each day, Coca-Cola sold their special "Pin of the Day" there at 11 a.m. Normally, the line would begin forming two hours earlier. Who would be crazy enough to line up in the middle of the night? It had to be 20 degrees Fahrenheit outside.

"Pitts-san. Are you there?" inquired the police officer, growing weary over the conversation.

"Yes. Yes. I'm here. I understand. I will be there shortly."

"Very good, sir. The permit costs ¥200,000 yen. You will need to bring cash."

The phone went dead. Bring ¥200,000? That was almost $2,000! Where was he going to find ¥200,000 at this time of the night? Scott knew of an ATM near his apartment. He ran over and put in his card. The maximum he could withdraw was ¥25,000. Eight ATMs later, Scott arrived at the police station with the money in hand.

Scott got the permit and finally made it back to his apartment. He put his head on the pillow. Before he knew it, the alarm went off … at 6 a.m. He hit the snooze button. An hour later, Scott reached for what he thought must be the alarm — and realized it was his phone again. It was 7:17 a.m. What could be wrong now? He hoped no one had started a riot or been hurt.

It was Jonathan. "Scott, I am sorry to disturb you, but you've got to get down to the Pin Trading Center. You won't believe what is going on." A short and precise summary of the situation followed.

"I'm on my way. Try to keep things under control until I get there."

Scott hung up and dressed as quickly as he could. Fortunately, he didn't have to think about what to wear. A Coke uniform lay strewn over the chair where he left it the previous night. As he walked up to the Coca-Cola Pin Trading Center he couldn't believe his eyes. The line stretched for blocks. Never in his imagination did he think that a brand licensing program would impel thousands of people to line up in the dark on a cold February morning for a simple Coca-Cola Olympic pin.

His thoughts flashed back 13 months to January 1997.

Now, allow me to pick up the story…

Scott had joined Coca-Cola after working on the 1996 Olympic Torch Relay. As the Midwest Regional Coordinator, he had been responsible for crowd-building along the relay route in his region. In that environment, things happen in a rush. About 90% of Torch Relay crowd-building occurred in the 60 minutes prior to the passing of the Olympic Flame. Scott and the rest of the Atlanta Torch Relay Team had successfully wrangled more than 20 million people to witness the Olympic Flame going by. Now he had joined Coca-Cola, one of the premier Olympic sponsors, and would get to be part of another Olympic Games.

I had just come off working on the Atlanta Olympics myself. As a Coke employee, my role had been substantially different from Scott's. Because the 1996 Olympics were in Coke's hometown, the company had pulled out all the stops. One of their initiatives had been to build a seven-acre theme park they affectionately titled, Coca-Cola Olympic City. It sat across from Centennial Park and would be open for 100 days. My job had been to negotiate contracts with Coke's suppliers to ensure the park was built on time and on budget.

This was my first Olympic experience. I found it exhilarating and wanted more. When Laurie Ann Goldman, head of Coke's worldwide licensing program, asked me to join her team to head up a newly formed event licensing group which would support Olympic sponsorships,[1] I jumped at the chance.

Scott and I were both newbies to the world of licensing and event marketing, but we were confident we could make up for our inexperience with our business skills, exuberance, and perseverance. We quickly realized we had jumped into the deep end. With the Nagano Olympic Games just over a year away and nothing started, we needed to complete 30 months of work in the span of 9. This meant running processes in parallel that normally functioned in series.

Our role was to create a co-branded merchandise program that integrated the Nagano Olympic and Coca-Cola marques. We decided merchandise would be sold at the World of Coca-Cola in Atlanta, Georgia, allowing us to ride a wave of momentum from the prior Games hosted in Atlanta. We would also target Olympic pin collectors based in the United States through a catalog. Furthermore, we would sell merchandise along the Torch Relay routes throughout the Nagano prefecture and at a Coca-Cola Olympic Pin Trading Center located in downtown Nagano.

---

1. I grew up mesmerized by the Olympic Games. As a child I would watch them for hours, often by myself. There was something powerful, almost hypnotic, about the Games and what they meant. While I would never be athletic enough to compete, it was my desire to someday get to be a part of the Olympic Games. As of 2017, I have worked on eight Olympic Games.

Expand, Grow, Thrive

However, first, we had to negotiate a program agreement with the Nagano Olympic Committee. That agreement would authorize us to create and sell the co-branded merchandise and set the terms for how the program would be run, including where the merchandise could be sold, what categories would be allowed, who could manufacture the merchandise, how product would be approved, the levels of royalties that would be paid, and finally, how those royalties would be split between Coca-Cola and the Nagano Olympic Committee.

We pulled together our plan and I flew to Tokyo to meet four members of the Committee. Through a colleague who served as my interpreter, we went back and forth for hours on the merits of a co-branded program. Because the Nagano Olympic Committee would be required to split the royalty revenue with Coke, the members were concerned that our program would cannibalize their existing program and deliver less royalty to them. I countered that it would likely bring in Coke-friendly consumers who would buy not only our co-branded merchandise but more of their Nagano single-branded merchandise. However, the Committee appeared to have no real interest in allowing Coca-Cola to create an additional merchandise program so close to the start of the Games. The objections continued. They didn't have any additional resources to put toward the program.

"Not to worry," I told them. "All you have to do is stick out your hand and collect the royalties and we'll do the rest." Still, they seemed to balk at my request.

With a wry smile, one gentleman asked, "Why would anyone want to buy Coca-Cola merchandise?"

I paused for a moment, and they must have felt they had finally won their argument and could politely escort this persistent American to the door. I then answered with as much confidence as I could muster, "I can't say for certain, but what I can tell you is that almost a billion

dollars of Coca-Cola branded merchandise was purchased worldwide last year."

That statement won the day! The Committee members agreed
to our program and I left for my hotel, and then a 14-hour flight
home. I was elated and exhausted! Our work had just begun.

With approval to move forward, the next thing was to identify
what categories of merchandise we would sell and who would
manufacture them. We knew that Olympic pins would be our
most important category. Coke had sponsored the first Official Pin
Trading Center in Calgary, Canada, in 1988. Since then they had
hosted a Pin Trading Center at each subsequent Olympics. Pins
had become the number one spectator sport at the Games so we
were banking on another big turnout of pin buyers and collectors.
In addition to the pins, we wanted to produce apparel, Coca-Cola
Polar Bear plush, commemorative crystal and gold-plated Coca-
Cola bottles, and other souvenir and collectors' items.

We almost didn't get approval for the plush. The Nagano
Olympic Committee felt the Coca-Cola Polar Bear might raise concerns. The Nagano mascots, known as the Snowlets, were four
cute little owls. Given that polar bears eat owls, there might be an
uproar from the public! We shared our advertising campaign with
the Committee and, thankfully, they quickly saw that the Coca-
Cola Polar Bear was only interested in sharing a Coke and promoting friendship. It seemed as soon as we gained approval from
the Nagano Olympic Committee that we started hearing from our
colleagues in Japan that building a Pin Trading Center in Nagano
was not a good idea. "The Japanese are sophisticated buyers. They
would have no interest in buying Coca-Cola branded Olympic
pins."

Oh boy! A large part of our budgeted revenue for the project
was tied to the successful sale of Coca-Cola Olympic Pins. If the
naysayers were right, not only would we not reach our targets, we
would also have an egg all over our faces. The road to Nagano
was getting narrower and more isolated by the moment.

To get an accurate assessment, Scott pulled together focus
groups in the United States and Japan and asked each whether

Japanese would want to buy and trade Coca-Cola Olympic Pins. It was a possibility, he was told, but only if the designs were right and we could appeal to enough people to build sufficient momentum. Many of the team from Coca-Cola Japan believed that the resources should go to other market initiatives. However, if we chose not to build the Pin Trading Center, we risked missing a big opportunity to connect thousands of new potential consumers with the Coca-Cola brand in a unique way. Not building might be the easy way out, but we believed deep down it was important for us to press ahead anyway.

Our next job was to find an event retailer who would believe in the opportunity enough to assume the inventory risk, pay for additional staff, and cover the additional expenses associated with selling the pins when the Center was open. We knew that W.C. Bradley had had a profitable event merchandising program helping Coke with the Atlanta Olympic Torch Relay. Would they be interested in being our partners again for a project that would be staged on the other side of the planet?

Fortunately, it didn't take much convincing to get the team from Columbus, Georgia, signed up. I thought about those Southern gentlemen doing business in central Japan and cracked a smile. It would be entertaining, if nothing else. We collectively decided that the best way to build momentum was to open the Pin Trading Center early. That way, people would learn the location of the Center and become familiar with the concept *prior* to the start of the Games.

Almost immediately we ran into another roadblock. Per our agreement with the Nagano Olympic Committee, we had to use the Japanese pin manufacturer which had acquired the licensing rights to sell Nagano Olympic-branded pins. Instead of having one company to create more than 100 different designs of pins, the Japanese licensee turned out to be a consortium of small companies. There was no way we were going to be able to meet our objectives if we had to deal with dozens of companies scattered all over the country!

Fortunately, the agreement between Coca-Cola and the Nagano Olympic Committee allowed us to choose an alternative supplier if the licensee was not able to meet our delivery schedule. With the approval of the Nagano Olympic Committee, we turned to Aminco, which had supplied pins to Coca-Cola for previous Olympic Games. Not only did they know how to deliver hundreds of quality designed pins on time, they could execute a program at world-class pricing.

Good. But we were about to be dealt with another major setback to our fledgling program. With all the challenges we had been facing, we had not seen that our "get it done" attitude had put a tremendous cultural strain on our Event Merchandising team member based in Japan. Miho[2] was a young professional woman with Japanese parents who had been educated in the United States so she had grown up speaking both Japanese and English. Bright and energetic, she wanted to help us be successful. However, from the outset she struggled to fit in with the male-dominated Coca-Cola Japanese team. As I had shared earlier, they did not wish for us to open a Pin Trading Center in Nagano. At the same time, Miho had to answer to Scott and me, who were asking her to move forward with the project. By April, it had become too much and Miho told us she was leaving the team. Literally our one line of communication in Japan had just been cut off!

We considered all the options, including sending Scott to Japan for the duration, but with all his responsibilities in Atlanta we knew it would never work. Moreover, Scott didn't speak Japanese. After a series of false starts we found Jonathan, an American who had grown up in Japan with missionary parents. Bi lingual, culturally aware, energetic, and enthusiastic, he was quickly signed to the team and sent to Japan.

Even though we had W.C. Bradley as our event retailer for the Coke Pin Trading Center, we still needed an event retailer for the other Coke Olympic-branded merchandise that would be sold along the Torch Relay route and during the time of the Games throughout the Nagano prefecture. This proved to be one of our biggest challenges. Few companies in general are willing to take

---

2. Our team member's real name has been changed to protect her privacy.

the risk of buying event-specific merchandise. While the payoff can be huge, the program is fraught with risks, including obtaining sales permits, staffing for the event, gaining merchandise approvals from the brand owners, selecting the right mix of merchandise, and finally, finding each of the exact locations for selling the merchandise where the crowds would be.

Event retailing just didn't make sense to most Japanese businesses. They would be happy for us to hire them, but they had no interest in signing up to own and sell the licensed merchandise. While Scott and I focused on getting our contracts signed with the Nagano Olympic Committee and the licensees who would manufacture the merchandise, we continued looking for an event retailer who would meet our requirements. The search proved elusive. Finally, after two months, we found a small company in Japan whose owner was entrepreneurial. After vetting them, we felt they were qualified in every way except one: financially. The owner's limited capital would put the program at risk because he would not be able to secure the entire inventory needed for the program to reach its full potential. We advised him accordingly and, to our delight, he went out and found a larger company willing to back him. This enabled us to close the deal. The pieces were finally coming together to deliver the merchandise by the time of the Games. Now the questions were: "Would they come?" and if they did, "Would they buy?"

The latter half of 1997 was a blur, as Scott, Jonathan, and I raced to approve the concepts, prototypes, and final projection run product that was being made by our licensees. Once Coke had approved the product, and we had gone through the Nagano Olympic Committee approval process, it still had to be tested for safety and quality standards. Having Jonathan on the team proved a godsend as he followed through on every task. He also settled in well with our Coke colleagues in Japan, which strengthened the chemistry between the two teams.

Construction on the Coke Pin Trading Center finally began in November 1997. Despite only wanting to have the building erected for 60 days, Japanese construction laws required that the center be built to the standards of a permanent structure. On

January 1, 1998 a small crowd of dignitaries from the Olympic Committee, the City of Nagano, and Coca-Cola senior executives gathered for the official opening. The center itself looked amazing. The exterior featured a 40-foot-tall Coca-Cola bottle with a large sign. Inside, the walls were stocked with brightly colored pins in all shapes, sizes, and colors, each commemorating something different: count downs; countries; sports pictograms; mascots; Nagano-centric; and all kinds of Coca-Cola pins. We had designs with delivery trucks, vending machines, six-pack bottles, and even coolers. Inside the center was a small stage for special events like the ribbon-cutting ceremony. Everything went off without a hitch and we got plenty of friendly media coverage, thanks to our hard working Coke colleagues on the Public Relations team.

The first day netted us a little over $10,000 in sales. Not a bad start. When sales dropped to about $2,000 the next day though, I got a bit concerned. We would never reach our budgeted revenue total if things didn't pick up dramatically — and we were being watched by consumers; Aminco, our pin licensee; W.C. Bradley, our event retailer; and our team at Coke. Sales barely reached $100,000 for the month of January. They were back up to $10,000 a day in early February but we were still a far cry from the $30,000 to $40,000 we needed on a daily basis to make our budget. Perhaps the pundits were right. Maybe the Japanese would never get into pin collecting and trading. We held our breath and waited for the beginning of the Olympic Games and what that would bring.

As Scott walked towards the Coca-Cola Olympic Pin Trading Center, the crowd went for blocks and blocks. Almost all the pins had been sold except for the Pin of the Day, which was held back. In fact, shipments of basic Coke pins had been couriered in the last couple of days from Atlanta to put *something* on the shelves. Over the 17 days of the Games, sales had jumped to over $40,000 on the opening day and increased ever since. Day 3 of the Games was Valentine's Day and Coke had made a special heart-shaped Pin of the Day to commemorate the holiday. The pin, which sold for the yen equivalent of about US$10, was selling on the streets of Nagano for over US$400 By Day 4, consumers were buying all 1998 pins that were allocated for each day along with many of the previous day's pins. There was nothing in stock. Every crowd projection and financial goal for the project had been reached by Day 7. Our business partners had exceeded their own targets and were also extremely happy. There was no time in the day when there wasn't a crowd in the Center and oftentimes there was a line formed outside. Sales on a couple of the days had soared to over $90,000 — unheard of for a 1,500-square-foot store. The Coca-Cola Pin of the Day program was a resounding success!

Scott pondered the size of the crowd lined up outside the Pin Trading Center. He was extremely concerned that the fans would be angry or disappointed when they learned they would not be able to purchase the Day 17 Pin of the Day. Too much goodwill had been earned and Scott was determined to ensure no one walked away with a negative impression of Coca-Cola or the Nagano Olympic Games. He decided he would count off the first 1998 customers in line. That was the least he and Coca-Cola could do. Inside, the W.C. Bradley team would merchandise the shelves with every piece of inventory in stock to make the purchase experience as rich as possible.

As Scott and Jonathan made their way along the line, the crowds were very happy and excited, despite the early hour and the cold temperatures. About 30 minutes later, he reached the 1999th person. There would be no more Pins of the Day available for anyone from that person on, which Scott estimated to be another 1000 people. He kept saying, "Why don't you go home, get warm and get some rest? You can come back at 10 a.m. when the Center opens." They just smiled and chose to stay.

Here are my closing thoughts on Nagano ...

When Scott's call came in that Sunday morning, I was at first startled and then irritated that someone would call so early. Who could be calling? In 1998, few home phones had Caller ID. Recognizing Scott's voice on the other end of the line, I immediately shifted from irritated to concerned. My military training kicked in, ready to hear whatever bad news he was about to share. Why would he be calling me at such an early hour? Scott started the conversation by saying that the police had called him in the middle of his night. I went into crisis management.

"Give me the details Scott." I said, as awake as I could muster.

"Pete, everything is OK."

I relaxed a bit and caught my breath. As Scott relayed what had happened, I began to feel the same emotions he had experienced 16 hours earlier. We had done it! A year before, the task had seemed insurmountable. Now, not only had we pulled it off, we had overcome the skepticism of many and blown through our best estimates!

Our success story didn't end there. In fact, we continued to sell Coca-Cola Olympic pins from our catalog for almost a year after the Games ended. Japan had fallen into a pin-collecting craze as never before. Today, I look back and wonder what else we could have done to fulfill their ongoing thirst for Coke Olympic pins instead of moving on to the next Olympic Games in Sydney. I am certain there is a special place in the homes of thousands of people who came to Nagano, a place where they keep and display their Coca-Cola Olympic pins and other merchandise. Perhaps those pins might one day become an heirloom passed down to children and grandchildren. For brands like Coca-Cola and the Olympics, it really doesn't get any better than that!

I love this story, and when I share it, everyone smiles. But logically, it doesn't really make that much sense. Where's the connection between the Olympic movement, a fizzy drink, and commemorative pins? And why would anyone in their right mind, never mind thousands of people, wait out in a queue in freezing weather to buy them? When people ask why I think this happened,

I smile widely and make this very simple point. The success of this program did not depend on its logic. In fact, the pin program at Nagano was so successful because people responded to what was being offered in ways that *transcended* common sense.

While the planning and implementation of every strong brand licensing program is carefully planned and meticulously detailed, an idea captures people's imagination, not because it's linear or even because it's well project-managed. Those things make the program possible, but they don't make it desirable. A program like this works because it's associative. It offers access to something people want to feel part of, and want more. That's why so many queued in the bitter cold that night in Nagano, and why they chose to collect pins as their souvenirs of the Games. They were collecting more than pins. They were deepening their association with an event they never wanted to forget.

I shared this story because, in order to understand how ideas take hold and why brand licensing is so powerful, you first need to understand how human beings assimilate ideas into their lives. And one way to get a better sense of that is to look at how and why people collect. You'll see what I mean in a minute.

Denise Gershbein and Nick de la Mare have also examined why people are so interested in turning things into collections. Their insights provide wonderful perspectives on how ideas work and why we are curiously keen to codify and assemble the things that happen in our lives.[3] Human beings, they say, have an innate wish to categorize the things that they encounter. We find comfort in perceptual order, and in extending that order. It's that wish to find meaning that drives us to connect thoughts and objects through stories, even between things that don't, at first, seem to make sense.

"When we envision emotional or historical relationships between seemingly disparate objects or experiences," they say, "we create narrative." That's how someone's idea becomes something that is shared with strangers, and how an idea grows into a phenomenon

---

3. http://productdesigngrays.blogspot.co.nz/2008/10/collective-instinct.html

among fans. We incorporate their idea, or thing, into our lives. It becomes part of us, and we weave a story around it that brings it even closer.

> "Collecting often begins with a personal affinity for one object or idea," the designers say. "We happen to come across a beautiful antique tin that stirs our aesthetic and nostalgic sensibilities or see a painting that unleashes a curiosity for modern art. Maybe we stumble upon a practical object like an eggbeater or a road sign that embodies some concept worthy of consideration, despite the mundane, or because of it. It is that feeling of affinity with an object and what it represents that makes us desire more of the same."

That's how it begins, and grows. That's why people collect plates, cars, toy soldiers, dolls, pins, and all manner of things. And they keep collecting and collecting, because, having entered a world of objects or ideas, the objects and ideas become part of their world. As Gershbein and de la Mare point out, "the act of collecting is more about discovery and accumulation than it is about completion." We want to feel surrounded, physically or mentally, by the things that give us comfort and joy.

When we interviewed Bill Jones, Chairman and Founder, and Bryce Jones, CEO of CollectorDASH,[4] a software company whose platform enables communities of collectors, they told us collectors are super passionate and social, willing to pay lots of money to fulfill their passion for a brand or thing. Whether their passion is for trains, dolls, coins, or Coke, all collectors have similar needs and characteristics. What brands need to do, Bill told us, is to tap into that human passion because it forms communities. That community may be social or mobile, specific to a place or group, but it is the connection that brings people together. For example, one of CollectorDASH's clients is trainz.com, the largest reseller of

---

4. Collectordash.com

pre-owned model trains in the world. They sell more than $5 million of products a year.

Programs like the Olympic pins link people with something they want more of — and their wish to have more, and to find relationships between the things that they are collecting, seeing, or buying, motivates them to become more and more involved. The success of brand licensing, in other words, just like collecting, stems from the relationships that people have with ideas, and their wish to bring those ideas together into forms and systems that they can surround with a personal story.

People love ideas that add value to their world. Brands are one of our collections: they are part of how we organize and link our lives.

Weight Watchers began as an idea — the idea that people needed support from other people in order to lose weight. That idea became a theory, then a belief. That belief was captured and expressed in a brand and it grew from there. To get some sense of just how powerful that belief has since become, consider this from the company's own website: Each week, approximately 1 million Weight Watchers' members attend over 40,000 Weight Watchers' meetings around the world and, in 2014, consumers spent approximately $5 billion on Weight Watchers' branded products and services. In 50 years that idea of companionship has become a multi-billion dollar global business comprising clubs, weight control systems food, and much, much more. Few people today would even recognize this as an idea that began when a woman named Jean Nidetch invited some friends over to her house and confessed her love for eating cookies.

A great brand licensing program isn't simply looking to extend a brand into new places, it's looking to work with what people know and love in order to change the *emotional scale* at which the brand operates. It does this by giving people more ways and new ways to interact as consumers. In Nagano, pins were the mechanism for consumers to extend their relationships with both Coke and the Olympics. In the case of Weight Watchers, the brand enables people to lose weight together and to feel part of a community as they do so. That's a powerful, powerful dynamic.

But what gets people interested in an idea in the first place? What does an idea need for it to even have a chance of making it?

Drs Nicole Dubbs and Kerry-Anne McGeary work at some distance from the world of marketing. They have been looking at why ideas take off specifically in the area of social change. Their observations about why people choose to embrace ideas are relevant to all of us. They point out that, while social networking tools and big data have increased the transparency of ideas and the rate at which ideas can be exchanged, the resulting flood of information has actually made it more difficult than ever to get mindshare and attention. There's the double-bind. There are more ways to air ideas than ever before, but there are also more ideas being aired.

They believe that if you want other people to take up, adopt, adapt, integrate, and ultimately champion your idea, there are four key things you need to understand:

1. You must know where and how to position your idea so that it has the greatest chance of succeeding. In other words, you must identify the "blockage points" that stand between hearing your idea and acceptance of your idea. Once you understand what people will recognize and like, and what they will struggle with, it's easier to remove the barriers that stand between your idea and acceptance of your idea.

2. The idea must be involving. It must invite people to do something or act in some way rather than simply reading, observing, or agreeing. If an idea does not engage this way, it remains too abstract for enough people to act on it.

3. The result must be clear and it must be something that enables people to include others.

4. Finally, people must believe in the vehicle — as they say, "there must be trust, authenticity, relevance, and salience in the message, messenger, and medium." The messages that people hear to support the idea must make sense and appeal to the listeners' priorities and judgment set. No idea will

fly if it doesn't make sense, even if that sense is more emotionally based than some people realize.

All of these observations about ideas for social change are applicable to the uptake of ideas in other contexts. As you read through the story of how my team and I brought pin-collecting and trading to Nagano, you can see how we encountered and overcame issues centered on all these points.

Those of us who read a lot may think they already have the answer to what makes ideas grow. In 2000, Malcom Gladwell published *The Tipping Point*, in which he talked about the power of influencers to take an idea from zero to hero. Gladwell identified groups of people — connectors, mavens, and salesmen — as critically important spreaders of ideas, alongside the stickiness of the idea itself, and the environment into which the idea is introduced. Many people still believe that this thought, the concept of an idea reaching a tipping point, is the key to an idea getting uptake. But is this the magic formula? Is it just about interest, momentum, and getting enough people to share?

Jonah Berger thinks not. In *Contagious: Why Ideas Catch On*, Berger says *The Tipping Point* has prompted many people to search for the right set of influencers to bring their idea alive, but ideas get taken up for reasons that are more complex and nuanced than selecting the right set of whisperers. Ideas explode, he suggests, because of six things: social currency, triggers, emotion, public, practical value, and stories. Those six characteristics help turn an idea from one person into something that more people are likely to want to share.

I agree. As I've just discussed, an idea in itself is not enough. The idea must make sense, it must add value for people, and it must trigger sharing in order to activate significant interest. It must also be framed in a form that resembles the brand: it must have a sense of entity, it must be tangible enough to be recognized, and it must have generated enough of that sense broadly enough for people to desire more.

As we've seen, brand licensing takes an idea that has growth dynamics and enables it to go to places where it is further welcomed. Brand licensing itself is not actually a growth strategy, in the sense that it won't make something grow that isn't growing already. It is, however, an expansion strategy. It can help a growing brand broaden its reach exponentially.

Was the pins program at Nagano a brand? No, in fact, it was three brands: The Coke brand, the Nagano Games brand, and the Olympic Games brand. The program worked because all the factors it needed to grow were in place to start with, and then once it was established, all the characteristics that would enable it to spread worked:

- The team and I were able to work through the roadblocks to make pins part of the Games.

- The idea of collecting pins did not require people to learn any new behavior or habit that was at odds with their current ones.

- People saw in the pins, the opportunity to take home a little piece of the Winter Games held in the city of Nagano.

- The presence of the Olympic and Coke brands provided proof that purchasing the pins was a good idea.

From there:

- The build up to the Games reinforced the value and desirability of the Winter Games.

- Time and the wish to be associated with the event acted as powerful triggers.

- Pride in hosting the Games and being at the events provided strong emotional affinity.

- The sight of crowds queuing and the overall public interest activated participation and, possibly, a fear of missing out.

- The pins were tangible, meaning they had practical value.

- The pins themselves were the subjects of stories and prompts for buyers to share stories with others.

The world we understand and feel at home in is not always the world of others. What excites them may surprise us — in good ways sometimes, and not so good ways at other times. I found that out, first hand, when I worked on the Nagano Olympics. My story is a study not just in what can happen when an idea takes off but how it can surprise even those who've been working with that idea for years. People may not see anything in your idea at all. Or they may take to it with a gusto that leaves everyone wondering what the hell just happened. And there are all sorts of reasons to suggest why that might be the case.

And that's why Scott Pitts found himself counting off 1998 people on that cold February morning. Word had spread. Time was short. The brands were highly familiar. Pins were limited. The price was affordable. And the memory was compelling.

The case for purchase didn't have to make sense. Because sense was not what people were hoping to buy.

Choose to Lead — How to Succeed in the Connective Economy

2

The bell curve of popularity has condensed to a frightening degree, generating a phenomenon that Mark Di Somma refers to as "fadar." Things, ideas, people, brands, scandals, and successes now rise to global awareness with immense speed, but fade just as quickly.

Cohesion is one of the toughest attributes to achieve in a brand. The brand itself must make sense structurally and strategically, but even more importantly, it must bind naturally and seamlessly to what consumers are looking for in their lives. It must also simultaneously account for shifts in competitive markets and, usually, within the accepted infrastructures of the time.

Brands work when they lock into people's needs: when they do what's expected in smart ways, at one level; and when they anticipate and surprise at another. And they can't just do that once, or even for a limited time. They must continue to evolve through changes in attitude and expectation, as consumers place emphasis on different priorities and as competitors bustle around them looking to gain their own footholds and upper hands. As we have discussed already, many won't make it.

The brands that thrive will come to form such an important part of our lives that, in the Western world at least, we see them as symbols of quality of life. We judge ourselves as trendy, informed, cool, in charge, well-off, and so much more, by the brands we have access to, those we can afford, and those our friends use too. Our brands endorse our aspirations as consumers and provide us with security and reassurance in our working lives.

That pan-life aspect, in itself, is relatively new. We used to judge brands in relation to other competing brands in the same sector. Now we judge them against our overall expectations of what will come our way and how. As a result, brands have not just taken on increased relevance (and attracted increased criticism and skepticism), they must also operate within a broader context than before now. Increasingly, they must compete not just to be included but to stay included. That's not easy.

Let's take a quick look at why. Brands are increasingly engaged in popularity contests. They must compete, not just against each other, but also with and against the sentiment of millions of connected consumers who can praise or condemn with frightening speed and force. Review sites, for example, are the new critics of many customer-facing industries. Social media sites act as megaphones, conversation drivers, trend spotters, and musterers of outrage, all simultaneously. The fabled six degrees of separation that once separated anyone from anyone has on the Facebook network at least, shrunk to just three and a half (and shrinking). Couple all that with the proliferation of devices that now keep everyone connected for more time and with greater ease than ever before, and brands find themselves in the midst of what we refer to as "the connective economy": omni-channel; synced 24 hours a day and continually updated; powered by trends; focused on experiences; linked by networks; and the stories that people tell each other. None of it shows any signs of slowing down.

As Thomas Koulopoulos and Dan Keldsen observed in *The Gen Z Effect*,[1] "Like it or not we inhabit an incredibly hyper-connected,

---

1. Koulopoulos, T., & Keldsen, D. (2014). Hyperconnecting: From me to we. In T. Koulopoulos & D. Keldsen (Eds.), *The Gen Z effect: The six forces shaping the future of business*. Bibliomotion.

information-saturated world, and we are suffering from a severe form of global attention deficit disorder as we are incessantly bombarded by more and more information and stimuli." Their research found that the connected world averages 2.5 cellular-enabled mobile devices per person. For consumers, this over-abundance of information is, perhaps not surprisingly, changing how we behave and what we seek. "We are not only con-nected; we are connected to a multitude of devices simul-taneously. This sort of disjointed connectivity does not lend itself to a collaborative set of behaviors. Instead it forces us to orchestrate an ever increasing and more complex set of connections."

In this environment, with its ready-made access to verification, trust in individuals, organizations, and therefore brands, is earned, and then endorsed in real time both physically through encounters, and online through sharing, ratings, and opinions. Increasingly, Koulopoulos and Keldsen predict that technologies will mingle to the point where there is no division between our online and offline worlds. "Far from being an either-or proposition, the two worlds will be integrated in a way that multi-plies people's potential and their opportunities to live, work and play."

The implications for brands in this evolving climate are signifi-cant. Many that continue to think and act vertically, within the context and frameworks of the sectors in which they identify themselves, will find it increasingly difficult to cater to the grow-ing "horizontal" bias of consumers. To succeed, they will need to rethink how and where they make their presence felt, and where they will expand in order to achieve that. Changing direction in terms of how they appeal could prompt many to think more late-rally about what they contribute to the lives of their buyers, what they could offer as a consequence, and who they could partner with to increase their relevance and reach. Making the move from hunting for share of market to appealing to share of life will require them to dig beyond the big data of what happens, and toward the behaviors, biases, and habits that motivate people to think and act the way they do.

Best-selling author Martin Lindstrom offers:

> As more and more products and services migrate online, and technology helps us understand human behaviour in real time at granular levels, many people have come to believe that human observations and interaction are old-fashioned and even irrelevant. I couldn't disagree more. A source who works at Google once confessed to me that despite the almost 3 billion humans who are online, and the 70 percent of online shoppers who go to Facebook daily, and the 300 hours of videos on YouTube (which is owned by Google) uploaded every minute, and the fact that 90 percent of all the world's data has been generated over the last two years[,] Google ultimately has only limited information about consumers … Google has come to realize it knows almost nothing about humans and what really drives us.[2]

One thing is certain: the brands that will flourish are those that are most connected to consumers' lives and patterns of thinking, and are specifically structured to cater to that.

The other significant pressure, of course, will be the lack of attention. Brands will be competing to hold the loyalty of generations that are quick to swipe and click the moment they are bored. The upside of this search for stimulation is that buyers now take their cues from many places and that it is now easier than ever for brands to win the world's awareness. But just as connectivity has made it easier for brands of all sorts to be discovered, so it has accelerated the rate at which consumers then lose interest. The bell curve of popularity has condensed to a frightening degree, generating a phenomenon that Mark Di Somma refers to as "fadar." Things, ideas, people, brands, scandals, and successes now rise to global awareness with immense speed, but fade just as quickly.

---

2. Lindstrom, M. (2016). *Small data* (pp. 12–13). St Martin's Press.

Heidi Klum's words that "[In fashion] one minute you're in and the next minute you're out" have never been more true.

The resolution, in part, it seems to me, is to use the first to counter the second — to build brands that are increasingly interesting because of how they morph. Apple, for example, may have built its name as a hardware company, but increasingly the company looks poised to use that installed potential fan base of over a billion active Apple devices around the world,[3] to expand its way into the services sector with offerings such as iTunes, iCloud, Apple Care, Apple Music, Apple Pay, and the App Store. Not only is this part of their business immensely expandable, it is also highly profitable, with an estimated near 60% gross margin. This is far higher than what Apple makes on its hardware products.[4] And of course much of the content and transactional traffic that drives this emerging business is not even produced by Apple. It's sourced from or through third parties that pay for the rights to be there. The result is a highly integrated ecosystem, purposely built to meet changing needs, where Apple buyers continue to be rewarded with access to new content and services on devices that continue to be upgraded to deliver those services better.

Over the past two years, I interviewed executives from dozens of companies that are grappling with how to build their brands in this bewildering new environment. Three stories illustrate what it takes to prosper.

Look Beyond One Income Source

As consumers expect more and more of what they used to pay for to be free, the requirement for brands to categorize what is worth paying for, and why, has never been more acute. For that to happen, brands need to look ever more closely at their value

---

3. http://www.theverge.com/2016/1/26/10835748/apple-devices-active-1-billion-iphone-ipad-ios?ref=il
4. http://amigobulls.com/articles/apple-services-a-giant-is-growing-within-apple-inc-aapl?p=n

propositions and their channels to arrive at models that are monetized around reward. When we spoke to Darran Garnham, currently CEO at MTW Toys and formerly of Mind Candy, he described many digital channels as "fantastic, but limited." Digital, he says, gains you reach and conversation, but it doesn't convert to cash easily. To do that, it's vital to offer physical products that take the digital offering to a new level of experience in exchange for money. In the case of Mind Candy, the revenue came from millions and millions in sales in Moshi collectibles and books.

Where brands often seem to go wrong is when they rush to digitize without thinking through how the revised revenue model will work, or they rely on investor funding to keep them afloat while they figure out a revenue model. Too many digital brands have focused on reach at the expense of conversion. Getting that right will require them to develop products at different price points ranging from free to premium. Nicholas Lovell has a great term for this: *The Curve.* It's a way of calibrating what you offer that helps consumers take the journey that Lovell describes as moving "from freeloaders into super fans."[5] His thesis is simple:

- Use free to find an audience;
- Use technology to figure out what people value;
- Let your biggest fans spend as much as they want on what they value; and
- Success lies in building relationships and community through variation and tailoring.

I agree. And that's all about knowing what must be free and what can't be. Mark Di Somma in an interview with sales guru, Mark Hunter, discovered that Hunter applied this philosophy to business-to-business sales. Social media, Hunter said, should get

---

5. Lovell, N. (2013). *10 ways to make money in a free world*. Portfolio Penguin.

a consumer to the point where they are calling a sales professional to find out more. But it should never go so far in terms of what it divulges that it makes the need for a sales visit unnecessary. In the connective economy, there always needs to be something to sell, to counterbalance what has been given away, and therefore every "give-away" must come with a call to action that ties what was enjoyed to what is also available. This must be done at a price.

Cater to Customers Across Their Lives

I'll talk in coming chapters about the need for a powerful and expandable idea that underpins your brand's promise. For now, let's focus on where your brand should be found, and what it should mean in those different places. That's right, I am talking about channel strategy! Do not just focus on media. Focus on where customers could "encounter" your brand across their lives and why those experiences would both reinforce what people know about the brand and how it would prompt them to see the brand in a new way.

We talked earlier about the need for brands to look for ways to push "horizontally" into people's lives. As brands look to extend how they make money, it makes sense that they should also investigate where that money is made. As we'll see in the later chapters, companies like Disney have transformed their properties into a full range of experiences that maximize the relationship between fans and characters. By doing this, they have been able to do business with buyers at the cinema, at amusement parks, at retail outlets, and much more.

But it's easy to take this too far. Just as a brand is not a logo, a name or logo alone does not automatically mean that consumers will welcome the brand into a different part of their lives. As Tom Oakley has observed about Virgin:

> Virgin used to have the image of being a rebellious brand ... but with Virgin Money and Virgin Trains, it

doesn't have that single message and association any more. Today, the host of sub-brands do not comfortably fit together in a way that Virgin can define itself as meaning something, which goes a long way towards explaining why Virgin isn't a leader in any of its industries. In the airline, broadband and gym industries to name just a few, Virgin is simply another player and fails to innovate in the way that a leader generally does.[6]

Virgin may not always get it right. Some would argue that Virgin's continued relevance owes more to its indefatigable leader than its business model. Having said that, Richard Branson's views on what it takes to have the right impact in people's lives serve as a great list of criteria for how brands should look to gain greater share of life:

- Add fun to people's lives through what you do;
- Deliver experiences that people want — not just that you think they want or that you are used to giving them;
- Enter areas where you can make a positive impact;
- Never be afraid to leave if things don't go to plan.[7]

Act Quickly

Continuing to meet the needs of consumers who expect to be wowed is tiring to say the least. And just as attention spans are shortening, so is patience. Brands must increasingly pace not just their product releases, but how they will fill the voids between those releases to keep interest high.

---

6. https://themarketingagenda.com/2014/10/25/virgin-unrelated-diversification/
7. http://www.businessinsider.com.au/how-richard-branson-maintains-the-virgin-group-2015-2?r=US&IR=T

Deloitte published a piece on how the insurance industry could look to overhaul how it introduces new policies to market.[8] It highlights how more brands should be looking to lift their agility by:

- Pinpointing areas of underperformance in your existing portfolio, and implementing product or pricing changes to make them more attractive;

- Rethinking your product development so that it is consistent, repeatable, and coordinated;

- Focusing on the overall competitiveness of the portfolio;

- At the same time, developing modular product architectures that allow brands to leverage a common structure and brand, and create tailored products more efficiently. This same principle should also enable brands to find new go-to-market arrangements built on that core architecture — e.g., licensing or joint ventures.

Of course, there's a balance to be struck here between speed, product quality, and market impact. My point is that brands with plenty to say need to back that up with the right amount of product/service to buy, and pace to elevate interest and meet demand. Success in the connective economy is literally about connecting the dots, but knowing which dots to join, where, when, with whom, and at what margin are the determining factors. For this reason, senior marketers need to be having more integrated discussions with their sales, product development, and licensing teams about how they can achieve the best brand presence possible in each market rather than relying on traditional launch-and-maintain strategies.

---

8. https://www.google.co.nz/url?sa=t&rct=j&q=&esrc=s&source=web&cd=12&ved=0ah UKEwjs1bS77ZfRAhWErJQKHbdGBD0QFghVMAs&url=https%3A%2F%2Fwww2.deloitte. com%2Fcontent%2Fdam%2FDeloitte%2Fus%2FDocuments%2Ffinancial-services%2Fus-cons-policy-admin-systems-speed-to-market-042415.pdf&usg=AFQjCNFHci3sd8RuJo-S-urzPn-lG5cUcQ&bvm=bv.142059868,d.dGo&cad=rja

In conclusion, here are 10 powerful motivations that cause people to think and behave differently, that companies can use to help people further connect to their brands. Understanding these motivators can help brands thrive:

1. Familiarity — Give consumers more reasons and better ways to grow their existing relationship with you;

2. Momentum — Give consumers more opportunities to participate in something they want to see happen;

3. Curiosity — Allow people to explore or engage with a brand they thought they knew in new and interesting ways;

4. Continuity — Bring back an idea that is deeply valued, but with a new twist;

5. Extension — Take an idea that people already like further than it has been taken before;

6. Advantage — Give people access to something they would otherwise not be able to get;

7. Immediacy — Speed up the time with which mundane things get done;

8. Community — Unite people behind an idea and give them the means to express or support that belief;

9. Capability — Make something happen for people that they have always craved in their lives. And do it in an unprecedented way;

10. Exclusivity — Offer people something that builds on what they already know, but let them experience it in ways few others will.

If you follow these principles you will not only stay connected to your consumers, you will also stay relevant and in demand.

Having identified the challenge to maintain growth, I've cited a personal example of how three brands connected powerfully with consumers and illustrated the necessity of staying connected. I am excited to now take a deep dive into each of the elements that comprise the LASSO Model. Together, over the next five chapters, we will explore the importance of each in meaningfully, purposefully, and profitably expanding your brand into new categories. At the end of each chapter I will provide you with a 5-point rating system within the LASSO framework by which you will score your brand. Thereby, you can assess how Lateral, Addictive, Storied, Scalable, and Own-able your brand is today. As you read Chapters 3–7, qualitatively benchmark your own brand against the illustrations I provide you so by the end of each chapter you can take a fair swing at ascribing an accurate score to your brand. While this may seem overwhelming or unfamiliar to you at the moment, I worked hard to make this book much more than just a group of great vignettes, and rather, a really approachable application you can use right now. My goal is to provide you with a worthy and useful tool to better your business, and once you learn this method, a tool you'll come to rely on year after year like a steady workhorse. In Chapter 8, I will show you how to interpret these scores to determine whether your brand's degree of extension and expansion are optimized. First, turn the page, and together let's take our first step to explore what it means to have a brand with Lateral attributes.

Lateral — Beyond Where They've Been

Every brand that is looking to go beyond what it is currently known for, regardless of the mechanism it intends to use, needs an expansion point — a pivotal characteristic that translates powerfully from one product variant to another, or from one sector to another, to give consumers even more of what they want from the brand.

Before I get started on discussing the specifics of what it means to have a "lateral" brand, I want to let you know that you don't have to be a brand expert to make use of the LASSO Model. The Model and its corresponding algorithm are designed for beginners and experts alike.[1] If you are a brand expert, you can begin to use the LASSO Model to help you prioritize your IP — which of your brands have the greatest potential to expand — so you can determine where to best focus your resources. If you are a brand owner, but not an expert, the algorithm can still help you determine how "expand-able" your brand is and what that may mean for your business. Finally, if you don't feel capable of assigning a score to your brand at present, the LASSO Model framework still can be a relevant and incredibly useful tool in running your business. As you plow into the next five chapters, I encourage you to

---

1. For an explanation of how this works, see the Appendences, which outlines the algorithm's methodology.

consider a brand you own, or would like to have the rights. Score the brand against each of the five elements of the LASSO Model and find out whether it is poised to expand, grow, and thrive. Let's get started.

"Lateral" is the first critical variable to a successful brand licensing program. You will recall from the Intro that powerful owners expand their brands into new territories while staying true to the idea for which they are renowned. Expanding a brand beyond its operating sector into wider life categories encourages customers to think of "their" brand in new ways. The challenge, however, is to strike the right balance between *surprise*, whereby the brand appears where it was not expected, and *alignment*, whereby the appearance of the brand in this sector makes sense because it mirrors what the brand already means. If the association is too "lateral," or if the brand isn't convincing enough, the whole arrangement appears wanting. It won't pass the smell test. Consumers will sense this as quickly as a predator picks up the foul scent of a skunk, and steer clear.

The lateral aspect of the LASSO Model is all about how far you push a brand away from its core identity in pursuit of additional opportunities and profits. Some brands, as we'll discover, can make that shift more easily than others. Others are much more powerful when they stay close to home. This decision is critical because it helps define not just where the brand is seen, but also where it is most profitable. Expand ambitiously and, with the right brand, you have a brand that can take on new meaning and new revenues. Get it wrong, and you have a brand that is confusing, laughable, or both.

We've all heard the horror stories. The brand extensions that failed to fire — the Vespa perfume, the Hooters airline, Smith & Wesson clothing ... So many have failed in fact that, as I alluded to earlier, it has caused many marketers to dismiss the very idea of brand extension as one reserved for brands that have run out of ideas or that simply want to squeeze every cent out of their fading IP. Some older statistics that I've seen suggest that more than 80%

of brand extensions will not succeed and, of those that make it, just over half can expect to be in place three years later — hardly encouraging.

Some notable brand strategists are equally dismissive. In their *22 Immutable Laws of Marketing*, Al Ries and Jack Trout argue vehemently, in law #12, that extending the equity of a successful brand is disastrous because ultimately such diversification makes a brand weaker. Instead, they argue for companies to maintain the courage of their convictions and to "narrow their focus until they build a position in the mind of the prospective customer ... The more products, the more markets, the more alliances a company makes, the less money it makes."

Why do brand extensions fail at such high rates? Nancy Wulz suggests four key reasons:

1. Lack of demand — The extension doesn't address a meaningful market need.

2. Uninspiring supply — The need may be there, but the extension itself does nothing to inspire consumers.

3. Relevance — There is a need and the answer is good, but it is ill-matched with the brand.

4. Execution — All the factors to make the extension work are in place, but the program fails through bad execution.

Ries and Trout's argument raises a valid point: if you're not extending or expanding your brand from a basis that consumers truly want, chances are you're doomed to failure. And Wulz's point, that any brand, regardless of the strength of its business case, will fail if it is not executed well, is absolutely true.

Before we go any further, let's draw some fundamental distinctions. *Brand growth* is when a brand expands the core business into a new geographic region or further saturates an existing region. It continues the business the brand is already in, offering more of the same to new audiences in different locales. It may do this as a self-contained business or through a franchise model. *Brand extension*, also known as line extension, is about building out a brand product portfolio. It's about continuation. For example, a whisky company extends its brand when it introduces a new line of malt or adds another style of whisky to its current portfolio. In effect, the brand offers its consumers access to more of the same, only different. Cereals are now formulated to meet a range of perceived needs such as gluten-free, low cholesterol, with premium ingredients, organic, and so on. Ries and Trout both argue that when brands extend in this way, they effectively create a "long tail" of choices that dilute what they stand for. For all that, I classify brand extensions as a lateral strategy because the brand continues to trade within the area within which it has hopefully built renown.

Brand expansion, which is also known as category extension, could be perceived as even more risky. Here, brands broaden their presence into markets where they have not built their reputation and, often, they rely on licensees to fill the experience and capacity gap on their behalf. They do this for a range of reasons. The most powerful is that, where brand extension looks to achieve product continuation, brand expansion is based on emotional continuation. The brands are in effect intending to carry the emotional relationship which they have built with consumers from one sector to another. It's a lateral jump, intended to achieve the greater "share of life" I referred to earlier.

Consider that Caterpillar has been able to carry its reputation for toughness into areas that are unexpected. In fact, according to Kenneth Beaupre, Brand Advocacy and Licensing Manager who runs Caterpillar's licensing program, the program is now active in over 150 countries and generates $2.8 billion at retail. This amount may be relatively small, compared to Caterpillar's $49 billion in core products and services, but it has allowed the business-to-business brand to build a very powerful direct-to-consumer connection over 25 years. Caterpillar's products such as safety shoes and eye protection have given the brand the credibility to extend into footwear, apparel, mobile devices in rugged cell and smart phones, toys, luggage, and watches.

Caterpillar's success points to the power of "building on your reputation." Every brand that is looking to go beyond what it is currently known for, regardless of the mechanism it intends to use, needs an *expansion point* — a pivotal characteristic that translates powerfully from one product variant to another, or from one sector to another, to give consumers even more of what they want from the brand. Coke was able to take its message to the Olympics through the label pin program because happiness translates perfectly to such a huge global event. Advertising people often refer to the pivotal truth at the center of a brand campaign as "the big idea," but to me, the expansion point of a brand is more than an idea — it's the single, most powerful emotion or association bonded with that brand that people have. In fact, they believe in it so much that they want to see it expressed for themselves across multiple aspects of their lives.

Take Ferrari's theme park, which opened in 2010 in Abu Dhabi. According to the company's website:

> Ferrari World Abu Dhabi was created in tribute to Ferrari's passion, heritage, excellence, innovation and performance. Each area and attraction in the Park brings to life a different part of the Ferrari story ... to not only showcase the best of the Ferrari brand, but to provide people of all ages with the most thrilling theme park experience in the Middle East.

The venture has been such a success that the company is now planning to put in more parks in Barcelona, China, and North America. Through this venture, Ferrari joins the theme park sector, effectively becoming a competitor to Universal Pictures and Disney, but it also gains access to millions and millions of people for whom the Ferrari brand would otherwise be completely out of reach. Everything about this theme park is scaled to take on that market: 20 rides across a 200,000 m^2 area featuring the largest Ferrari logo in the world, including four rides designed specifically for children. Ferraris may not be family cars, but the Ferrari Park has offers for drivers and non-drivers alike.

Contrast the success of the theme park with the other initiatives by Ferrari to expand its brand, particularly where it has sought to pitch its licensed products against the likes of Hermes and LVMH.

I'm not surprised at all that Ferrari's fashion expansion got off to a slow start. Timing didn't help. Ferrari made its move into the luxury market at the very time that the luxury sector itself was under stress after terrorist attacks in Europe. But there's more to it than that. The expansion point is wrong.

Ferrari may have aspirations to be a full-fledged luxury brand, but the essence of Ferrari itself has nothing to do with luxury or style in my perception, even though these are both words that Ferrari might wish to lay claim. Ferrari is all about speed. Unreasonable speed. Linking the brand to the world's fastest rollercoaster makes complete sense from an associative point of view, and it enables Ferrari to form a lateral connection with the theme/ amusement park sector: a sector that is growing, global, and in which consumers are always looking for new thrills. By contrast, that speed association doesn't work with luxury goods, and the luxury market itself is already bulging with great brands that offer beautiful, high-quality products. This is where truly understanding how consumers view the brand is critical. If you start an expansion program from the wrong expansion point, everything about the journey is going to be an uphill battle.

Neuro-marketing expert Sandra Pickering believes Ferrari's attraction derives from fundamental archetypal thinking — the need for freedom from control. Ferrari consumers find unreasonable speed deeply attractive because they love the idea of something being untamable. They will give the brand permission to tap into that because of Ferrari's personality and the meanings that consumers link with the brand. It *makes sense* for Ferrari to be fast. And because that link is emotively based, rather than specific to a product or sector, Ferrari can take their brand into unrelated markets, as long as they trigger the thrilling emotions that consumers associate with the brand.

In 1994, Sridhar Samu of Indiana University looked at the role of brand associations in successful brand extensions. Consumers' relationships with brands, he suggested, were an expression of the associative memory concept of nodes and links. Brand names, he said, are stored as nodes in our memory, and the various associations consumers have with that name are stored as links. Exposure to the brand name activates these nodes and links and that activity, in turn, strengthens the associations consumers make with the brand. The types of associations consumers form, Samu continued, can be broken down into product class- and non-product class-related groups.

Where the association with a brand pivots around a product, the consumer tends to associate the brand directly with that, and the directness of that association, in turn, makes it hard for the brand to successfully expand that association. However, it may well enable the brand to further extend its product lines within the segment. For example, Sandra Pickering says that the Mars brand is associated deeply with the product experience. That association makes it relatively straight forward for the brand to extend its products along similar lines but not to venture beyond that. This helps explain why brands like Suzuki, for example, extend and expand their brands in different ways than a lifestyle brand like Harley-Davidson. By contrast, where a brand is less directly linked with a specific product type, the brand may find it easier to encourage consumers to associate with the brand across a range of sectors, meaning there may be expansion opportunities.

While Samu's article was written some time before brands set out to consciously broaden their mandates through purpose, story, and experiences, the principles still hold true. If a brand is "closely held," in other words, if it is deeply and singularly associated by consumers with a singular sector, then, as Pickering confirms, it will struggle to break out of the box where consumers consign it. If, on the other hand, the brand is associated more broadly with an idea, a ritual, a mythology, or an aspiration, it will probably find it easier to form lateral connections. That's one of the strengths of Virgin, she says. It is associated with rebellion rather than a specific product or sector.

It's fine when consumers and brands agree on the parameters of the association. The difficulty for many brands is, while they may see themselves as having a broad mandate, that may not be how their customers see them. Samu's point, that brands only have the latitude afforded to them by consumers, is as relevant today as when he first made it, and underpins my point about the need for each brand to fully evaluate its basis for expansion.

More recently, Dr. Edward Tauber, President of Brand Extension Research, and John Parham, President, Director of Branding, Parham Santana, have explained associative success as a direct correlation with "Opportunity, Fit and Leverage." Brands that are looking to expand are best to look for a beachhead opportunity in a large category, they say, because by doing so, they create instant scale for themselves. But simply identifying that large market is not enough. A brand should only enter that market if they have fit or "permission" from consumers to go there — in other words, as per earlier, their brand is forging a presence in markets that "fit" with where consumers expect to see them. Tauber and Parham add that a brand should only exercise that fit if it can do so with leverage, whereby the brand can use its good name and attributes to achieve a competitive advantage.

That's difficult enough, right? But wait, there's more. "There's an inverse relationship between fit (consumer permission) and leverage (competitive advantage) ... Consumers might give a brand permission to be in many categories. But if they don't perceive the new products as credible and superior to existing competitive products, it's a bad business decision." In other words, the greater the number of sectors a brand has permission to enter, the lesser the chances that it will compete meaningfully across all, or even any of those sectors.

A good example of this inverse relationship is Rubbermaid. When I worked at Newell Rubbermaid, market research revealed that the Rubbermaid brand had consumer permission to expand into a plethora of categories. The internal criteria initially for doing so were "as long as the products were made of plastic or rubber and were used in and around the home." On this basis, I found that Rubbermaid had extended its brand via licensing into categories that ranged from cleaning chemicals to garden edging; from mailboxes to automotive floor mats and wiper blades; and from ready-to-assemble wood furniture to pet accessories including food storage, dog house, and litter boxes. But because the brand did not have a competitive advantage in "all things made of rubber and plastic" the sales in these licenses were not significant and they left the consumer wondering exactly what the Rubbermaid brand meant. In 2006, I worked with the Rubbermaid brand council to redefine the Rubbermaid brand pyramid and positioning, honing in on the brand's core equities of "storage and organization." From that point, under my guidance, the brand extended into categories that reinforced this positioning, including those it had once created, ranging from kitchen tools and gadgets to garden dumping carts and kitchen step ladders. Each of these "new" categories not only performed exceptionally well commercially, but they also added measurably to the brand's equity.

Expansion is not a license to go wherever a brand feels like going. In fact, quite the opposite. Brands should look to expand into sectors where they will have a specific advantage because of how consumers perceive them. That expansion may be obvious in some under served markets, or it may appear completely left-field. Success will depend on whether consumers "follow" the leap. And knowing that comes down to a deep and proven understanding of how consumers see a brand in their lives.

A great example of how understanding consumer associations can impact a brand is evident in Turner Classic Movies (TCM). TCM has found ways to expand into cruises, wine, and film festivals. But, to do this effectively, Jennifer Dorian, General Manager at TCM told us, they've been prepared to say "No" to a whole lot of offers and they've stayed open to what may or may not be on-brand, because, as she says, it isn't always obvious. On the face of it, the shift into wine for example, risks being exactly the kind of brand expansion we talked about at the beginning of this chapter. But what Dorian and her team found when they really looked deep into the passions and interests of their audience was that wine was a significant shared passion among the TCM community. In fact, TCM viewers liked nothing more than to enjoy a glass as they watched a movie, therefore making the relationship more obvious made complete sense. Cruises may seem a strange association at first glance — but again, people who love classic movies are deeply drawn to the idea of cruising. Maybe it's another way to get away, or, maybe it's the thought of watching a classic film on the open ocean that's striking. Whatever the motive, it led the company to instigate a cruise brand that has proven highly successful, adding new value to the brand and giving fans new experiences that reinforce their affinity for TCM.

Even brands that are currently using licensing effectively see further potential to shift their association laterally through new ventures and partnerships. When we spoke to Meredith Corporation's Vice President of Brand Licensing, Elise Contarsy, she talked about how the organization, the second largest licensor in the world, with reported licensed product sales worldwide of $22.8 billion in 2016, was continuing to look at ways to maximize its branded assets to move beyond its core publishing business.[2]

For example, Better Homes and Gardens Real Estate is a franchised brokerage service run by Realogy Corporation that operates through a license agreement with Meredith Corporation, the publisher of *Better Homes and Gardens*. It's an astonishing 100-year deal, made up of two 50-year terms — certainly the longest licensing deal I had ever heard of, but one that reflects the long-term nature of the property sector. The business, Contarsy says, is going strong because there's a very strong partnership in place, the brand stewardship is robust, and the CEO of the real estate business is a leader in that industry who is passionate about the brand and utilizing its attributes. The license works because the core brand and the licensed brand are both focused on the needs of the next generation of homeowners.

John Parham of the Parham Santana agency, who has worked with Meredith on *Better Homes and Gardens* licensing deals at Walmart, says that what makes these arrangements work is when there is a genuine alignment of agenda. In the case of Walmart, he says, the company had a flourishing backyard furniture business but wanted to shift indoors. The tie-in with *Better Homes and*

---

2. http://www.licensemag.com/license-global/meredith-teams-lifestyle-mag

Gardens enabled them to reach out to house-proud consumers and find new ways to fall in love with their home again. The success of that initiative enabled *Better Homes and Gardens* to cultivate new product lines with new customers, and helped Walmart to change the conversation they have with this consumer group from one focused on the practicality of polyester to one based on aesthetics and entertainment. Consumers can now make decisions in-store that enable them to bring their desired lifestyle home in order for their home to look more like the magazine.

Here's another example. The firm, Bulgari, founded over 130 years ago by a silversmith is well known for making jewelry and accessories. However, it did not gain this reputation until the 1950s and 1960s when Rome's large film studio Cinecitta took off. The movies *Roman Holiday, Ben Hur, War and Peace,* and *La Dolce Vita* were all shot there. As a result, a parade of film stars and producers discovered the Italian brand during the filming, which helped the Bulgari brand gain global recognition. Some suggested at the time that Elizabeth Taylor, who fell in love with the brand, knew just one word in Italian: Bulgari.

According to Chief Executive Jean-Christophe Babin, this burgeoning international reputation drove the company to expand beyond Europe, opening its first flagship store in New York in the 1970s. At the same time, Bulgari began extending its brand into watches. Later in the 1990s, Bulgari moved into fragrances and eventually bags — all of which Mr. Babin said fit with the firm's "mission of making the lady more unique, more special."

I'm taken with Bulgari's Creative Director Silvio Ursini's statement that a brand should only venture into a market when it has something distinctive to say. Babin has elaborated on this idea, saying that to follow your competitors into a sector out of fear, or just to keep up, would be disastrous. Still, Bulgari has made what many might consider a surprising leap by venturing into the hotel business through an arrangement with Marriott via their Ritz group.[3]

---

3. http://www.bbc.com/news/business-35857946

Bulgari opened its first hotel in Milan in 2004, and has since opened two more, with three more openings planned. In 2009, I traveled from my home in Atlanta to Bali, Indonesia, for my honeymoon. And here is where the Bulgari brand expansion gets personal for me. I had heard amazing stories about Bali from my days flying in the Pacific and Indian Oceans while serving in the U.S. Navy. Having always wanted to see it myself, I convinced Emily, my wife, to honeymoon there. One day, while we were exploring, we came across a magnificent resort. It was my first encounter with the Bulgari hotel brand. The resort stood atop a cliff and from our viewpoint we could see the villas below, each with its own garden and pool overlooking the Indian Ocean. It formed a powerful memory.

This example is important for two reasons. First of all, although I was surprised at seeing the Bulgari name, the idea of a Bulgari hotel did not clash with my preconceptions of the brand. It was indeed a jewel. Secondly, because of that experience, my understanding of the whole of the Bulgari brand has changed — it is now more than a brand that sells expensive jewelry.

When brands truly understand their consumers they create opportunities for special experiences to happen. And when those new experiences happen, they create new opportunities for the brand to consider further lateral steps.

Idea Channel describes modern-day brands as a cross between "personality, design and purpose": brands are culturally dependent tools that people seek for things to consume and with which to align. All these aspects are critical to understanding how, where, and why a brand can successfully make a lateral leap:

- The new expression of the brand must fit with the personality and the qualities that consumers know and treasure;

- It must make sense from a design point of view in that the brand must look the part in the new sectors in which it is seen;

- It must align with what consumers see as the powerful driving force of the brand;

- It must be something consumers want more of in their lives; and of course;

- The brand itself must be one they want more of in their lives ... more on that in later chapters.

Licensing strategists have often positioned brand licensing as a powerful and cost-effective way to develop new products. I absolutely agree. But, as the Ferrari example shows, new products cannot survive in isolation or even on their own merits. Products need a thriving environment in which to prosper and must bring a perspective to that environment that has been missing up until now.

It's one thing to know that you should expand. Just as important is knowing where to expand. Very few brands are in sectors where organic growth is increasing enough for them to hit their targets. That means they must either acquire other companies, joint venture, or take market share off others in order to achieve within-sector growth. If those options are not available to them, then the need and temptation to expand into faster-moving, higher-value sectors makes a great deal of sense. Ferrari's luxury good play has struggled because they not only looked to build presence in an already competitive and fulfilled market, they also looked to do so at a time when luxury goods themselves were at a low ebb. By contrast, the decision to participate in the theme parks' market has been helped by the organic growth dynamics of that sector.

I'll deal with the specifics of whether you're ready to license, and the process for doing so, in later chapters. The key consideration at this point is *where* should you expand and *why* should you do so? To decide that, think carefully about the inherent growth characteristics of that part of the economy:

- How quickly is the sector growing? And what are the predicted growth patterns over the next five years?

- How long are the economic cycles in the sector? How tightly does the sector typically mirror changes in the wider economy? In other words, are economic cycles heavily influenced by consumer and market confidence or are they more consistent?

- What types of brands do best in the sector — luxury or budget, for example — and is there direct alignment between your brand positioning and the positioning of those that thrive in the lateral sector? If they're not aligned, it's probably not a good decision to expand into that sector.

- What other factors, beyond the sector itself, affect demand and profitability in the sector? For example, is it sensitive to changes in commodity prices, is it subject to a high level of convergence, or is the pace of technological change so rapid that you are likely to be outpaced if you attempt to enter?

- What are the regulatory barriers to entering that sector? Is there anything that actively prevents your brand from participating in that sector?

- What is the current political environment and how will it impact growth? What cultural factors exist and how should they be taken into consideration?

Ken Favaro's examination of companies that have successfully diversified reveals two critical consideration factors. The diversification must materially improve the overall value proposition of your brand and your business; and there must be enough of your company's distinctive capabilities present to give you what Favaro calls "a right to win" in the new market.

When IKEA decided to start selling televisions, he says, they didn't see themselves as entering the already-crowded television market at all. Instead, they were looking to solve the common furniture challenge of fitting all the technology we live with today seamlessly and neatly into a room. That was a challenge they were qualified to solve, he says, so it made sense for consumers.

But like Jean-Christophe Babin, Favaro counsels brands to:

> resist the alluring temptation to pursue adjacencies to compensate for slowing growth in your core businesses, exploit a hot growth market, keep up with others, or upgrade your company's growth or margin profile. Such come-ons are what drove airline companies into car rentals, led steel companies into buying construction aggregates, and seduced pharmaceutical companies into consumer products. These adjacency moves all failed because their motives were wrong, and so those companies missed growth opportunities in their core businesses while also diluting their overall coherence.

This advice is echoed by Laura Ries in a very good analysis of why brands will grow and fads will fail. The secret, of course, is knowing whether your brand is a passing interest or one that will bloom as consumers see more of it. Ries gives the example of the Crocs shoes brand, which burned bright for some time before collapsing under its own weight.

The brand did several things wrong, she says. First of all, they ramped up production to meet what they perceived as mass hysteria only to find themselves in a hole when consumers moved on. Secondly, they extended their lines to include a variety of shoe styles and then other gear that didn't align with the Crocs ethos. In the process, says Ries, they turned themselves into just another brand. Thirdly, they went "broad-brand" with their distribution to be more available, but again, in doing so they diluted what made Crocs special. Fourthly, they looked to appeal to everyone and so they lost appeal and focus — shifting from an audience that should have been kids, athletes, and workers to one that didn't know who it was trying to reach. And finally, while they invested well in manufacturing and distribution, they paid too little attention on their global marketing.

Ries may not be a fan of the brand expansion ethos — in fact, she uses the Crocs example to argue against extension — but her points about why Crocs went wrong are absolutely valid. I may respectfully disagree on the conclusion, but I absolutely endorse her cautionary note. Brand success is never just about momentary surges. If you are not bringing something to a new sector through the associations and expectations that consumers have of your brand, you have no business being there. On the other hand, if you are entering a sector with opportunity and your brand can bring in a missing perspective and approach that consumers will welcome, and if you have the time to develop the market into one that works for all those who have invested, then I would suggest you should do so.

Ries says that probably won't happen, and that's why so many brand extensions and expansions fail. Management forget to think associatively. Instead, she says, they apply the logic of "more" and the self-indulgence of perceived success. I agree. The discipline here is to be able to see past the thrill of the chase, and beyond the deal, to understand the need. Many companies will back themselves to do that but a lot of them will fail, because in the excitement of the hunt, they will lose sight of the priorities and perspectives of the customer.

While I agree that there is plenty of reason for hesitancy, and these decisions are too big to simply rush into, let's end this section on an up note with two brands that have done it well. They have expanded to connect with people in new ways, enabling them to take their brands where they had never been, to grow new styles of partnership, and to shift how consumers were able to stay close. If Crocs demonstrates how and why extending your brand can fail, Harley-Davidson and Mickey Mouse show what is possible.

Let's start with the big bike. The company has built one of the most successful brand licensing programs in the world, and they've done it through a simple brand expansion point: access. Harley-Davidson understands that not everyone will own one of their notorious road bikes, but they also understand that the spirit of the brand — the lifestyle of freedom and rebellion against unquestioning conformity that it represents — is one that many people crave access to, in some form.

Harley-Davidson's licensing program is that key: it opens the door to being part of that world to whatever degree, and at whatever price point, feels comfortable. You can buy a "Harley" burger in Manhattan, choose a shirt, buy the perfume, or hit the road ... and through those or hundreds of other purchase decisions, consumers can sign up to the ethos. They can make it part of their lives — for lunch or for life. The pay back for Harley-Davidson is obvious: they extend their reach, and therefore their customer base, far beyond the motorcycling community by imbuing a whole range of other goods and services with the brand's particular stamp of rarified cool. It works because consumers crave to be part of that. They also establish a platform for some of those people, who might not be in a position to buy one of their bikes now, to do so at a later point.

They've been able to do this because, although their product is iconic, the associations with the brand are deeply emotive. Even then, to pull off their program successfully, Harley-Davidson must negotiate a path between two contradictory ideas: rebellious enough to feel delightfully unorthodox; and yet broad enough for all who wish, to be able to subscribe their way.

Now — another happy ending, but a very different story. Possibly the most famous licensed character of all time, Mickey Mouse, was created in 1928 by Walt Disney and Ub Iwerks, and rapidly became a cultural icon. In 1934, at the height of the Depression, General Foods, the makers of Post Toasties, paid $1 million for the right to put Mickey Mouse cut outs on the back of cereal boxes. It's said that in one day, Macy's New York sold a record 11,000 timepieces featuring the Mickey Mouse image.

So far, so good. But things haven't always been smooth sailing. In 2003, when Tim Kilpin, former Executive Vice President for Franchise Management at Walt Disney managed Mickey, the character was turning 75. America's favorite mouse had lost his connection with consumers and needed to be revitalized. Andy Mooney, former chairman of Disney Consumer Products, saw an opportunity to use this birthday occasion to increase Mickey's relevance through a new apparel line. So Disney collaborated with the hottest designers to create a high-end vintage program through upscale Los Angeles-based clothing retailer, Fred Segal. To promote the line, Mickey was seated with celebrities who wore the clothes at marquee events and was featured in top shows including *Sex and the City*. All this activity created tremendous buzz and the Mouse was back! But the program did more than revive the character. It actually changed the perceptions of Disney as a company, so that it is now viewed as a major fashion player, consistently ranking on *Women Wear Daily*'s WWD100 list of most influential fashion brands. Even more compelling was that the apparel program had no specific entertainment aspect. The program was created simply to remind consumers why they love Mickey Mouse.[4] It's a wonderful example of a brand using the breadth of its appeal. I'll share a conversation I had with Tim Kilpin about his experiences at Disney in more detail in the next chapter.

Key Takeouts

- A brand will fail to expand successfully if there is a lack of demand, uninspiring supply, the brand itself is not seen as relevant, or the growth plan is badly executed.

- Brand growth is about growing what you already have. Brand extension focuses on building out a brand product portfolio. Brand expansion is about taking the brand into new and unrelated markets.

- Every brand needs an *expansion point*: a pivotal characteristic that gives the brand an emotional basis for growth.

- Where consumers associate a brand closely with a product, the brand is more likely to be successful looking to extend its product lines within the segment.

- Where a brand is more closely linked with an emotion, it may be easier to expand the brand beyond its initial category.

---

4. http://articles.baltimoresun.com/2003-07-27/business/0307260289_1_mickey-mouse-walt-disney-donald-duck

- Brands should only look to expand into sectors where they will have a specific advantage because of how consumers perceive them.

- If you are going to expand, expand into sectors that have healthy growth potential. There's no point in expanding into a stalling market.

Look before you leap; here are seven searching questions to answer before you decide where to extend or expand:

1. What exactly is the problem that you're solving for buyers? And why would consumers look to you to solve it?

2. Is your brand closely linked to a specific product set or to a more general idea? If it's the latter, what qualifies your brand to take ownership of that broader idea?

3. Are you big enough and well known enough to extend or expand? What makes you more than a "fad" in the minds of those who buy into you?

4. What do consumers want more of from your brand, if anything? Will the association make sense to them? Will it change their world for the better?

5. How does your brand fit into the lives of your core consumers? What latitude will they give the brand to take up more space in their lives?

6. Do the dynamics of the sector(s) you are looking to expand into warrant your presence?

7. How will you counter the downsides of being more widely available?

Your Turn

Professor Kevin Keller's book *Strategic Brand Management: Building, Measuring and Managing Brand Equity* includes a very good Brand Extendibility Scorecard. Mark Di Somma and I were so taken with his idea that we adapted it for the LASSO Model using a spider web evaluation tool. We'll build one for your brand over the course of the book.

All you have to do for now is to think about your answers to the seven questions I just asked and score your brand on its literal/lateral potential by using the scale on the next page. There are no right or wrong answers. Some brands will feel that they are at their strongest when they stay close to what they do now. Others will see opportunities to take their brand into radical new territories. Take a moment now and choose the number on the Lateral Expandability Score chart on page 53 that best describes your brand's potential to shift sectors.

Were you able to select a Lateral score that best matches your brand? Good! Jot it down in the margin for easy reference. Once you're ready, turn to Chapter 4 and get ready to evaluate your brand from an Addictive perspective, the second element of the LASSO Model.

Lateral Expandability Score Chart.

1	2	3	4	5
We will only ever stay in the one category.	We could extend our brand to include new or evolving opportunities, but still within our core category.	We could extend our brand into a number of related categories.	Our brand has enough latitude to expand into a new and unrelated category with strong growth characteristics. We have the Opportunity, Fit and Leverage to do that successfully.	Our customers align with our brand on emotive much more than product lines. As long as we stay consistent with that emotion, we can take the brand into a range of different and unrelated sectors.

Lateral — Beyond Where They've Been

Addictive —
Growing to Love

In order for a brand to be addictive, there needs to be the right combination of frequency, intensity, and access.

"Addictive" is the second critical variable to a successful brand licensing program. Once you have established how Lateral a brand can be, how easy it will be to extend or expand, you want to determine its level of addictiveness. Does the brand encourage consumers to choose it wherever they find it? Do they want to return time and time again to experience the brand? Does the next experience build on what they already know? If so, have you created a repeatable model? If not, what elements are missing that could enhance its addictiveness? Addictive ensures that the brand has bankability enabling the relationships themselves to be proactively managed to keep customers constantly looking out for new opportunities.

Addictive brands are the ones in which consumers cannot get enough. It may be because they love what these brands stand for, or that they want more of the experience that they are offered, or that they want to be more involved in what they see as the brand's world. Whatever the incentive, these brands play to people's sense of "more." They excite us.

There are five reasons why certain brands exert such influence on people's lives:

1. Pursuing them is fun — "finding out more" and "not missing out" have become hallmarks of pop-culture living. Everyone wants to be up with the play.

2. Now is everything — ideas come and go so fast today that consumers want access to the things that are current, for as long as they remain current. After which, they move on.

3. Availability — hyper-consumerism has encouraged all of us to buy now, and to use readily available credit to do so.

4. Curiosity — together, the factors above give rise to a strong sense of curiosity. They encourage buyers to want and expect new things all the time.

5. Hyper awareness — ready access to the Internet means consumers are over-aware of the world around them. We live in a world of trends, likes, and connections. Brands are now part of wider and bigger conversations, and tides of popularity.

Perhaps no sector better exemplifies the power and profit of addictive brands than entertainment. Even if you had never before heard of the brand Pokémon, by now you have become aware of the insanely addictive game called *Pokémon Go*. Launched in July of 2016, *Pokémon Go* became the summer's most popular distraction for millions of kids and young adults alike throughout the world.[1] The key to its success is, in fact, the marriage of new technology and augmented reality (AR), to an established and trusted brand name, Pokémon. Having started as a video game in Japan in 1996, it went on to become the number two best-selling video-game of all time. Pokémon then quickly extended through licensing into a trading card game with 21.5 billion trading cards now in circulation as well as a very successful animated TV series and film franchise. Moreover, in the 20 years since it launched, the brand has expanded via officially licensed merchandise into every conceivable category.

---

1. https://tfmainsights.com/pokemon-go/

Nintendo, who owns Pokémon, coupled that emotional appeal with the technological innovation of a mobile game that utilizes AR to create a pop-culture phenomenon that has caught on like wildfire.

According to Steven Ekstract, Group Publisher, *License! Global* magazine, "What *Pokémon Go* teaches us is that marrying a strong [addictive] brand to a new technology is a way for millions of consumers to adopt new technological concepts." Niantic Labs, the game company that created *Pokémon Go* has had a similar AR game in the market since 2012 called *Ingress*, which achieved more than 8 million downloads between 2012 and 2015. By contrast, *Pokémon Go* achieved 100 million downloads in 26 days with estimated revenue in its first 30 days topping $200 million. *Pokémon Go* has become so addictive that it has had to post warnings such as, "Do not trespass while playing *Pokémon Go*," and "Do not play *Pokémon Go* while driving," and "Do not enter dangerous areas while playing *Pokémon Go*" because injuries incurred while playing the game or complaints received about people trespassing in front of homes and businesses by "Pokémon trainers."[2]

"The brand has pushed the game into a different demographic; *Ingress* players are dedicated gamers, while *Pokémon Go* players are more casual. The game continues to generate an estimated $10 million per day, spending power is driven by the fact that 78% of players are 18- to 34-year-old," adds Ekstract. To emphasize the power of this addictive brand, Nintendo, the parent company of Pokémon, had an increase in market value of $9 billion just five days after the release of the app.

What this shows us is the power that branding has in mainstreaming new technology in the consumer product business. Nintendo rightly understood that the Pokémon brand equity is key to successful product marketing and in keeping a 20-year-old brand fresh.[3]

---

2. http://www.ew.com/article/2016/07/31/pokemon-go-new-safety-warnings
3. https://tfmainsights.com/power-of-brand-licensing/

The power of Addictive can be seen as far back as 1930 when Stephen Slesinger purchased the U.S. and Canadian merchandising rights to A.A. Milne's Winnie the Pooh character as well as the television, recording, and other rights. Within a year the loveable bear was a $50 million business; that is almost $700 million in today's dollars. Slesinger would go on to license Pooh and his friends for the next three decades, creating a panoply of Pooh dolls, records, board games, puzzles, and films, before the rights were acquired in 1961 by the Walt Disney Company. Today, Winnie the Pooh is known in virtually every country and literally thousands of different Pooh products have been manufactured under license, generating billions of dollars in revenue.

By their very nature, addictive brands are part of our everyday lives. They are brands that buyers have easy access to, that reward on a range of levels, and that are uplifting and/or comforting in some way, which is what gives them their addictive quality. For these reasons, they tend to be consumer-facing and many have a strong media and social media profile that gives them ongoing presence in consumers' lives. What's particularly interesting from a brand expansion perspective is how these brands use that presence not just to grow their consumer base but, as we shall see soon, to actively enhance their revenue model.

Today, the licensing models of major blockbusters are so deeply ingrained in how major film studios publicize and market a work, that it is easy to forget that this fully integrated model took some time to develop. Sure, there had been plenty of successful licensing programs dating back to the first half of the 20th century, but the game plan for turning films into expanded platforms really hits its straps on May 25, 1977 with the release of *Star Wars* by 20th Century Fox. The George Lucas series would prove a tipping point for expanding the scope and ambition of film revenues, paving the way for other successful franchises including *Batman*, *Transformers*, and *Frozen*.

Around the time the first *Star Wars* film was due to be released, Marc Pevers was Director of Business Affairs, working in the licensing section for 20th Century Fox,[4] which held the rights to the Star Wars brand. Charlie Lippincott, who worked for George Lucas, was responsible for promoting the release. In the build up to the premiere, Pevers says Lippincott negotiated a *Star Wars* comic book deal and then went to Trekkie conventions to get the word out about the new release.[5]

While Lippincott seemed to feel that the movie would do well with sci-fi buffs, Pevers was not so sure. "Lucas, who was keen on licensing as a way to grow the brand, let me see a rough cut of the release despite my relatively low position." During the two-and-a-half-hour showing, Pevers observed that several children, who had accompanied their parents to the viewing, sat transfixed. To Pevers, who had witnessed children fidget through hundreds of movies geared to an older audience, this was nothing short of remarkable. "At that point, we knew it was going to be great for licensing."

But while Pevers may have formed a view of how he could take the brand global, film director George Lucas was not interested in making the job so easy for him. Pevers needed to be able to show the film to prospective licensees to stimulate sales, but Lucas, he says, insisted on secrecy. With his hands tied, Pevers could gain very little interest in the film at the 1977 Toy Fair, which took place in February that year. He left emotionally and physically exhausted with no major deals, despite having what he knew in his gut could be one of the greatest box office releases ever made. "Lego wouldn't touch it. We couldn't get on the Tonight Show back then. No one knew who Mark Hamill or Harrison Ford were." Pevers was stuck.

Fortunately, one company saw the potential. Bernard Loomis, who ran Kenner Toys, was prepared to spend a lot of money on TV and other advertising promoting an action-figure licensing program. It was a great match. "As a big company, Kenner could

4. Responsibilities included the rights to the original *Star Wars: Episode IV — A New Hope*, Shirley Temple film merchandise and any publishing activities.
5. These are Star Trek Conventions.

ensure there was a uniform look and packaging," Pevers recalls. "They could also afford to not over-produce; they were in it for the long haul."[6] As the launch loomed, Kenner faced a narrow selling window. Pevers and Fox wanted the toy company to have an action figure program ready for Christmas 1977, but Kenner was not able to produce the tool and dyes in time. Instead, the company released "an Early Bird Certificate package" that consisted of a large envelope of 12 action figure cutouts with a certificate kids could mail to Kenner and redeem for four *Star Wars* action figures. The package also contained a diorama display stand, stickers, and a *Star Wars* fan club membership card. Loomis knew this would connect with the young audience and buy Kenner sufficient time to produce the action figures on their timetable and without inventory risk.

Pevers says it was a brilliant concept, selling 50,000 figure sets in the first run. "For a kid back in the 1970s, getting something in the mail was like a gift that gave twice, once on the day you opened the present and the second time when the toys finally arrived." In fact, demand for the action figures and accessories was so high that even Kenner had difficulty fulfilling it. Sales of Kenner's *Star Wars* action figures reached 40 million units in 1978, accounting for revenue of $100 million.[7] To put that in perspective, that same year Fox grossed $40 million in total royalty revenue from all its other releases.

Total box office revenues for the original six *Star Wars* motion pictures would go on to exceed $5 billion, putting the series right up there with *James Bond* and *Harry Potter*. And while the movies themselves were hits, it was the earnings from the associated merchandising that forced a mindset shift at the studios. "Back then" says Pevers, "with the exception of Disney, studios didn't realize

---

6. In Pevers experience, small companies that had limited resources tried to extract as much revenue from their license as possible by producing licensed product to meet their most favorable projections. This offer saturated the market with too much licensed product.

7. *The Free Lance—Star* (1980). Toymakers are ready months ahead of Santa. *The Free Lance—Star*, February 18, 1980; *Ellensburg Daily Record* (1980). Killer Toys. *Ellensburg Daily Record*, June 19, 1980.

the importance of licensing." For many of them, this was a side business to help drive awareness of the real hero, which was the release itself. Any consumer products licensing revenue was considered gravy.

"Disney is the largest consumer products licensor in the world. Across so many categories and properties, Disney sets the pace," declares Tim Kilpin, former Executive Vice President at Mattel and Disney toy business executive in the early 2000s. For Disney, the consumer products business, which oversees all licensing, is an important pillar in their overall growth strategy. This is how they bring brands like Mickey and Pooh to life. "Disney always takes a holistic approach to managing their properties."

When Robert Iger, Chief Executive Officer of Walt Disney, negotiated the acquisition of Marvel Entertainment for $3.96 billion in 2009 and then, Lucas film in October of 2012 for $4.05 billion, many pundits in the entertainment industry thought the company had paid way too much for these properties. However, Disney knew the real value of both studios because they had factored in the consumer products royalty revenue they would generate on the portfolio of brands in addition to the box office revenue. According to Kilpin, "*Star Wars* is a brand and Disney thinks about it as such, just like they would any other brand. It is one thing to talk about *Star Wars* and Marvel as characters; it's another to understand each brand's full value."

Marvel Comics had been founded in 1939 by Martin Goodman as Timely Publications. Its first publication, *Marvel Comics #1*, was published in October of that year and introduced the superhero, the Human Torch, and the anti-hero, Namor, the Submariner. Marvel would go on, of course, to create some of the most memorable and licensable characters in entertainment, including Spider-Man, Iron Man, the X-Men, Wolverine, the Hulk, Fantastic Four, Captain America, and Ghost Rider. So while others may have evaluated Marvel on what they thought it was worth at the time, Iger considered the value of the wider Marvel universe. He saw opportunities to bring characters together, cross-reference and tease audiences into deeper levels of involvement.

Iger proved to be absolutely right. Since the buyout of Marvel, Disney has generated over $8.5 billion in global box receipts from the property with surprises like *Guardians of the Galaxy* grossing $774 million.[8] According to *The Licensing Letter*, *Spider-Man* leads the pack of brands with global retail sales of $1.3 billion in 2013. *The Avengers* brought in $325 million that same year. Meanwhile, *Star Wars Episode VII: The Force Awakens* has generated over $2 billion since it opened in North America through the month of December 2015.[9] Though the movie is expected to earn big bucks at the box office the real moneymaker for Disney is *Star Wars* merchandise. Analysts predict it will generate some $3 billion in sales in 2015, and $5 billion over the next 12 months.[10]

Disney wasn't the only ones to benefit from *Star Wars*. Hasbro's deep lineup of toys related to the blockbuster film led them to a 35% sales increase in their boys segment, helping overall revenue rise 13% to $1.47 billion, driven by a surge in demand for lightsabers, action figures, and other related toys. In fact, Hasbro's Chief Executive Brian Goldner has said the company's overall *Star Wars* business for 2015 was "very similar" to the nearly $500 million the company made in 2005 when the last installment of the original series hit theaters, and the company forecasts sales for 2016 to be around that level again.[11] Now that's an addictive brand!

Disney's rival Warner Brothers also has a long history with addictive licensed characters, including Looney Tunes and Scooby Doo. The *Looney Tunes* animated cartoon series began its run in movie theatres in 1930 and continued until the late 1960s. It would

8. http://www.newsarama.com/24999-disney-s-4-billion-marvel-buy-was-it-worth-it.html

9. http://www.boxofficemojo.com/movies/?id=starwars7.htm

10. http://www.forbes.com/sites/natalierobehmed/2015/12/16/how-disneys-star-wars-merchandise-is-set-to-make-billions/#3a1d2f7541a4

11. Ziobro, P., & Hufford, A. (2016). 'Star Wars' is the force behind strong Hasbro sales. *The Wall Street Journal*, February 8, 2016.

produce such highly recognizable and heavily licensed characters as Bugs Bunny, Daffy Duck, Porky Pig, Elmer Fudd, Sylvester, Tweety, Wile E. Coyote, Road Runner, Foghorn Leghorn, Yosemite Sam, Pepe Le Pew, and Speedy Gonzales. More recently, Warner Bros has acquired the character stable of what was once DC Comics to build what is dubbed "The DC Extended Universe."

DC Comics was originally created in 1934 and would ultimately become one of the largest and most successful publishers in the comic book market, developing and popularizing such characters as Superman, Batman, Wonder Woman, Green Lantern, Captain Marvel, and Catwoman.

In 1932, Jerry Siegel and Joe Shuster created the fictional super hero Superman and in 1938 sold the character rights to Detective Comics, Inc. (now DC Comics). With his distinctive red, blue, and yellow costume, cape and large "S," Superman was one of the early superhero characters and ultimately launched an entire superhero market for comic books and related licensed products as well as related characters, e.g., Supergirl and Superboy. The earliest Superman licensed product appears to have been marketed in 1939 as a button signifying membership to the Superman Club of America. In 1940, Superman featured for the first time in the Macy's Thanksgiving Parade. During World War II, the U.S. Navy Department mandated the inclusion of Superman comic books as part of the supplies provided to U.S. Marines at Midway. In that decade, licensed Superman merchandise included jigsaw puzzles, paper dolls, bubble gum, trading cards, and wooden or metal figures. Today, of course, Superman is still a global success — and the two mega-universes, Marvel and DC, are at war for billions of dollars in film and ancillary revenues. It is literally a fight for control of the known world between two vast leagues of superheroes. More on that soon. Still, with the launch of the *Wonder Woman* movie in 2017, generating record sales at the box office for more than $620 million in its first three weeks, DC Comics may have tipped the balance back in their favor. In fact, some analysts predict *Wonder Woman* will also overtake Disney's *Frozen* movie, made in 2013, which generated $1.28 billion in ticket sales.[12]

According to Kilpin, a successful execution never just takes the form of movie or television content. Merchandise plays a critical role and can fill apparel, home furnishing, or even kitchen categories. The key thing he says is that in choosing categories, brands need to tie their programs back to a consumer perspective. "For long-lived characters, the brands must execute consumer research to understand which demographic is most connected to the brand and how," he says. "Brand owners look [carefully] at gender *and* geography. For example, Donald Duck in France does incredibly well." Disney, he says, looks at brand equity scores to evaluate its brands and conducts proprietary work to glean information.

They use these to determine if a brand is dormant, what its latent qualities are, and which categories and retail partners are needed to engage the brand in a fresh way. Regardless of what program or brand is being considered, *everything* starts with the consumer.

As a result, their returns, by every yardstick — whether you look at brand equity performance measurements, gross revenue, net operating profit, or stock price — have outperformed the other studios.

Simon Waters, General Manager of Consumer Products at Hasbro, says it's about recognizing successes and then giving consumers every opportunity to play and engage with those characters, and universes, in ways they enjoy. "We are in every category you can imagine: fashion, home goods, bedding, stationery, location based entertainment, and Hasbro live theme parks, each expressing our brands all the way around the consumer. Expansion takes consumers on a journey."

To be successful, a property must be about more than just familiar characters though. It has to offer authentic storytelling or play

---

12. http://www.bbc.com/news/entertainment-arts-40398892

value that engages people to want more. Once consumers connect with a brand, Kilpin says, they are prepared to purchase over and over again for as long as they see value in doing so. And while brands may place their faith in research, the fact remains that some brands simply take off for reasons that only buyers know. "No one could see that Minecraft would be a half a billion-dollar property," Kilpin observes, "but once consumers saw the value, it took off. Equally, no one would have called *Frozen* or *Angry Birds*. *Minions* is another example. NBC Universal's *Despicable Me* developed *Minions* as breakout characters. Now after three movies, *Minions* is its own franchise."

But the play for addictive brands is more than just a wish to lift customer loyalty. Drill a little deeper and it becomes clear that it is also an integral part of the revenue model. In a three-part examination of the film industry, Matthew Ball explains that only 4 of 18 blockbusters in 2013 actually grossed enough at the box office to actually cover their production and marketing budgets. The major studios, he says, have invested more and more in each picture each year. Between 2003 and 2013 those increases in investment generated a 22% increase in ticket sales, but production and marketing spends also doubled in that time, meaning in effect that cost per ticket grew at twice the rate of net revenue.

On the face of it, this looks like a disaster: movie studios overspending by millions of dollars. So why do they keep investing? Because, says Ball, box office receipts only account for 52% of revenue for the average blockbuster film. The rest comes from ancillary revenue: home video sales, pay-per-view, licensing, syndication fees, and merchandising; and this has fundamentally changed the role of the core product. Movie releases are no longer required to make all the money in order for the studio to make its revenue. Today, while they are focused on recouping as much cost as possible, the real interest of every potential blockbuster is in building the addictive interest needed to sustain and feed a multi-platform media experience. "The majors have successfully transformed their products into truly mass audience 'event films'. While these films typically do not deliver a positive return … they establish a platform through which entertainment becomes a recurring service."

There's the key word right there: *recurring*. If you're looking to grow an addictive brand, you're looking to take engagement beyond the 'one-off' encounter. Having established a primary relationship, the goal is to broaden and deepen the involvement of consumers beyond the point of entry. In the case of movies, for example, that's about extending the relationship the consumer has with the brand beyond one seat at one session.

In other words, the films set the scene, so to speak, for what follows. Everything is about ecosystems. The business side of movie-making today is about creating characters that people are drawn to and that they will continue to interact with, through further films in the series, through spin-offs featuring individual characters, and through broader experiences such as rides and toys. That's why the characters and the play worthiness of the different experiences are so important. They are the expansion point for the business model and the connection point for consumers. They provide the motivation to see and do more.

That idea is equally applicable in the digital space. When Darran Garnham, currently CEO at MTW Toys and former Chief Commercial Officer of Mind Candy joined Mind Candy in 2009, it was just a small start-up with a handful of employees. At that point, the company had no licensing. "In the beginning, they used to relegate me to the end of Board meetings and call what I did 'toys'." These days everyone at the company takes licensing a lot more seriously. Over a period of 18 months, expanding its brands into other sectors grew to become 50% of Mind Candy's overall revenue. Today, the company generates $1 billion of retail sales in video games and collectibles, predominantly in the UK market.

Mind Candy has two very well-known brands: *Moshi Monsters*, the original game on which the company built its fan base, and then in 2015, *World of Warriors*, a freemium game aimed at core gamers young and older. Later that same year, to accompany the launch of the mobile game *World of Warriors: Duel*, they introduced a range of 120 action figures along with

World of Warriors' battle gear weapons and accessories, and a range of publications including action-adventure books.

All of this is about immersing fans deeper in the worlds of their favorite characters and enhancing the experiences Mind Candy delivers its digital fans. Garnham told me that digital can be fantastic for dealing with a fan base, but it also has its limitations. The reason Mind Candy has looked for ways to engage beyond its digital platforms was because they understood the need to give fans new opportunities to interact. They also recognized opportunities to monetize their audiences away from digital channels. Ironically, by doing this, Garnham said they also attract more digital users to the brands. "Digital may be the core of our business, but unlike a lot of digitally-based companies we don't only focus there. We see physical as an intriguing piece of the process. It helps consumers come on a journey with us, and pay to stay on that journey over time."

The channels may be changing, but the human emotions that drive how and why consumers get hooked on brands are much more durable. Ted Larkins, SVP/General Manager at CPLG North America, says it's all about creating new things and that means you need to stay open to the possibilities, communicate clearly with all parties and know your intentions. A prime example of seeing and seizing the opportunity occurred in Japan way before the days of sophisticated product placement. Pink Panther was one of the studio's properties. "One day, one of the team spotted a paparazzi photo of a Japanese pop star, Namie Amuro, with a Pink Panther keychain hanging out her pocket," Larkins remarked. "Someone else said they had contacts at the star's management company. So the team put together a box of Pink Panther merchandise and sent it over."

Clearly, it struck a chord. When the singer released her next album, *Queen of Hip-Pop*, the whole theme was Pink Panther. She even had a Pink Panther in her likeness and a key video from the album also used the character. Things exploded from there. With the studio on board, the team was able to build a multi-million dollar Pink Panther program around the album with the help of 30 different licenses. There was even a Pink Panther store. "It took a lot of work," Larkins remarked, "and it certainly doesn't happen all the time like that, but if there's an opportunity to capitalize on interest this way, everyone benefits."

"What consumer products do," adds Kilpin, "is that they allow people to touch and feel the brand in new ways." And that's what builds the intrigue and delivers the emotional rewards. It's the search for those things that fires the changes in human behavior that brands depend on when they look to move closer to consumers' lives.

Let's take a closer look at that concept. Dr. B.J. Fogg has developed the Fogg Behavior Model to explain what it takes for humans to behave in certain ways. Each behavior, he says, requires three things: motivation, ability, and a trigger. Motivations can range from high to low depending on the activity. Ability, in turn, is dependent on the individual. Something is either hard to do or it is not. And triggers impel action or they fail to do so. It makes sense, based on this model, that in order for something to be addictive, the motivation and ability need to be aligned, i.e., there needs to be the right balance of willingness and feasibility and there needs to be sufficient triggers for people to want to take ongoing actions. When that happens, an action can take place. As consumers take more actions, and the more rewarded they feel through taking those actions, the more likely they are to repeat the same action and/or respond to a similar trigger.

In the world of entertainment, we're drawn to characters and personalities because they engage us: they may entertain us; they may outrage us; they may express or capture something we agree with or that excites us. That engagement creates intrigue. We become determined to find out more. And that demand generates the motivation needed to follow a character for as long as they remain interesting.

Ability is generated by access. Our abilities to "follow" a person or a character, emulate them, learn more about them, or take up their next invitation, are directly proportional to their visibility in our lives. The more we see them, and the more we like what we see, the more inclined we are to want more.

The triggers come through opportunities to participate: to see them in concert, to go to the movie, to buy the limited edition set, to buy the merchandise, to attend the convention ... and to join the many others who are also involved.

In order for a brand to be addictive, there needs to be the right combination of frequency, intensity, and access. I've talked a lot here about the addictive nature of the entertainment properties, but the quality is equally applicable to other sectors that intersect frequently with people. Technology, for example, has become a "must-have" industry as the big brands look to lock consumers more tightly into their ecosystems, thus the power of *Pokémon Go*. Professional sports have also played to the passions of their consumer bases, giving fans plenty of ways to express their loyalty and relive the joy of their favorite games.

At the same time, there are those who argue, with some justification, that the movie industry is in danger of becoming so formulaic in the way it works within its universes that it removes the very quality that it is looking to build. A number of people raised concerns with me that some of the films they had seen were closer to long film trailers for upcoming releases than quality stand-alone experiences in their own right. Their concern draws attention to a quality that I think is essential in keeping people involved in a brand: surprise. There needs to be enough elements of 'new' in where and how brands extend and expand that they entice customers down those paths in search of something about which they're intrigued.

At the beginning of this chapter, we talked about the fact that curiosity is a key driver of addictiveness. It's fascinating to look at some of the science behind why we're drawn to want to know more. Apparently, our natural curiosity as humans and our wish to explore can be linked to a trait called neoteny. Neoteny means, in essence, that as humans we retain key characteristics from our childhood, including an insatiable appetite for wanting to know more. While structure and routine are part of the way we each organize our lives, distraction gives our brains something else to think about. As Tom Stafford observes:

> Curiosity is nature's built-in exploration bonus. We've evolved to leave the beaten track, to try things out, to get distracted and generally look like we're wasting time. Maybe we are wasting time today, but the learning algorithms in our brain know that something we learned by chance today will come in useful tomorrow.

Building an exploration bonus into your brand makes the hunt worth it, and brings each of us back for more. It also builds buyers' cognitive memories and understanding of the brand.

How does Addictive tie into the rest of our Model? If the purpose of Lateral in the LASSO Model is to ensure that the brand has the right presence in the right markets to make the most of its product lines, the Addictive quality is all about driving up demand and revenue by providing buyers with more and more reasons to grow their interest, and investment, in the brand. It's a quality that is particularly applicable today because of how much brands give away through their freemium models. The Addictive element locks all that free or limited-purchase activity into revenue models that reward brands for all the work they're now expected to put in upfront. It's what drives returns because it motivates consumers to spend in a world where they increasingly expect so much to simply be delivered to them.

For corporates looking to find new ways to engage with their consumers, and keep their attention, there are opportunities here to shift beyond just promotional involvement to partnered license deals that grow the market for all involved, in the way that Hasbro and Disney have done with *Star Wars*. Another example is the partnership between Microsoft's 343 Industries and Mattel, which resulted in a Master Licensing arrangement in 2016 under the Halo MEGA Blocks franchise. "The success we've seen with the Halo MEGA Blocks franchise over the years laid the foundation for this partnership," said Bonnie Ross, Microsoft Corporate Vice President and Head of 343 Industries. "We're excited to work with Mattel to bring innovative, quality and, most of all, fun products to old and new Halo fans alike."[13] Each benefits from the involvement of the other by growing the overall "access" that consumers have to the brand, and each brings a perspective to the end line up that keeps consumers interested. I talked earlier about the fact that Lego showed very little interest in the initial release of *Star Wars*. Today, Lego is a key partner in that franchise's universe, bringing its own dimension of play, and fascination, to the series. Remember too, my pin trading story from Chapter 1? That's another example of brands working together to deliver consumers a unique line up that they were willing to queue to acquire.

The Addictive quality should also be of real interest to smaller companies looking at how they can leverage the qualities of a known brand to gain a foothold in key markets. Traditionally, licensees have looked to provide an item or a small number of items to a wider range. They have, in essence, contributed to the catalog. But if they want to take their business beyond being inventory suppliers, what they may want to look more closely at is a line up of related items that talk to the master brand and at the same time have addictive qualities in their own right. In other words, use their specialist knowledge but also build an exploration bonus into what they're licensed to produce, because that's the only way that a smaller company can continue to contribute new aspects, grow business in its own right, and establish a reputation for adding value creatively not just logistically. I believe Niantic Labs, the game company that created *Pokémon Go*, is a perfect example of this type of creative growth strategy. Leverage and delight, don't just supply. The former is what you're paying for the right to do. The latter is what you will end up doing if you don't have a clear plan.

---

13. http://news.xbox.com/2016/02/12/343-industries-and-mattel-sign-master-licensing-agreement-introduce-new-halo-toys/#iJw7BvFIwpp6rDcd.99

Building an Addictive brand is about building powerful connective tissue between the parts — hints, cues, rewards — that play to people's curiosity and incite them to take the time to explore. It's all about thinking through what consumers would like to see happen next; what would add to the pleasure they get from the brand now. Building out an Addictive Thought-Map in this way allows you to build connections for consumers in fascinating ways that in turn drive more and more involvement. This is how you keep people glued to your brand in the iterative economy. It's also how you distinguish an enduring success from a fad. Only time will tell whether *Pokémon Go* has what it takes to defy Ries' prediction of inevitable decay, mentioned in the last chapter, or whether it can indeed continue to engage players at historically high levels.

Key Takeouts

- Addictive brands play to people's appetite for "more." Consumers are driven by the thrill of pursuit, the wish to be current and the fear of missing out, the expectation of availability, the strong sense of curiosity we're all born with, and the hyper awareness of the world around us that social media, in particular, has created.

- Addictive brands tend to be consumer-facing and many today have a strong media and social media profile that gives them presence in consumers' lives.

- It's easy to confuse the subject matter with the appeal. *Star Wars* may have been located in space, but its addictive quality for audiences extended far beyond the sci-fi genre.

- Extending or expanding your brand requires taking a holistic approach to managing your branded properties in order to realize their full potential. What more do people want exactly?

- Invest in categories that fit with the brand, but that also align with how and where consumers want to buy.

- Characters can make a brand addictive. However, what adds value and stickiness is authentic storytelling and/or play value.

- Sometimes consumers will hook into properties and ideas that take even the most skilled veterans by surprise. That's the power of serendipity.

- Everything today is about ecosystems. Increasingly addictiveness is part of the financial model not just the customer relationship model.

Keep them coming back; here are seven searching questions to judge whether you have a highly addictive brand:

1. What more does the brand deliver that people want — escapism, distraction, adventure, authority?

2. Will consumers see the connections between the various expressions of your brand? How will you direct them from one activity to another?

3. Do you understand the overall playbook? On what journey are you taking consumers? With what part of that journey are you involved?

4. How long do you want to keep customers buying? Is your involvement with the brand tied to a specific time frame or project, or is it longer?

5. Does your program have the best mix of frequency, intensity, access, and surprise?

6. What's your exploration bonus?

7. If you are the brand owner, is your core business inherently profitable? How dependent are you on ancillary revenue to hit your growth targets? And therefore, how big does your licensee community need to be?

Your Turn

In the previous chapter, we asked you to rate your brand's ability to extend or expand. Now let's do the same thing for Addictiveness. Please think about your answers to the seven questions we just asked and score your brand on its addictive potential below. Once again, there are no right or wrong answers. Some brands will feel that they are not addictive and have no interest in becoming addictive. Others will see opportunities to make a lot more frequently recurring income. Take a moment now to choose the number that best describes your brand's potential on the Addictive Expandability Score chart located on page 75 to keep buyers coming back for more. We'll come back and get this number later (see next page).

Were you able to select an Addictive score that matches your brand? If so, great job! Let's keep the momentum going. Now that you're assessed how Lateral and Addictive your brand is, when you're ready, turn to the next chapter and get ready to evaluate your brand from a Storied perspective, the third element of the LASSO Model.

Addictive Expandability Score Chart.

1	2	3	4	5
There are only limited opportunities to interact with our brand. We tend to work on an "as-required" basis.	We need to find new ways to involve our customers more within our core category. We need to give them more reasons to come back to us.	We could be more inventive in how we involve people with our brand. We need to forge stronger links between what we continue to give them and what we ask them to continue to pay for.	Our brand is compelling enough to expand into whole new areas and to take our audiences with us. We'll change our revenue model by continuing to surprise and delight via what they can access.	Our "core business" is just the starting point for a highly inclusive, engaging journey with our customers that spans all sorts of touchpoints. That journey is where we generate the real money.

Storied — The Power of Heritage in a World of Action

5

Without [story], there's a very real risk that a brand will become a mono-lith: a towering presence, dispossessed of soul and humanity, and one that consumers find hard to align with.

Stories are now an accepted part of marketing. Narrative works because it is a way of explaining an idea in a way that naturally makes sense to humans. Storytelling and story listening are intuitive. So it will come as no surprise that we agree that the ability of a brand to tell a story, or stories, that people connect with is vital to its success. In fact, I would go so far as to suggest that any brand wishing to add value to what it offers probably needs to add a story if it wishes to enhance how it is perceived.

In *All Marketers Are Liars*, Seth Godin said that successful marketers deliver stories that people want to believe about themselves, about others, and about the world as they see it. The huge power of stories, he pointed out, was that they enable us to process information in ways that capture our imagination.[1] As he says about Coke, "We drink the can, not the beverage."[2]

---

1. http://www.summary.com/book-reviews/_/All-Marketers-Are-Liars/
2. http://fourminutebooks.com/all-marketers-are-liars-summary/

Here are five things that make people believe that something has merit:[3]

1. They trust what is being said — in other words, it comes from a source they know and that others trust in. Powerful brands tell powerful truths because of the credibility they carry.

2. There is consistency — the story adds up. It is coherent. There is a clear logic that holds it all together, underpinned by a central premise that speaks to the consumer. That premise may be rational or emotive. The key thing is that it is powerful and motivating, and everything about that idea, and that springs from it, aligns.

3. There is detail — specifics add to the sense that something is real. Evidence, such as numbers, is very powerful in that sense. It makes the story concrete by adding to the truth and consistency of what we are being told. Combined with other evidence such as examples and backstory, it adds to the perceived value of what we are being told.

4. The story is concise where it needs to be — brevity brings surety. It portrays confidence, where overstatement or elaboration can feel like a brand is trying to explain or justify itself.

5. The story mirrors something of the way we all live — when a story is about something that people know, or deals with situations or emotions for which they have a strong attachment, people build affinity with what they are hearing. It feels real to them, because the story "talks" about something they believe is real.

Another brand rich in story is Chupa Chups. According to Christine Cool, Area Licensing Manager at Perfetti Van Melle (PVM), "Salvador Dali designed the Chupa Chups brand back in 1968. Since then the lollipop has become an icon for consumers. There is a huge emotional value of our brands for consumers who remember their experience and feelings."

---

3. http://www.dougcarter.com/six-simple-ways-to-increase-your-credibility/

How stories work, and why they work, hasn't changed. But how we tell stories — and more particularly, how brands choose to tell their stories — has evolved considerably. Think about how we consume TV now. Television series used to tell stories in stand-alone chapters. These chapters happened on set channels at set times, with set interruptions for commercials. But the "Netflix effect" is changing all that. For a start, many of us no longer sit on a couch at an appointed time to watch a show. Binge watching and mobile watching have changed the way shows are structured.[4] Increasingly, those making series for TV are using product placement rather than commercials to monetize their models. And that, in turn, has changed how viewers get involved.

Storylines are becoming more episodic. Look at the series like *Stranger Things, Orange is the New Black, Suits, or The Americans*. They now include more in-jokes, returning characters, recurrent themes, etc. to draw people in and make them feel that the series is part of their world, one of the things they experience. By doing this, series makers are inviting people not just to watch once or when they can, but to catch the whole series at a time and in ways that suit them best. Can't watch now? OK, watch later. Enjoyed an episode? No problem, stay there and watch another ... and another ... with no commercials, and with complete viewer control.

That has created new problems for the TV industry and for marketers, of course. As *The Guardian* observed:

> by weaning audiences from live viewing and teaching them to binge on their own schedule, all without commercials, Netflix is killing the goose that laid the golden egg. While audiences are watching more television than ever, they're watching less of it live, causing ad revenue to shrink. A big part of the problem is an ad buying system built around live viewing and the

---

4. http://fortune.com/2016/03/11/netflix-changing-game-network-tv/

Nielsen ratings to measure it ... That mistake is compounded by the ad industry's inability to work out how to serve up a similarly robust ad load ....[5]

The problem for many brands is that while they are good at telling stories, most have yet to learn how to "live" a story. That's because brands have tended to use stories for communications, and they have told those stories in short bursts and in campaigns. As a result, brand stories for many years have been expressions of media flights. A campaign with a story. Then another campaign with another story. Many in response to a business wish, or a strategic change. With very little to hold them together or to tie back to the new sense of story that now interests consumers. That hasn't really changed in the shift to digital channels.

More recently, some brands have looked to craft what David Aaker refers to as "signature stories":[6] stories that are intriguing, involving, authentic, and have a strategic message. Lifebuoy's "Help a Child Reach 5" and Always "Like a Girl" are stories and they are campaigns, but they also point the way for a brand to do more interesting things. They signal the commitment of both brands to look to achieve change in the world. While the cynic may say that they are heart-warming narratives that still lead to the sell, they can also serve to focus a brand on what it intends to contribute and how it wishes to be valued. This is next-level storytelling where stories try to help change the world, or at the very least to better define the world that the brands see as desirable to them.

But beyond that still, companies like Disney have spent many years taking storytelling to a completely different place. They have, in effect, constructed whole universes: connected storylines happening in defined worlds that revolve around a group of characters for whom people care. A universe can be described as the

5. https://www.theguardian.com/media-network/2015/feb/05/netflix-subscription-services-television-ad-revenues
6. https://www.prophet.com/thinking/2017/01/higher-purpose-programs-make-powerful-brand-stories/

scope of what you do. It provides the context for a series of immersive experiences, multimedia and/or multi dimensional, that happen inside that world. The characters of DC Comics, for example, congregate in the DC Universe.[7] *Lord of the Rings, Avatar, 1984,* and *Star Trek* all take place in defined universes. While the idea may seem relatively new, it is in fact as old as Sir Thomas More's *Utopia.*[8]

Each universe is, in turn, governed by a set of rules or principles. Peter von Stackelberg has a lovely term for these. He calls them storyworlds.[9] A storyworld is "the governing principles and parameters by which occupants of the Story-World (characters and events) will adhere."[10] By way of example, Batman operates within clear rules of engagement in Gotham City. He doesn't trust the police and the police don't trust him, but they share a goal of getting rid of crime, and that principle extends across much of the Batman canon.[11] As a result, there is a consistency and a predictability to how Batman behaves that makes the character believable. A storyworld extends a framework for the interactions that characters have toward each other. Its role is to help build a powerful mythology: an understanding of the world and its purpose that attracts people to the universe.

Danny Simon, owner of The Licensing Group Ltd, had the privilege of working on the 1991 *Terminator 2: Judgment Day* (*T2*) film, which was a sequel to the movie *Terminator* that was launched in 1984, and whose mythology is rich and powerful, with a universe that is as deep and defined as any created in recent history. In the first movie, Arnold Schwarzenegger, stars as the Terminator, a metal endoskeleton with a mimetic polyalloy covering programed to assassinate, who is sent back in time from 2029 to 1984 to kill Sarah Connor (played by Linda

7. Read about the DC Universe in more detail here: https://en.wikipedia.org/wiki/DC_Universe
8. https://en.wikipedia.org/wiki/Fictional_universe
9. http://transmediadigest.blogspot.co.nz/2011/11/storyworlds-what-are-they.html
10. http://blogs.aftrs.edu.au/screenculture/?p=690
11. http://convergenceishere.weebly.com/storyworlds.html

Hamilton), to prevent her son, John, from becoming the leader of the Resistance against the machines in a post apocalyptic future. In *T2*, Sarah and her young son, John, are pursued by a new, more advanced Terminator, the liquid metal, shape-shifting T-1000, sent back to kill John Connor and prevent him from becoming the leader of the human resistance. Schwarzenegger's character, an inferior model in *T2*, is reprogrammed and must now protect John against the T-1000. He will do anything to save John Connor:

> *Terminator 2* would be the property I worked with the longest in my career. I started a year before it began filming through 2011. We licensed a wide range of products from toys to apparel, to books, to very expensive collectible products that were replicas of iconic pieces of the film such as the Endoskeleton and the Endoarm.

With a powerful universe and mythology to leverage, the merchandise program thrived despite losing rights to the Schwarzenegger image shortly after the film launched, as Schwarzenegger went on to star in other films. Simon elaborates:

> Left without rights to the film's star, we revised the licensing program to feature the Endoskeleton. T2 was an extraordinary movie. It broke ground in many ways certainly in the technology area where things like *morphing* were created; for licensing, it reached a level of success that very few R rated films attain.

Much of the retail success attributed to the *Terminator* property can be attributed to the indomitability of its universe and the allure of its mythology. Approximately, $1 billion of retail licensed merchandise sold worldwide for *T2* alone.

In the context of a brand, the universe is probably the ambition or purpose of the brand. The mythology encompasses the ideas, rules, and beliefs that hold that universe together and drive it forward, making it expandable. For example, Intel built its mythology on Moore's Law. Apple built theirs for many years around the vision of Steve Jobs. That mythology serves to build, and align, the brand's reputation. For B2C brands, the mythology may focus on the product itself or on the vision of the world that it inhabits. For B2B brands, it may be driven by a wish to change how business happens, how people work, what gets accomplished, or even how history is shaped.

"Start with the mythology," Simon Waters, General Manager of Consumer Products at Hasbro, urged when I spoke to him. Understand the biggest impression you are seeking to build, based on the core DNA of the brand. What could it be? Where could it go? Who else could be involved? What could happen? Build a story for the brand that goes far beyond a game, an event, or a product, and that only becomes stronger and more powerful as others contribute and partner. Through storytelling, Waters says, a brand like Hasbro looks to take consumers to a different understanding, one with which fans are passionately engaged. "Organizationally, I would say that we are great storytellers. Once you tell a great story it is really easy to fit all the chapters together. You kind of know where it is headed," remarks Waters:

> We continue to do such a good job of telling our brand franchise story. We are thinking of them not as a product, but actually as a story. I think that has helped coalesce the company against the story. Storytelling is a medium [people] have used for hundreds of thousands of years to transfer information. There is no better way to do that then telling a story.

Gaming and entertainment brands understand these concepts intuitively because they must literally create and populate the worlds in which viewers and players are invited. They then look to their partners to bring those worlds to life in multiple ways. One of the most interesting aspects of this was the time frames in which these brands worked. John Friend, Head of Consumer Products and International Expansion at 343 Industries, the company behind the Halo franchise, told us their storylines and outlines for the game are 10—15 years ahead of the current action. Releases, updates, and new products are slotted into these storylines as and when they fit. When Mark Di Somma and I visited John and the 343 team at their office in Redmond, Seattle, the immediate impression on entering their building was that we had literally stepped into the Halo world. From the huge sculptures of the characters to the museum that tells the story of Halo so far, the gameosphere, if we can call it that, was a living, breathing, action-packed entity. Intrigued, we peered longingly down forbidden corridors and up stairwells, wondering what on earth was being created and perfected on that day alone.

One of the great benefits of operating a universe is that stories do not need to be linear. A universe gives creators the space and environment they need to roam, uncover, segue, revert, focus, elaborate, etc. Storylines can also be cross-referenced. For example, one of the intriguing things about the way Pixar has built its universe is that characters from one film make cameos in others.[12]

Universes can even change. *Rogue One*, which we referenced earlier, is part of a complete redefining of the *Star Wars* universe.[13] The Expanded Universe that had been developed to take George Lucas' vision beyond the three original movies was superseded in 2014 as Disney set about in-filling the saga with new stories that fit in and around the chronological episodes. That Expanded Universe as termed by Lucas was built on narratives that took the characters that moviegoers knew many years into the future, and at the same time revealed new personalities who had stories of their own. Now, new books and programs have been released that add new layers, and new revenue streams, to the *Star Wars* universe. According to the Bloomberg article:

---

12. http://www.stuff.co.nz/entertainment/film/88583015/disney-release-clip-exposing-the-pixar-universe-all-the-characters-are-related
13. https://www.bloomberg.com/news/articles/2016-12-16/-rogue-one-is-just-a-first-step-in-a-larger-star-wars-world?cmpid=BBD121616_BIZ

... many of the new books also follow the old Expanded Universe formula, filling gaps in the main storyline or looking into secondary characters that drew fan interest. A trilogy dubbed *Aftermath* is part of a 20-title effort to address the gap between *Return of the Jedi*, the sixth episode of the primary films, and *The Force Awakens*, the seventh.

The search for wider and more cohesive involvement isn't restricted to storytellers in the entertainment sector. It's an intrinsic need for all brands as they grow today because virtually no one can do so alone. As Ron Adner points out in *The Wide Lens*,[14] the scope for success has broadened. Once everything depended on channeling volume efficiently and effectively down supply chains to market. Today though, solutions are multi dimensional, integrated and require the inputs of a range of suppliers. A car can't just be a car anymore, he points out. Today, it must house state-of-the-art connectivity, navigation, safety, and sound systems. Some of that may be original equipment manufacturer (OEM). Some may be ingredient brands. Either way, the product itself, and the brand it represents, is no longer a single output from a single source. And in order to deliver what's required, and to do so to the quality and with the speed and consistency expected by today's consumers, brands must have a masterful ecosystem strategy.

Companies tend to focus on their own execution according to Ron Adner.[15] But to innovate successfully, they need to broaden their viewpoint to include co-innovation (i.e., who else needs to innovate for my innovation to matter?) and adoption chain (i.e., who else needs to adopt my innovation before the end customer can assess the full value proposition?)

---

14. Adner, R. (2013). *The wide lens: What successful innovators see that others miss.* Portfolio. Retrieved from https://www.amazon.com/Wide-Lens-Successful-Innovators-Others/dp/1591846293/?tag=thwilebo-20

15. http://thewidelensbook.com/excerpt.html

What has been fascinating is watching how Caterpillar, the B2B company, was able to connect with a whole new class of future customers by creating a line of consumer products through licensing partnerships. Kenny Beaupre, Brand Advocacy and Licensing Manager, told us:

> When we think about where our strategy started, we are kind of an unusual story. We are basically a B2B brand. We sell our core products and services to dealers. They in turn sell them to consumers. For us to be a B2B brand with a B2C connection it is actually different and not something many other B2B brands have been able to do. Some of the others that license very well have already been in a B2C space. This is a little bit different. Some of it comes from the success of our licensees. We have been able to partner with some great companies that have done a lot to build the brand in their respective categories. 25 years ago when we started, we asked what kind of products would a tractor owner need to do their job? We got into safety shoes, work wear and eye protection. We were able to cross over. Consumers gave Caterpillar permission to extend into new categories. Anyone can logo slap and put a brand on anything. What has been successful for us is when we have used our brand and marketed to our brand attributes — to the strength, to the durability, to the quality, to the rugged, to the tough. Whenever we have stayed close to our core attributes, that's when we have had success.

It's time to move beyond stand-alone projects and to collaborate with others. The days of autonomous innovation are over. "Winning in ecosystems requires winning more than the execution race," says Adner. "It demands that you create coherent alignment among a network of partners, each of whom will succeed in their own execution, and each of whom is willing to collaborate productively with the other partners."

Storying offers a powerful way to do that. It provides a powerful means to bring people together and to forge a common view of
what is required and how it can happen.

Perhaps nowhere is the layering of stories clearer than in brands
that have a long and proud history. These brands have heritage on
their side, so they are trusted and they have the consistency and
detail that provide belief. But increasingly they must find ways to
tell their stories briefly and in a manner in which people can relate.

NFL is a juggernaut. In any given season, some 17 million people
will attend a game in person and hundreds of millions more will
watch at least one game on TV.[16] What started out as a meeting of
four teams in an Ohio car showroom in 1920 is now a multi-billion
dollar, multi-channel business. Storytelling has played no small
part in driving the legend of the NFL. Steve Scebelo, who runs business development and licensing for the NFL Players Association
(NFLPA), sees it as his job to give fans a greater opportunity to follow their favorite players and to experience those players outside of
the traditional football game. This enhances the story. One way the
NFLPA has done this is through Madden NFL.

> EA Sports has been a licensee for longer than NFL
> Players Inc., the licensing and marketing arm of the
> NFLPA has been in existence, which has been 24 years.
> Madden NFL has put out its 27th edition. EA clearly
> saw and understood the value of having the players'
> rights included into its product. We have grown that
> relationship along the way. The traditional console
> games continue to drive the business, but it's been
> encouraging to see how many people are continuing to
> play the game digitally, downloading it directly through
> their Xbox [as well as] those who are playing the game
> year round by doing the online upgrades. Draft night is
> especially great to see. Jameis Winston gets drafted by
> the Bucs and you can have him playing as a Buccaneers'

---

16. http://www.shmoop.com/nfl-history/summary.html

quarterback that night in uniform in EA. You don't have
to wait until August when the console release comes out
to play. You can download the update and go.

By building up the history of the teams and the players, the
story has become about more than the game. It has become a live-
to-air struggle between brands determined to win. But it has also
given an elite sport a very human face. The entertainment, the
signings, and the results mean the story is continually refreshed.
Stats and opinions add interest on the day, especially in a Fantasy
Football crazed world. Scebelo expounds:

> What is interesting to us too is how Fantasy Football has
> played a role in helping drive business. We see more
> fans who are fans of players. It's because they have
> them on their fantasy team. Even though they might be
> in a specific geographic area they may find themselves
> rooting for a player who is on a different team because
> he is on their Fantasy team.

And beyond that, the epic struggles, the historic rivalries, and the
plays and games that everyone deliberates have provided a wider
context within which to build the mythology that this is the most
gargantuan of games.

It's interesting to look at how Wimbledon, the oldest tennis
tournament in the world, is changing its game, so to speak, to
ensure that it can balance prestige, history, and tradition with relevance. Held at the All England Club in London, Wimbledon is one
of the four Grand Slam tennis tournaments. It has an estimated
global audience of 1 billion people. Today, social media plays a
critical role in getting all sorts of brands to engage with the event,
and of course to engage their customers.[17] In addition to social
feeds that follow the build up to the event itself, the arrival of the
stars and the big games, Wimbledon increasingly serves as a

---

17. http://digitalsport.co/how-social-media-enhanced-wimbledon-2016

staging post for other brands to tell stories about themselves in a Wimbledon context. IBM may highlight the data they have compiled. The various sportswear brands show their gear in action on some of the biggest names in tennis. Sponsors like Lavazza coffee create events and footage around the event that enables them to feel part of the action. The goal, as the Club's head of communications, content and digital, put it, is to make the virtual experience of Wimbledon "the next best thing to being here."[18] And that has nothing to do with selling tickets, because the event itself is 10 times oversubscribed. Rather it's about future-proofing the heritage of Wimbledon; it's about making sure that, as their audience ages, younger viewers across the world enroll themselves in following what is happening at the only major tennis event played on lawn.

Of course, there's a very long list of heritage brands in sports alone that are doing this: Formula One; the All Blacks; Major League Baseball; the NBA; the Olympics. All have seen that longevity provides a bank of backstories that give a brand status. The power of heritage is uniquely revealed through this story that Rick White, President at Atlantic League of Professional Baseball and former CEO of Major League Baseball Properties shares:

> Around 1989 some retired firemen opened up a bar in Brooklyn called the "Brooklyn Dodger." Peter O'Malley, the owner of the Los Angeles Dodgers couldn't believe this could happen. The Dodgers, however, had never trademarked their rights to the Brooklyn Dodgers and had little recourse.
>
> O'Malley said to me, "How can I ever prevent this from happening again?"
>
> I told him, "There is only one way to do this. You need to create products that says Brooklyn Dodgers and sell it in interstate commerce."

18. http://www.usatoday.com/story/sports/tennis/2016/07/10/wimbledon-social-media-brings-fans-closer-action/86920326/

He said, "Well, I don't want that to happen."

I said, "Then you are going to have to deal with Brooklyn Dodgers bars and merchandise going forward without any say."

O'Malley ultimately agreed.

Today, when you see people who wear retro-inspired merchandise, this is the story of how it originated. Out of that discussion we invented what is now known as the Cooperstown Collection. In our first year, the Cooperstown collection, driven largely by the Brooklyn Dodgers, generated over $30 million in royalties. If you extrapolate the royalties, it generated $600 million in revenue out of the box. This was the beginning of throwback products. From the collection, we had this incredible arc in terms of growth. The Cooperstown Collection was the kind of innovation borne from necessity that drove the growth for MLBP.

Fashion brands too have seen opportunities to combine the long stories of their history with the short stories of seasonal releases. But there are still many brands, even in this age of increased content marketing, that have fallen short in creating a rounded, fascinating, dimensioned portrayal of who they are, who they've been, what drives them, and what they do that entices buyers' engagement. The fact is that it is simply not enough today to make a film, post something groovy, or run a series of attractive, but disconnected, campaigns held together with a logo.

Increasingly, brands, particularly expanding brands, need to paint a storied world in the minds of shoppers and viewers that is intriguing and involving. Social media does not create that world. It may provide glimpses into it, and it may even open doors. But the world itself must come from the vision and the imagination of those involved.

This is true even when the subject matter itself is awesome and inspiring in its own right. Take this interview with Matt Walker, in which he talks about how BBC Earth has continued to adapt:

> BBC Earth originated as a television brand. We broadcast programs and expected people to turn up to watch. But digital media has transformed the way we distribute our content. Even online, we can no longer publish to web pages and expect audiences to come and find us. We have to place ourselves where our audiences are; and interact with them on their terms.[19]

As per Ron Adner's points about the need to co-innovate, brands may create universes, but increasingly they cannot do so alone. They need to work with other brands that act as innovators and inhabitants. And they need to work with customers. John Friend, Head of Consumer Products and International Expansion at 323 Industries, the company behind the Halo franchise, has a great description for this phenomenon. He talks about "Consumer 720." Brands must build stories, with others, that consumers engage with and in which they feel a part. But they must also be open to letting consumers create matching worlds or to expand the universe itself. The "720" stems from the interaction between two rounded worlds: the view that the brand has of itself; and the view that consumers have of the brand and its potential.

In the case of Halo, the brand is in real-time contact with its community through social media — and they are left with no doubt about whether an idea is good or not.

> "Our community is hugely engaged," says Friend, "to the point where we are not measuring success by the number of consoles sold but rather by how many people are playing our game on a monthly basis. Engagement is our #1 metric because we want to grow sustained

19. http://webbyawards.com/news/matt-walker-editor-bbc-earth/

interest and participation. In fact, we often say that we are in the engagement business, not the transaction business. We want people staying as long as possible, and as often as possible in our universe. A key responsibility for us is to make that happen."

"That carries through to our 360 franchise strategy. When we think about rolling out new product lines, we want them to deliver the benefit of driving repeat purchase and collectability; but we also want the theme to tie back to, and add to, our stories. If you're a Halo fan, we want you to join a fan group, to dive deeper, building new friendships and connecting with other people, and trying new things. Social media has turned people into authors. They want to have an influence and input. If they have a voice, they will be connected to you, and of course it is much easier to hear voices today because there are so many ways to do so."

"We get people playing games and commenting in real time through a chat bar. That means that at any time we can see not just how many people are playing, but also how they are reacting. Contrast that with cable TV where you broadcast, get ratings and wait for research. We get feedback the way it is truly experienced: in real time."

Many brands struggle with this, John told Mark and me, because they're concerned about brand management and ownership rights. They don't want the uncensored feedback. They want to be able to run their brands the way they believe is best. But what Halo has found is that involving others outside the brand can bring new dimensions to how the business thinks about its universe and its future. The meeting of Halo's whole world and the whole worlds of participants adds a new dimension to the story-making.

The crucial contribution that story brings to a brand is involvement. Storying gives people a narrative to interact with that none of the other aspects of the LASSO can deliver. I'll discuss the role of scale in the next chapter, but for the moment, consider this: if you add scale to your brand, but don't expand your story to match, you will add weight and footprint to your presence, but there's a good chance you will do so at the expense of interest. Story doesn't just bring a brand to life, it adds to the vitality of a brand as it grows by keeping the brand exciting. Story enables a brand to take people with it as it grows. And, as in the case of Wimbledon, it enables others to join in and bring their own perspectives and communities. Without that, there's a very real risk that a brand will become a monolith: a towering presence, dispossessed of soul and humanity, and one that consumers find hard to align with.

Key Takeouts

- Great marketers tell stories that people want to believe. We can argue about how literal they are about that and about the level of loyalty that inspires, but the fact remains that brands cannot simply go to market today with a narrative that's just about features, benefits, and price and be sustainable.

- In order to continually reach buyers, have something interesting to say at all times, and use the platforms available to you to make your brand heard. To do that consistently, there needs to be a central story underpinning what you talk about and how. That doesn't mean you can't sell. It does mean you need to find ways to keep people interested beyond just buying.

- If you're going to build a connective story, then you need to provide people with multiple ways to connect with that story, and you need to provide them with control over the aspects of the narrative that affect them.

- Use short stories to bring people to the brand, like Volvo Trucks did with its Van Damme videos. But don't stop there. Make that story part of a bigger story that brings people to Volvo looking for answers. Tie the strands together.

- Bring in partners that add to the story and help form the wider ecosystem.

- Know your own backstory. Stay true to what you were, and connect that with the story of who you are today. Shuttle back and forth through your history to connect your past with what shapes your brand today. Connect pieces. Bridge gaps. Explain mysteries. That's how you build a true mythology.

- Think long term rather than just campaign to campaign. And, if you're a brand in multiple markets, think anecdotally. Tell stories people relate to, not just those that make you feel comfortable. Link your world with theirs through story.

Inviting people in; here are six searching questions to assess the state of your story:

1. What do people most want to know about that pertains to what you do? If you work in a high-interest sector, how will you compete for attention? If you have a low-interest brand, what can you do, say, stand for, or talk about that will get people leaning toward you?

2. How are you expanding how people perceive your brand through storytelling?

3. Where will you tell your stories, and how will you use the channels to shuttle between the immediate and your wider world?

4. What role do customers have in helping to shape and influence your story?

5. How will new partners change your storytelling? How will their stories blend with yours?

6. How have you connected your storying to your selling? How accurately can you measure how and when conversion occurs? Which of your storylines are most profitable?

Your Turn

Is your brand building its story into a rich mythology? Please score your brand on how powerfully you think your brand is framed in the minds of consumers below. Once again, there are no right or wrong answers. Some brands will feel that storytelling is just part of how they explain themselves; others will see it as a way to continually redefine and refresh everything they represent. Take a moment now to choose the number that best describes how your brand connects and explains its actions and viewpoints on the Storied Expandability Score chart located on page 96. We'll come back and get this number shortly (see next page).

What is the Storied score that matches your brand? Mull it over and then decide. You've come a long way! I hope you have been diligent and honest in evaluating your brand in the LASSO Model along the Lateral, Addiction, and Storied attributes. When you're ready, turn to the next chapter and get ready to evaluate your brand from a Scalable perspective, the fourth element of the LASSO Model. You're almost there!

Storied Expandability Score Chart.

1	2	3	4	5
We don't have a continuous story. It's campaign- or product-focused. The stories we do tell make our products more accessible but we have not extended beyond that yet.	We're starting to extend our story through content marketing into various channels. We're engaging with our customers to help us do that.	We have a sense of our wider story, and we are working with partners to connect everything we have in ways that will make sense for our customers. We'd like to involve them more further down the line.	We have a purpose that drives us as a company. Our portfolio of brands reports to that ambition, but right now they do that as separate brands. Each brand has a fiercely strong tribe of customers.	Our brand is a multilayer, multichannel, multi-partner universe held together by principles that make it consistent and that enable us to work together to build out what we stand for and to shuttle stories back and forth across a range of time frames. Everything we do takes place within this context.

Scalable — Achieving Your Best Size

6

Scalable today is about achieving the critical mass needed to achieve critical presence.

Now that you know your expansion point, the behaviors you will cultivate to be addictive, and the storylines with which you will engage, the next thing to do is to set limits. How far will you go to deliver your brand? Recalling from the Intro, the hardest point of scalability is knowing which parts to make even bigger and which to adapt or omit. Brand licensing should be viewed, from a scalability point of view, as a form of merger and acquisition. You are merging the brand of one sector with the momentum of another sector in order to achieve new levels of growth and scale to create a hybrid presence, which is more powerful and effective than either expansion would have been alone.

Once, brands looked to globalize everything. The goal was to be bigger and get there faster than anyone else: the first brands to the ends of the earth won. Or, so they thought. Oftentimes, senior management, hell-bent on growth, failed to consult with the brand team to confirm that the global expansion into new regions, markets, or channels actually fit with the brand plan. In the military, this is referred to as having proper air cover.

Armies don't want to invade a country with ground troops and infiltrate their towns and villages without knowing they have air supremacy. Similarly, a brand which launches an extension into a new market without critical mass or sufficient resources to sustain the launch is set up for failure. Furthermore, even if the brands do have sufficient air cover, do they bother to check to see that the consumers there even want them in their market? Do they even care? Back to our military example, has the invading country even bothered to check whether the people believed to be oppressed actually want to be liberated?

Let's assume our brand team could even get it right on both counts. The problem is still that not everyone's convinced it's about reach and one-brand-for-everybody anymore. In fact, there are plenty who believe we are now competing in a post-globalization world. Here's why.

Let's start with the shifts in expected economic rewards. The whole concept of globalization was born out of a wish for economies that depended on foreign earnings to be able to trade freely and openly with others. After World War II, with manufacturing running strong, American companies recognized that they could export to, and invest in, the recovering world, and that they stood to gain greatly from doing so. At first the German economy recovered, and then the Japanese economy boomed, and free trade and the expansionist policies that supported it made sense. A number of assumptions underpinned this ongoing success, and according to *The Atlantic*[1]: "There needed to be fixed exchange rates, full employment, an absence of international flows of labor or capital, an absence of economies of scale, and perfectly competitive markets." As profits rose and American median household income and per-capita income surged, everything looked rosy.

But then, others began to catch up: productivity in other countries overtook that of the United States and America's debt

---

1. https://www.theatlantic.com/business/archive/2016/12/globalization-trade-history/510380/?utm_source=feed

increased with imports. As containerization revolutionized transport, and manufacturers across the world began using economies of scale to compete directly with each other for the same foreign markets, the very basis on which globalization had worked began to change. The introduction of free-trade arrangements, and the rise of China, India, and parts of Asia as manufacturing powerhouses, saw the U.S. trade deficit jump, the departure of production to other parts of the globe that were deemed less expensive, and a growing sense of resentment among local populations that others were taking jobs they saw as rightfully theirs. All of this has diminished the business case for expansion for expansion sake in the minds of many.

Then, there are the social and technological effects. Rich Lesser, Martin Reeves, and Johann Harnoss have looked at what it will take for companies to move forward from here.[2] While the world has never been more prosperous than it is today, nationalistic sentiment and an ongoing distrust of business, globalization, and technology have the potential to undermine future prosperity. Not only have the rewards changed, so have the expectations that there will be a pay day.

> "The division between those who have captured the vast majority of the benefits from global integration and technological progress and those who haven't runs between major cities and smaller communities, between young and old, and between people with different levels of education," the authors observe; "And it's not just Great Britain — 70% of the US workforce has experienced no real wage increase in the past four decades. Similar patterns can be observed in Canada, Germany, and other European countries. Wealth concentration has also increased globally, with

---

2. https://www.bcgperspectives.com/content/articles/strategy-globalization-saving-globalization-technology-from-themselves/

around 1% of people controlling 50% of the world's assets."

Globalization can work, the authors insist, but it will need to change course to do so. The next wave of globalization could well be more decentralized, more geographically differentiated, more digitally interconnected, and much more aware of the need to achieve social impact and build capabilities. We could see smaller companies involved in ecosystems that deliver broader economic returns. And there will be less pressure on obsessive short-term profitability as organizations find new ways to measure what they are achieving.

Finally, there's the view of marketers and customers. There's now a feeling among some marketers that the "think big" model has reached its "best before" date. Even global marketing expert Martin Lindstrom has expressed doubts that the pursuit of world domination is the way forward for most,[3] and that's because of a change in customer intimacy. Customers now expect a much more one-on-one level of attention than most mass models can afford.

> "Suddenly, borders are popping up everywhere," says Lindstrom. "Not long ago, we valued global markets; but now we want to protect our local communities, farmers, growers, stores, and tradesmen. They once defined us; then, we forgot about them; but now we admire them again. In this regenerated appreciation for the local, you'll find the epicenter of emotions setting the tone for a new (and disturbing, if you're a global brand builder) trend: the death of global brands as we know them."

All we have to do is listen to President Donald J. Trump's inauguration speech given on January 20, 2017, to understand his isolationist view of "America first" coming on the heels of UK Prime

---

3. https://www.linkedin.com/pulse/end-global-brands-martin-lindstrom?trk=hb_ntf_MEGAPHONE_ARTICLE_POST

Minister Theresa May's commitment to a complete Brexit from the European Union.

Whether you agree with these sentiments or not, the point is that the scalability of tomorrow will not be what got us to this point. In many ways, the scale debate is a little like the extendibility debate. People tend to take sides and argue either for local/regional relevance or for scale. Many multi national brands have pursued a "glocal" strategy with varying degrees of success, looking to marry an international brand and infrastructure with a service model that is tuned to the specifics of each market, but Larry Light has suggested that in the years ahead brands will need to reconcile three forces[4]: the reach of globalization with its appeals of coherence, reliability, and certainty; the call for increased localization, as people become more protective of local differences and celebrate variation and diversity; and increased personalization, as consumers resist one-size-fits-all service models and the categorization of them as demographics rather than individuals.

None of this should detract from the fact that there are still plenty of brands that are huge. Amazon, for example, depends on its size and scope to assert its competitiveness. Facebook and Google dominate the lucrative world of online advertising. Airlines, telcos, utilities, large parts of the financial industry, and many other sectors still rely on volume to underpin their revenue models. No one's suggesting that this will change any time soon. In fact, the CEO of Emirates has said that his company still sees huge scope for network growth globally. The airline already has the largest available flight kilometers of any international carrier and in absolute size, is in the top three behind American and United Airlines. But Sir Tim Clark says the airline has

---

4. http://www.brandquarterly.com/globalization-meets-localization-meets-personalization-new-era-brand-leadership

modeled up to 60,000 places in the world that could be linked, including little-known cities in China and Latin America.[5]

Like the lateral factor, there is a continuum rather than a strict divide: a point that will be different for every brand where they have access to the right markets at the right levels of intensity to achieve their business goals. Scalable today is about achieving the critical mass needed to achieve critical presence. Some, as I've said, will rely on all-pervasive physical or online presence to make their brand models viable; others can or should remain much more compact. Just as Lateral is about knowing how far you can expand your product into the same or other areas of lifestyle, Scalable is about working through where you need to be found and your capacity to deliver there.

Of course, we always look at Scalability and Lateral movement from a brand lens. Does the brand exhibit the characteristics or attributes to move laterally from one category to another? Is it poised and positioned to scale from a few consumers to a large number, or from one country to many? Finally, does the brand have permission to move laterally or to scale, and if so, would that extension or expansion reinforce the brand's position and promise?

In my Rubbermaid example earlier, I shared that consumers gave the brand permission to enter almost any home or garden category where a product was made of plastic or rubber. However, the brand is restricted in scale by its regional awareness. Conversely, LEGO, is limited laterally, but has almost infinite scale. If we think of Lateral being the *breadth* of a brand, then Scalable would be the brand's *depth*.

Irrespective, all the elements of the Model are interrelated; i.e., the moment one changes, the others are affected. I will be discussing in Chapter 8 how to apply the LASSO Model in the

---

5. http://www.nzherald.co.nz/business/news/article.cfm?c_id=3&objectid=11728908

context of my 8-Step Brand Licensing Process, which is covered in Chapter 9.

What brand owners may want to do is rethink what Scalable means. Traditionally, scalability has been based on footprint: you establish a beachhead, you gain orders, you add infrastructure to fulfill that demand. More and more though, brands are rethinking how this happens. A tiny vineyard in New Zealand, Invivo, managed to massively expand its audience not by installing itself in England but by persuading hugely popular talk-show host Graham Norton to make their wines the official wines of his show. As a result, they achieved massive awareness, celebrity endorsement, and whole new markets on a miniscule budget.

How else should brands consider scaling? There are at least three other options:

1. *Audience Expansion* — your brand looks to engage with people it has not engaged with before, because they now see something in you and/or who you are associated with that draws them closer. Traditionally, brands have looked to reinforce demographics by partnering with brands that extend an offering to a defined group. Increasingly, particularly in areas such as licensing and through joint ventures, brands see opportunities not just to use their name, but to draw on their core expertise to make the tribe larger. Nintendo took its highly successful gaming experience and, through Wii, set out to expand its place in the fitness market by gamifying how people could exercise. Bang & Olsen took their knowledge of sound and partnered with HP to change the audio experience that laptop users enjoyed. Moleskine's partnership with Evernote changed the technology of journals, bridging a barrier in new ways. Steve Scebelo, Vice President, Licensing & Business Development at NFL Players, Inc. says it best:

   EA has done a great job of refining its mobile game. This version reaches a younger audience. It's a simplified version that lends itself well to a younger audience. It helps build the next group of Madden fans.

2. *Experience Expansion* — your brand delivers a new level of experience than it has delivered, or it delivers a range of experiences that change how people feel about the brand. Ferrari's decision to brand the world's fastest rollercoaster in Abu Dhabi is a great example. It not only changes how people think about Ferrari, but also redefines what Ferrari can be and who can experience the Ferrari promise of unreasonable speed.

3. *Media/Channel Expansion* — as we continue to explore new media options such as virtual reality, and artificial intelligence exerts more influence on what customers expect, brands will need to find new ways to bring themselves to life. I'm not talking here about simply jumping on the latest social media fad or about how to better cater for more mobile customers, but rather how brands will further integrate themselves into what consumers do and need in ways that are thoughtful, delightful, and distinctive. We have only to look at how banks and airlines have completely changed how they use the Internet to interface with their customers to recognize that the connective economy will continue to re write how consumers and brands connect, and therefore how brands can expect to expand. The My Mercedes program, for example, is redefining not just how drivers monitor their cars, but also how automakers partner with drivers to keep their vehicles in optimum condition.

Choosing the expansion mode that is right for your brand will depend on what's feasible, what your consumers are looking for, and how you can sustain the advantage you gain by investing in your chosen mode.

Some brands will want or need to do the exact opposite: to concentrate their diversified assets more tightly so that they are clearer, stronger, and more defined. While most brands do this now in the context of a restructure, I see it as a way to dynamically manage brands for effectiveness, margin, and returns. You'll see more about this in the next chapter. It makes sense that just as brands should expand to seek out new markets and customers under the right conditions, they should also look to sell down their portfolio if it doesn't hit key metrics or if refocusing the range and structure of brands would deliver greater yields.

A number of people, including Mark Di Somma, have written about treating brands as investments and running brand architectures in much the same way that companies run their investment portfolios. This makes strong sense if you agree that your brands are assets, not just marketing costs, and should be treated that way.

One thing is clear. Diversification for its own sake will not work. A prevailing temptation referred to in a McKinsey article is that companies continue to broaden their brand portfolios with ever more variants of the same brand idea, which quickly clump into a mass of look-alike offerings that only serve to confuse consumers. A great example of this was the former, larger, General Motors (GM) that included Chevrolet, Pontiac, Oldsmobile, Buick, and Cadillac. Many of the models under one brand were virtually the same as those under another brand. With the Recession of 2008, GM eliminated Pontiac and Oldsmobile greatly diminishing the duplication:

> It's easy to see why marketers resist the portfolio approach to brands … managing them has become more difficult, since companies in maturing sectors have not only used new brands and products to pursue continued growth but also resisted pruning existing ones, in hopes of maintaining market share, cash flows, and long-lived consumer franchises.[6]

While brand managers may like to think this approach makes them more appealing, in fact, the opposite is true. Where each of us has been involved with companies that have multiplied their number of brands simply to increase their footprint and deliver more consumer choice, the recurrent result has been that overall

---

6. http://www.mckinsey.com/business-functions/marketing-and-sales/our-insights/making-brand-portfolios-work

revenue and volume (especially per brand) hasn't kept pace. The new brands that companies have piled on have also increased the workload and cost of brand owners because they have required more and more work from finite resources to get them to market. As the McKinsey article explains, and contrary to what many brand owners believe, more brands don't necessarily mean greater market share or even greater market reach. Instead it can often add up to greater confusion, more dilution, more cost, and lower returns from each brand.

To counter this temptation, brands should be identifying and catering to a nuanced set of consumer need states rather than basing their decisions on demographics or their own views of how the market is tiered, economy versus premium. For example, different parts of the market may have multiple need states that a company can cater to through various brands, or it may have none. The trick is knowing which brands to keep, which to reposition, which to rebrand, and which to remove to achieve the best returns.

And that, renowned brand strategist Sandra Pickering told us, is about recognizing the difference between brand meaning, which focuses on the emotional significance of your brand for each customer, and brand architecture, which is how your brands are structured and designed to form a system. Portfolio, she explains, is how you arrange your brands within your architecture to make them as meaningful as possible. In other words, your brand must be expandable in its own right, but it also needs to be structured in ways that allow it to grow to its full potential, and it needs to be managed within a portfolio that continually monitors that architecture for its effectiveness.

———

The critical question this all leads back to of course is: what exactly are you trying to grow here? In a speech Mark Di Somma gave in Miami a couple of years ago, he identified five types of brand:

1. Global players — companies like Heineken that have had a worldwide mindset for many years and have consciously pursued a policy to be readily available to everyone.

2. National/regional players — companies that have focused on being powerful brands in their parts of the world, at least for the time being. Many emerging Chinese brands are currently in this category. Examples include Cheetah Mobile, which offers free mobile security software, and Hisense, which makes white goods and electronics like TVs and tablets.

3. Challenger brands — the brands that challenge the establishment. These are the up-and-comers that are looking to fight their way into a position of strength. Virgin quite often looks to take this position in a marketplace.

4. Niche brands — the brands that go after a particular part of a particular market. This doesn't necessarily mean they are small, but rather that they have adopted a specialist approach. Examples include Whole Foods and Fresh Market in the U.S. market and Star Sports, a subsidiary of 21st Century Fox division STAR TV, serving the Indian sport enthusiasts.

5. Cult brands — the brands that are powerful through word of mouth. These are brands like Deus ex Machina, Yeti, and Sriracha: known to the people who love them, but operating generally below the marketing radar, and proud to do so.

In his presentation, Di Somma talked about the fact that these five types of brand could be divided into two broad groups: monsters and upstarts. But Di Somma predicted that this stratification wouldn't necessarily last and that we would see a merging of characteristics as the bigger brands looked to gain influence through a more agile approach and the smaller brands looked to gain dominance by finding ways to lift their visibility and presence. The time was right, he suggested, for monstrous upstarts and upstart monsters. Scalability, going forward, may well stem from how brands choose to think of themselves. How should you be thinking about the character of your brands? How should they be behaving in order to mean the most to consumers, sit within a coherent system that minimizes friction and cannibalization, and work to capacity?

Here's a final question as you think about scalability. What's the catalyst? The days of advertising your way to scale are long gone for many. How will you encourage easily distracted consumers not just to pay your brand attention but also to transact with you? Will you advertise, sponsor, or build your brand through association, media presence, or placement? A lot of that comes down to the nature of your brand. Monster B2B brands will work their contacts and their reputations; B2C brands, on the other hand, may look to leverage pop culture. The critical factor here is that you must find a way to capture consumer interest beyond the immediate. Apple does this exceptionally well. In today's world, with its emphasis on views and trending topics, the temptation is to build a brand on exposures. Sure, having your brand featured on, or with, a celebrity will earn your brand interest and increased sales, but the effect is often momentary.[7] Ultimately, your brand needs an intention that acts as a through-line for all your marketing initiatives. For example, do you want your brand to be seen as a tastemaker, a revolutionary, a simplifier, a hero, an inspiration ...? And how does that stand your brand apart from everyone else around you? Why will that bring people flocking to your brand, not just in the moment, but for an enduring period of time?

This is harder than it first appears. For example, so many B2B brands I've spoken to say they want to be seen as a thought leader. Brows quickly knit, however, when they are asked how many of their competitors also want to be seen as thought leaders — they concede that everyone has the same intention. In this context, thought leadership is not a catalyst. It's table stakes.

Perhaps no brands better exemplify how to be a catalyst than today's celebrities. Not so long ago, brands hired celebrities to endorse them. Increasingly, celebrities are packaging and

---

7. http://licensingsource.net/indepth/the-power-of-celebrity-seeding/

marketing what they do as brands: monetizing and expanding their popularity not just for who they are but what they are seen to stand for. Martha Stewart led the way, building out a brand that stood for effortless homemaking into the publicly traded entity Martha Stewart Living Omnimedia.[8] Jamie Oliver and Gordon Ramsay have done the same as celebrity chefs, with Oliver expanding his "Pukka" ethos into a network of restaurants, franchises, publications, cookware ranges, and cooking products across the world.[9]

The concept of bankable qualities is not just confined to the living. Deceased superstars like Marilyn Monroe, Frank Sinatra, Elvis, Audrey Hepburn, Michael Jackson, and others are part of an estimated $3 billion business. In fact, since his death in 2009, Michael Jackson's estate has generated more than $1 billion in revenues by licensing his name, likeness, and music.[10]

According to Anthony Effinger and Katherine Burton of the *Washington Post*, "Jamie Salter, the branding guru who owns a majority of Elvis's estate, is planning a 'live' show in Las Vegas with Presley appearing as a hologram, much like the one of Michael Jackson that appeared [in 2014]."

"Today, deceased icons from pop culture's heyday are enjoying unprecedented success, out-earning even their former flesh-and-blood selves," says Salter, one of the new breed of brand managers using technology to wring big bucks from dead superstars. The celebrities are profitable in part because of their huge mass appeal when they were alive plus the ability for licensing agents today to connect what made them great with audiences of today.

Salter bought the Elvis estate, including Graceland, and the rights to the singer's image and music, from Core Media in November 2013. By 2015, Salter's Authentic Brands' profits rose

---

8. http://www.cnbc.com/2014/04/29/martha-stewart-its-all-about-branding.html
9. http://www.thetimes.co.uk/tto/life/food/article4499218.ece
10. https://www.brandingstrategyinsider.com/2016/07/10748.html#.WGr6Xly5rm4
   Also worth reading because they may inform this:
   http://www.nytimes.com/2017/01/02/business/dealbook/mergers.html?_r=1
   https://hbr.org/2016/04/pipelines-platforms-and-the-new-rules-of-strategy#

by 25%, thanks to Elvis-themed bathrobes, calendars, cookie jars, cuff links, luggage, and, oh yeah, music.

Salter began working with dead celebrities in 2010, when he bought the majority of Marilyn Monroe's estate for more than $30 million. Since then Salter purchased the balance of the estate and owns the Monroe brand outright. Previous to his involvement, "the Monroe estate brought in less than $3 million a year through 300 licensing agreements for low-end products such as shot glasses and T-shirts." Focusing on the Monroe brand position and a less-is-more strategy, Salter reduced the number of licensees by two-thirds and earned $17 million in royalties in 2015. Marilyn Monroe branded products today include spas and nail salons, a line of lingerie, hair spray, and eyeliner — all in keeping with her image of beauty and allure. Monroe appeared in a TV ad in 2015 for Chanel No. 5 comprising archival footage overdubbed with an interview. "They ask you questions," she says. "… What do you wear to bed? Do you wear a pajama top? The bottoms of the pajamas? A nightgown? So I said, 'Chanel No. 5.'"[11]

As Robert Strand observes, people are drawn to iconic celebrities partly because of the memories they have of them, and because they often represent a lifestyle or dream that is exciting or inspiring. This gives brands incredible scale. Of course, partnering with a celebrity has its risks, as all humans have character flaws and can engage in nefarious behavior that can hurt the brand. You might recall Tiger Woods' cheating scandal while married to Elin Nordegren that occurred in 2009, Michael Jackson dangling a small baby from a balcony in 2010, or more recently Olympic swimmer Ryan Lochte vandalizing a convenience store in Rio De Janiero during the Summer Games.[12] Oftentimes consumers will forgive these missteps if the celebrity is remorseful and changes their behavior. Still, episodes like these can hurt the brand for a

---

11. https://www.washingtonpost.com/business/and-the-brand-played-on-agents-help-dead-celebrities-maximize-their-afterlife-earning/2015/01/08/02182086-9447-11e4-927a-4fa2638cd1b0_story.html?utm_term=.0dbbb055462a

12. http://www.thesportster.com/entertainment/top-13-hottest-tiger-woods-mistresses/

significant period of time. Of course, deceased stars by definition cannot make any additional missteps their living counterparts can.

The takeout for brands looking to expand their presence goes far beyond whether they should employ a celebrity to endorse their brand.

The key questions in terms of arriving at a catalyst as follows:

- What will consumers look to you for, in terms of making a change in their own lives?

- What can they always rely on you to do for them?

- And how will your delivery of that help your brand expand?

Key Takeouts

- Consistent reach is rapidly becoming a historic metric. The years ahead will see a shift not just in how brands scale, but also in what they look for from scaling.

- The next era of globalization will need to reconcile not just new markets, but also local and individual relevance, and it will need to do so in ways that make smaller businesses part of the new way that brands build capacity.

- Expect "the world" to increasingly give way to "my world" in terms of where brands need to deliver.

- We will still have, and need, huge brands — but the criteria every marketer should be striving for is critical mass, which is access to the right markets at the right levels of intensity to achieve their business goals.

- Brands will scale in different ways — some will use the leverage of others, some will change who they reach, some will expand what consumers can expect, and some will find new ways and new places to make themselves heard.

- Scalability is not just about growth. Some will choose to expand their profitability by scaling back.

- We'll see more hybridization of character as brands explore how they will grow. Get ready for more monstrous upstarts and more upstart monsters.

- Scale is nothing without a catalyst to drive and maintain it. I like this thought. The biggest challenge brands face, as they look to scale, is their ability, ironically, to stay true to what they are.

Your Turn

OK, by this point you know the drill. Time to assess how Scalable you need to be as a brand and how far consumers will allow your brand to go. Please think about your answers to the six questions above and score your brand on how you intend to take your brand forward and what that will mean for your availability on the chart below. As always, there are no right or wrong answers. Some brands will feel that there are still plenty of room for them to grow; others will see that a more focused approach will enable them to gather the best returns. Take a moment now to choose the number that best describes how your brand expands geographically from the Scalable Expandability Score chart. We'll come back and get this number shortly (see next page).

Does a particular Scalable score represent your brand well? Once you have settled on the right number, you are ready to contemplate the final LASSO element, that of your brand's degree of Own-ability. Up to now you've run a steady race, contemplating how Lateral, Addictive, Storied, and Scalable your brand is today. If you're feeling a little unsure of yourself, please trust the process and plow ahead. If you're feeling pretty good, then let's roll forward to Own-able, the final element of the LASSO Model. Ready? Then, let's get started.

Scalable Expandability Score Chart.

1	2	3	4	5
We have a very small number of brands that are growing strongly. We generate intense profit out of keeping things condensed. We're looking for constant and controlled growth.	Our brand portfolio achieves growth by expanding to meet changing market demand. We're looking to keep pace with the prevailing rates of change.	We dynamically manage our brand portfolio across a growing number of countries. We buy, sell, create, and discontinue brands to achieve our revenue goals. We judge our success by how much each brand in our portfolio exceeds metrics.	We look for opportunities to grow our presence through arrangements with others, such as licensing, joint ventures, and project partnerships. We're looking for agreed rates of return from these initiatives.	Our brand portfolio is global, and spread across multiple sectors via many different arrangements. We use this diversified approach to make the most of rapidly growing markets and to counter downward movements in others.

Own-able — How You Expand and Stay True to Your DNA

7

You don't need to own every aspect of a brand in order to have an own-able brand.

Own-able is the final critical variable when looking at whether, and how, to expand or condense a brand. In some ways, it's the most important because how you structure a brand decides its form. Form influences not just where a brand can go, but also how easily it can meet the demands of consumers, and where it can be found. Own-able even influences the brand story because unless your brand can lay claim to a unique narrative, chances are it's underpowered.

Own-ability is how a company transcends commodity status. Own-able brands are the ones that lay claim to what they see as theirs, and that defend that property with passion and gusto. They recognize better than others that until an idea is attributed to you, the chances of making money from it are diminished.

Own-able itself exists in several states:

- It's what your brand owns legally;

- It's what you own emotionally;

- It can be what you have access to territorially; and

- It's what you get to monetize, and how you get to monetize it.

An example of how important it is for a company to protect its brands can be found in the case of *Louis Vuitton versus My Other Bag*. My Other Bag sells everyday canvas tote bags with drawings of various luxury brand handbags on one side and "My Other Bag" in large cursive print on the other side. Louis Vuitton took offense at My Other Bag's products that imitate a number of Louis Vuitton bag styles and commenced a lawsuit claiming, among other things, trademark infringement and dilution. The district court, however, did not see this as infringement and granted My Other Bag summary judgment on all of Louis Vuitton's claims. The court saw My Other Bag's products as parodies and, as such, the bags were not actionable sources of trademark infringement or dilution. In response, Louis Vuitton appealed the decision to the Second Circuit Court of Appeals only to lose again.

According to Oliver Herzfeld,

> The key here is that My Other Bag is not using Louis Vuitton's trademarks solely to increase sales of My Other Bag's products by inducing consumers to mistakenly believe the totes are Louis Vuitton bags or somehow sponsored or endorsed by Louis Vuitton. Instead, My Other Bag is primarily using the trademarks to parody Louis Vuitton's high-end luxury image. On that basis, the Second Circuit affirmed the trademark dilution part of the district court's award of summary judgment in favor of My Other Bag, too.

The takeaway is that brands today feel they must do everything in their power to protect their trademarks even if it means going after a company that is treating their marks as a parody. And, while in this case there was no perceived impropriety, brand owners should diligently protect their trademarks from infringement, dilution, and other misuse that may harm the owner's goodwill and business reputation. For it is this reputation and brand equity that gives the brand permission to extend, expand, and grow. And while brand owners may not win all cases, taking a posture of rigorous protection can prevent a weakening of an owner's marks, loss of distinctiveness, and brand dilution over time.[1]

For many years, we have assumed that ownership is how value is created and owned. So not surprisingly, many traditional expansion models presume actual ownership. But digital models are quickly disrupting that presumption. Just as "the cloud" now means companies can outsource acquisition and maintenance of significant parts of their infrastructure, the ways in which value can be created — and the relationships between a brand and the people who create that value — are changing. Uber and Airbnb have challenged who has the right to drive people places or play host. The increasing use of freelancers and contractors has called into question whether people need to be permanent members of a workforce in order to contribute to the work itself. Brands like Apple have now entered into communal relationships with developers to drive product development and enhancement on multi-billion dollar platforms like iTunes. All of this is changing not just what a brand is, but also how a brand is organized and how it is perceived.

As much as it is critically important for brand owners to protect the ownership of their trademarks, and to prevent outside companies from infringing on the use of those marks, I concur with Martin Lindstrom's assertion in his book *Brand Sense* that the "concept of branding is already undergoing dramatic changes," with the ownership of brands shifting from the companies with the trademark registration to the consumers who use them on a daily basis. Lindstrom, who first saw the shift appear in the late 1990s, documented this phenomenon in BRANDchild[2] and named it MSP, the Me Selling Proposition. MSP brands, according to

---

1. http://www.forbes.com/sites/oliverherzfeld/2017/01/06/louis-vuitton-v-my-other-bag-no-license-required/#af0fde941c64
2. http://www.dualbook.com/aboutbc.php

Lindstrom, are no longer owned by the manufacturer, but rather by the consumer.

According to Lindstrom, technology can be attributed to this phenomenon as manufacturers have shifted from mass production to mass customization. A great example of this customization can be seen in the Share a Coke campaign which was launched in 2011 in Australia. This campaign allowed consumers to purchase cans of Coke where the label is swapped out with popular first names. Share a Coke was so popular that by 2015 more than 50 countries offered consumers the chance to buy cans with their favorite names on them. By 2016, Share a Coke was in 70 countries tapping into consumers' desires for personalization and customization.[3]

> The concept of interactivity has forced us to rethink each and every communication, evaluating and designing it for the ever-demanding consumer. Technological innovation paved the way for MSP brands, which saw consumer taking ownership of the brands. The Canadian brand Jones Soda is a good example of this phenomenon. Consumers design their own label, which Jones Soda guarantees to distribute in the designer's local area. Nike and Levi's websites offer to customize any of their models exactly to your need and size.[4]

And it raises the question that every brand owner should be asking: How do you build a profitable model in a world where ownership itself is under threat? For many brands, that's a real grapple: trying to understand what's theirs today and for how long. The question that too often gets asked is this one: How long can we keep making money the way we have? In other words, how long can we keep working with what we know?

---

3. http://www.beveragedaily.com/Processing-Packaging/Coca-Cola-launches-Share-a-Coke-and-a-Song
4. Lindstrom, M. (2005). *Brand sense: How to build powerful brands through touch, taste, smell, sight & sound.* London: Kogan Page.

Similar questions are being asked around how work is organized. According to author Jacob Morgan,[5] there are five types of organizational structures today.

1. *The traditional hierarchical structure is a waterfall where power and control descends from the top to the bottom in a clear, and often unquestioned, chain of command.* It's a system that thrives on unquestioning loyalty, a clearly defined pecking order, bureaucracy, and certainty of structure. In this model, there is little or no emphasis on innovation, leadership is in command, and there is little chance of responsiveness beyond the inclination of that leader to drive it.

2. *The flatter model, as its name suggests, has fewer layers than the traditional structure and places greater emphasis on collaboration and communication through robust technologies that enable people to work anywhere/anytime.* Companies like Cisco, Whirlpool, and Pandora use this structure to encourage workplace participation, worker support, and greater flexibility around work hours and location.

3. *Flat organizations have no formal corporate structure.* Instead everyone is seen as equal and the work is run as projects through teams. According to Morgan, this arrangement tends to suit smaller and some medium-sized companies that prefer a more free-form way of working.

4. *A flatarchy is a hybrid structure that uses a combination of hierarchical and flat structures.* It may, for example, have a more traditional structure with specific "flat" teams or it may work in teams that are more structured. This approach suits organizations that have internal incubators or innovation programs and that place a strong emphasis on new ideas.

---

5. http://www.forbes.com/sites/jacobmorgan/2015/07/08/the-5-types-of-organizational-structures-part-2-flatter-organizations/#23231ec4bca7

5. *Finally, there is the holacracy model, practiced by the likes of Zappos, where teams are built as circles and where decision-making is distributed through interactive groups.* Information and issues are processed and decided during ongoing meetings. It may not be working perfectly yet, but the fact it's still on the table shows that seemingly radical models are still in play and are still developing.

These organizational options demonstrate just how much structures are continuing to change. My feeling is that brand structures will mirror this trend, moving to more open, federation-style models to keep pace with the demands of the connective economy, and embracing ways of developing the brand that are time-, project-, region-, or outcome-specific.

A number of people have been surprised when I've raised ownership as one of the looming debates of brand. After all, it seems so straightforward. Ownership is about who bought and paid for the rights to the assets, developed them into something valuable, and therefore gets to set the rules, right? What is a brand but a literal statement of ownership?

Actually, ownership is more complex than it first appears because, from a brand point of view, it's not just about who owns the shares or how they are structured; it's about what your brand is associated with, how closely your assets are held, how they're connected to your intellectual property, and how the wider ecosystem is able to work. Different ownership structures also have implications for what is pre decided and where decisions get made. And changing ownership structures or arrangements can affect all of that.

Let's take a moment to look at three ownership models and their implications for brand expansion.

If your brand is structured as a franchise, then your model for expansion depends on four things: the brand, the system that brings it to life, the footprint of that system, and the inclination of consumers to seek out what you offer. Subway has built a global empire out of promising food that tastes good; that represents good value; and that is fast, healthy, and tailored for local tastes within the clear and universally understood concept of sand-wiches.[6] Those sandwiches might have been different in taste and ingredients in Japan than they were in the United States or in New Zealand, but the basic format of six-inch and foot-long options underpins what consumers see and what they recognize.

Subway has been a success story because it jumped the fresh ingredients trend early on; it changed the meaning of what "fast food" could be; it was able to gain access to markets that were unavailable to its more unhealthy rivals because of that; it intro-duced the whole ritual of "food prepared in front of you"; and it told a human story about a big guy who lost weight eating their food and it cultivated huge loyalty with its network.[7]

But more recently, Subway has struggled to maintain that growth trajectory, and the reasons for that are also, in part at least, about ownership of a different kind. Subway hasn't been able to hold onto its ownership of "fresh" in consumers' minds, because the word itself has changed meaning in the past decade.[8] And the downfall of Jared Fogle has eliminated their ownership of a success story that made Subway one of the most powerful weight-loss brand stories in the world. Shifts like that put immense pressure on the system because they diminish the competitiveness of the brand.[9]

Franchises are all about presence. They work very well if you have a brand that needs to systematically expand to meet demand, and that demand requires a turn key, proven answer that people can learn to operate. Sadly, as many other franchises, particularly in food, have discovered that can also be their weakness. There's a limited focus within which to innovate once the system itself stalls. Like its competitor McDonald's, Subway finds itself with an extended network that looks more like an older part of the

---

6. https://www.qsrmagazine.com/interviews/how-subway-went-global

7. https://www.entrepreneur.com/article/219062

8. http://adage.com/article/cmo-strategy/subway-s-strategy-discount-ads/301938/

9. https://www.washingtonpost.com/business/economy/the-rise-and-fall-of-subway-the-worlds-biggest-food-chain/2015/05/29/0ca0a84a-fa7a-11e4-a13c-193b1241d51a_story.html?utm_term=.94a15efe52ff

landscape rather than the game changer it once was. Tweaking the brand to make it appear younger and extending the product lines to make them feel more in keeping with the times will help outlets turning over product, at least in the short—medium term, but ultimately reach in itself won't be enough.

After tasting the initial success of its turnaround strategy, primarily on back of the success of its *All Day Breakfast* initiative, McDonald's is now working on several initiatives aimed at enhancing customer experience to drive revenue growth in the future. The company has begun pursuing additional opportunities to keep this growth momentum going, including innovation in food items, improved menu boards, as well as quality and improvements in the overall restaurant experience.[10]

Going forward, improving food quality will be a top priority, Easterbrook, McDonald's CEO said. "In the last five years, the world has moved faster outside the business than inside. The business cannot ignore what customers are saying when the message is clear: We're not on our game."

Nevertheless, franchisees, which make up more than 80% of McDonald's sales, remain unconvinced. "The system is broken," one franchisee wrote in response to a survey investment firm Janney Capital Markets. "There is no leadership, no plan, no respect for operators or their investment or bottom line." Another wrote: "The future looks very bleak. I'm selling my McDonald's stock. The morale of franchisees is at its lowest level ever."[11]

Mergers and Acquisitions (M&A) have been a staple of corporate expansion since the late 19th century. We have, according to Patrick Foulis,[12] the *Economist's* New York bureau chief, seen no less than seven waves of deal-making in that time, from the firms that created national giants in commodities and consumer goods to the $18 trillion of transactions that have taken place since 2012 as companies ranging from chemical and food giants to healthcare

---

10. http://www.forbes.com/sites/greatspeculations/2016/05/03/how-mcdonalds-is-effectively-executing-its-turnaround-strategy/#c46eb02d917c

11. http://content.time.com/time/magazine/article/0,9171,1963755,00.html

12. http://www.theworldin.com/article/12757/waving-goodbye?fsrc=scn/tw/wi/bl/ed/

companies sought to cut costs, export tax bills, and create global monopolies. But this era will come to a close too, says Foulis, as antitrust regulation tightens, localism rebounds, and the deals themselves fail to live up to expectations in terms of returns on investment.

No one's ruling out M&A completely just yet. While the success rates around M&A, particularly of large organizations, are not great, McKinsey cites five ways that large brands can use acquisitions to derive untapped organizational value.[13] They work with varying degrees of success at a brand level.

M&A can help improve performance by reducing costs — but while the returns here are easier to gain for companies with low margins and low returns on invested capital, this can quickly evolve into an efficiency-hunting-only exercise if brand investment is not retained. Efficiencies may improve, but at the expense of brand value as the brands themselves will almost certainly face commoditization pressure.

Consolidation of capacity is a good generator of value because it helps keep supply and demand in check and this in turn should help brands keep margins and perceived value higher. Scarcity is a powerful driver in brand modeling because it returns power to brand owners. However, it can also encourage other players to enter a market to alleviate "supply pressure."

- Accelerating market access by acquiring smaller companies and then applying the resources of a larger buyer works well for brands looking to drive sales into under developed markets. It can be a particularly useful strategy when a brand has strong brand equity and intellectual property but lacks the momentum to address market need as quickly as it should. Many of the larger digital companies like Facebook and Amazon have built their ecosystems this way. Danone's acquisition of Stonyfield is an example of this; however, in

---

13. http://www.mckinsey.com/business-functions/strategy-and-corporate-finance/our-insights/the-five-types-of-successful-acquisitions

Stonyfield's case, they required autonomy as part of the acquisition.[14]

- M&A offers opportunities to acquire skills or technologies faster or more efficiently than developing them yourself. Cisco has used this approach to advance its presence and brand, and, as I'll discuss shortly, this is also a highly effective approach in the hands of companies like Apple. Brands with a strong sense of where they're going and the skills and resources they will need to get there will find this a highly effective way to fast-track market presence.

- Finally, McKinsey points to identifying winners before they are evident and bringing them onboard. That's worked well for Facebook and Google and failed for Yahoo. Speculating on what the market will require and seeing how it will integrate into the brand you're building is risky, but that's the whole point of a strategy such as this. And it's not just small companies that can be acquired for this purpose. When Disney bought Marvel, many people thought they had paid too much for the comic brand, but Disney recognized that, for their business model, the opportunity to apply the Marvel portfolio to how they structure their entertainment would work brilliantly. They were proven right.

Recently, Ryan Caldbeck suggested that an avalanche in the areas of consumer and retail brands was imminent.[15] His reason? Big consumer packaged goods companies (CPGs) are finding it increasingly difficult to convert a new generation of shoppers to their brands. In part, he says, that's because their marketing models are not working as well as they used to in the past. But the key issue, he says, is that these behemoths cannot innovate quickly enough. Their solution, he suggests, will be to circle the wagons

---

14. https://web.archive.org/web/20070110034106/http://www.stonyfield.com/AboutUs/MoosReleases_Display.cfm?pr_id=36
15. https://www.linkedin.com/pulse/we-verge-consumer-ma-avalanche-ryan-caldbeck?trk=hp-feed-article-title-like

by buying up brands that show promise, and merging entities to squeeze greater efficiencies out of their operations.

At one level, this helps alleviate an issue; at another, it creates a new set of problems. When Marriott International acquired Starwood Hotels and Resorts Worldwide, they created the largest hotel group in the world, with more than 1 million rooms worldwide. The new company now operates 30 hotel brands globally, including such global icons as Sheraton, Westin, The Ritz Carlton, W Hotels, and Marriott. But as Mark Ritson so rightly pointed out,[16] volume is no longer the competitive force it once was:

> Not so long ago, owning and operating a large portfolio of brands made sense ... [but] the fascination with adding more brands has been reversed in recent years ... Compare the brand portfolio of any major organization today with how it looked a decade ago and, almost without exception, you will see a leaner and less diversified list of brands than was once the case. Everyone from P&G, and Coca-Cola to Ford, has moved away from multiple brands and sub-brands towards a simpler, more parsimonious brand architecture in which the number of brands is as tight as strategically possible.

Bigger is not always better. Sometimes it's just more complex. That's not to say that brands should rule out M&A as a way to strengthen their profile and presence, but rather that it's not the only way to build an expanded brand that people want to feel is theirs.

Meanwhile, Foulis predicts that mergers themselves may need to morph for the next round of deal-making which he believes will peak around 8–10 years from now. Unbundling foreign operations is likely to occur, as firms take the focus off presence and onto the markets where they perform best. We're also likely to see the rise of regional champions, he suggests. And everyone should

---

16. https://www.brandingstrategyinsider.com/2016/12/sound-brand-architecture-requires-killing-the-weak.html#.WFyoAly5rm4

be keeping an eye on China, because that's where the outbound deals will spring from as Asian companies look to diversify out of the markets they're known in and into the wider world.

My key concern around M&A revolves around speed. In the time that it takes to ferment and seal a large deal, ratify it with regulators, and implement all the changes, chances are the market itself has moved on. Companies that have forked out billions can easily find themselves playing catch-up as consumers shift attention to smaller brands that seem to better represent what they want.

What are the alternatives? If you have a large brand and you want to stay current, maybe you should look at co-branding. This powerful expansion tool brings two or more names together to create a presence that transcends what each brand could have achieved separately. From fashion to audio, sports to film, brands are increasingly working together to broaden their appeal and drive new interest in what they do.[17] Adidas, for example, has teamed with everyone from Raf Simons to Kanye West. Alexander Wang has worked with H&M. Mac Cosmetics has partnered with Disney. And, of course, LEGO has joined forces with *Star Wars*. In each case, not only has the partnership created new products, it has enabled both partners to gain interest and leverage that they would not achieve otherwise.

The partnership has changed consumer perceptions of both brands while enabling them to retain their individual identities and to pursue simultaneous campaigns in new places. There are risks to such a strategy, of course. Consumers may see the pairing as unsuited, or one party may lose favor and sour the relationship for both. But a hugely advantageous structure is garnered for those large brands that can both retain ownership and simultaneously extend interest.

According to Hitesh Bhasin, there are six different types of co-branding[18]:

---

17. http://www.trendhunter.com/slideshow/strategic-cobranding
18. http://www.marketing91.com/co-branding/

1. Same company co-branding — where products from within the same company are teamed to complement and cross-sell one another, like GoPro and RedBull in the "Stratos project," or Bonne Bell and Dr. Pepper when they created flavored lip balm.

2. Joint venture co-branding — where two brands join forces to produce a new product, such as an Air New Zealand branded credit card.

3. Multiple co-branding — where a range of companies come together in a branded initiative such as when Unilever's Lagnese brand launched the Cremissimo ice cream line, and then partnered with Milka Kuhflecken, and then later, Kraft Foods' brand Toblerone, the liquor company Batida de Coco, Italian coffee maker Lavazza Latte Macchiato, and marzipan maven Niederegger Marzipan.[19]

4. Retail co-branding — where different retailers tie up with each other to make the most of each other's resources such as Yum Brand's Taco Bell and KFC, which often share their brick and mortar space.

5. Ingredient branding — where a core part of the end product is independently branded and delivers specific value as a result — think about Intel with Dell, for example, or Gore-Tex with North Face.

6. Co-ventures — where two name brands come together to deliver an experience that would not normally be available otherwise. Bhasin cites the example of the BMW I8 car, which came with Louis Vuitton bags, thus building brand equity for both participants.

Whether it is a joint venture arrangement or a licensing deal, I am a strong advocate for these types of ventures, because when

---

19. Beckman, I., and Willas, K. (2005). *Multiple co-branding: From the consumer's point of view* (pp. 33–34). Diplomatica Verlag GmbH, Hamburg, Germany.

they are done well, their cumulative reach and appeal makes them highly attractive and credible. But there are a few rules to getting these ventures right:

- The right partners in JVs are crucial — the association must make sense as a business proposition but it must also make sense to consumers. It must bring together partners who are of equal strength, have loyal audiences, and have a common ethos.[20] On the other hand, hot new startups and younger companies like GoPro, which everyone is clamoring to get a piece of, will often leverage the name and likeness of a top Olympic or other professional athletes to drive product sales.

- There must be agreement on how the partnership works and how it is communicated — so there must be a common viewpoint on why the parties have come together and what is said.[21]

- The co-venture must offer access to something valuable that wouldn't be available otherwise (or else, it is more likely to be seen as a sponsorship arrangement).

- Co-branding works best when the pairing feels timely and can be linked to something that consumers care about or are afraid of losing. When I ran Coke's co-branded merchandising program, I proactively looked for brand attribute alignment and leveraged that to drive relevance. Both Coke and the Olympics stood for authenticity, nostalgia, and timelessness. Co-branding is much less effective when it feels like one party is trying to ride on the coattails of the other.

Intellectual property lawyers have their own view of what's own-able. They will often tell you that brand ownership is about

20. http://www.managementstudyguide.com/co-branding.htm#
21. https://www.hausmanmarketingletter.com/back-to-marketing-basics-co-branding-strategy-in-the-digital-age/

trademarks and patents, copyright, trade secrets, and the like. It's about knowing what you can rightfully and often globally put your name on, to the exclusion of others. It's about having an identified and tangible intellectual base on what to buy and sell, develop, trade, license, and deal. Ownership is about knowing what you have the right to protect and defend. And, just as importantly, it's about knowing what others already lay claim to, and therefore is out of bounds to your company. But most importantly, it's about knowing the basis on which you can move forward, while being confident that others will not, or cannot follow.

Perhaps no company in recent times has better understood the power of using what you own to your advantage than Apple. According to Alexander Poltorak,[22] Apple has successfully implemented a range of strategies to acquire patents in order to maintain its innovative position and expand into new sectors. First of all, Apple has embarked on a vigorous innovation program, applying for and being issued patents for technology that it develops in-house. For example, Poltorak says, Apple was granted over 2000 U.S. Utility Patents in 2014 alone. Second, the company continues to acquire patents that align with its future growth plans. Third, it buys companies, such as Beats Electronics, that own patents that it may wish to use in the future. And finally, it buys companies that are obsessed over nascent, pre-patent research and development. With the Beats Electronics purchase, Poltorak says, Apple acquired one U.S. Utility Patent, fourteen U.S. Design Patents, thirteen Canadian Patents, two European Patents, four U.S. patent applications, and five PTO applications. Through those acquisitions, the company is well armed to take on the likes of Spotify and Pandora, perhaps by boosting or revamping its own iTunes product.

Clearly, Apple views IP as a cornerstone of both ownership and expansion. By protecting its own innovation and acquiring the rights to ideas that could help shape its future, Apple is able to maintain greater control over what it sees as its future. Apple is

---

22. http://www.generalpatent.com/node/2368

also not afraid to take on others who it believes may be infringing its patents, and their reasons for doing so may be about more than just ownership disputes. For example, Apple sued Samsung in a hallmark case back in April 2011. Apple alleged that Samsung had "copied" the designs of the iPhone and iPad. Samsung counter-sued Apple in June 2011, saying it had infringed on Samsung patents around wireless communications and camera phones. The jury, made up of seven men and two women, awarded Apple in August 2012 nearly $1.05 billion in a "sweeping victory" over claims that the Korean electronics maker copied the designs of its iPhone smartphone and iPad tablet. The jury said Samsung was entitled to "zero" in damages on its counterclaims.[23] Alberto Galasso observes that while managers can see patent litigation as a way to protect what is being copied, companies like Apple have also used it as an effective marketing tool to declare their rights and intentions in the media and to ward off those who come too close.[24]

Efrat Kasznik has described the tussle for IP rights as a combination of turf wars via global litigation and land grab via acquisitions motivated by multi-billion dollar IP-focused transactions.[25] In a global market where it is taking longer to file patents and the chances of success are nowhere near as high as people imagine,[26] some companies see corporate ownership as a fast-track way of acquiring valuable ideas in a shifting, dynamic, and global market.[27] Thus, ownership is not just about what you develop or acquire, but, just as importantly, what you are committed to protect.

23. http://www.forbes.com/sites/connieguglielmo/2012/08/24/jury-has-reached-verdict-in-apple-samsung-patent-suit-court-to-announce-it-shortly/#1d5f55ff1d44

24. https://hbr.org/2014/06/are-apples-patent-wars-a-marketing-strategy

25. http://www.slideshare.net/ForesightValuationGroup/are-patents-promoting-product-innovation-the-role-of-ipstrategy-in-the-global-marketplace

26. http://ipscience.thomsonreuters.com/product/virtual-ip-office/?utm_source=Linkedin_LSU&utm_medium=paid&utm_campaign=VIPO

27. Fascinating article on this here: http://www.theatlantic.com/business/archive/2012/07/why-there-are-too-many-patents-in-america/259725/

A quick glance at the stats shows just what's at stake. The trade in counterfeit goods is estimated to be worth $462 billion a year, with more than 63% of those knockoffs originating in China and most involving famous American brands.[28] Key sectors impacted by counterfeiting include clothing, luxury goods such as watches and jewelry, medications, cigarettes, toys, sunglasses, technology, cosmetics, and accessories.[29]

When Mike Dunn founded Octane5, he did so because he saw that many companies with licensing programs were failing to resource compliance around their properties. Companies weren't taking enough control of their assets; they had no analytics; their supply lines were opaque, and the brand was being executed in sloppy ways that led to misuse and misrepresentation. Most interestingly, though, was that Dunn said failure to take ownership at this level quickly led to deeper risks. For example, companies that don't take control of their licensing programs are also likely to be less vigilant about things like counterfeiting because they are operating in a vacuum that separates them from their customers and keeps them at arm's length from their supply chains.

"IP strategy can determine a product's success, market share and profitability," Kasznik says, "... [and] a failure to properly address IP issues can result in loss of market share, margin erosion, and reduced market competitiveness." It's vital, therefore, that companies set themselves clear goals around what and why they protect, that they manage their litigation exposure, and that they are resourced to enforce their IP and manage their royalties.

That's one side of the IP debate. Then there's the other side: companies like Tesla give away their IP in order to promote faster mainstreaming of electric vehicles; Google makes their Android system available to one and all; Mozilla and Firefox work with developers to continually improve their browser capability; and

---

28. http://www.msn.com/en-us/money/companies/the-worlds-most-counterfeited-brands/ss-BBsVVXu
29. Also worth reading: http://brandandcommercial.com/articles/show/brand-building/214/counterfeiting-the-challenge-to-brand-owners-and-manufacturers1

universities like Stanford, UC Berkeley, MIT, and Harvard offer free courses online.[30]

In summary, own-ability is defined as much by what your brand chooses to take ownership of, as it is by what you claim. This includes balancing many issues that put a brand at risk, jeopardize its competitiveness, or serve to make it more accessible.

Most brands should start by making the most of what they have at hand. Ask yourselves: Have you maximized the potential of what you own already? Many brands have assets that they have under utilized because they haven't seen their potential.

Tom McGuire, a one-time VP at Coke, told me that when the company decided to explore the assets in its archives, it led to a $40-million-a-year business opportunity built around its stores, The World of Coca-Cola, its experiential brand destination, and licensing. McGuire conveyed that the deals he and his team generated took a brand that was built on attitude and experience, and gave consumers new ways to interact beyond the drink itself. Originally, The World of Coca-Cola had been a museum for Coke memorabilia. By transforming it into a branded encounter, they changed the role of The World of Coca-Cola and the stores, from a place you went to browse, to a place where consumers could have an experience.

Coke stores, for example, started to stock incredibly expensive Coke cans that were encrusted with jewels and cost about $5000 each.

> "Because the can cost $5,000, it really boosted the value of everything else in the store," McGuire told us. "As a consumer I might not have $5,000 for the can, but I do have $45 for the sweatshirt. In fact, during the 1996 Olympics, the Crown Prince of Qatar bought not one,

---

30. Some great insights here on the push to open strategy: http://www.strategy-business.com/article/00075?gko=e1727

but seven of these cans. The reason, we found out later, was because he had seven wives and he couldn't take home just one can."

It's a classic example of how brands should be thinking laterally and find opportunities that will monetize well. By taking designs it already owned and re interpreting them in new ways, the brand was able to generate new revenue and to revitalize how people felt about Coke overall.

> "The whole idea of connecting a licensing program to the archives was really powerful," according to McGuire. "It enabled us not just to forge a link between consumers and the history of the brand, but also to link something of what the company was with not just where the brand was going but also with where consumers were at."

Such an opportunity would not have been possible if Coke had not owned those assets in the first place or had chosen to preserve them. It begs the question: What has your brand got, or has had, that could be reintroduced and/or re interpreted to give consumers a refreshing new sense of what you represent?

Companies that operate with a smaller range of products, particularly those that wish to resource and oversee how they take those brands to market, will choose to keep their assets close. With that comes a dependence on internal resources: you are, in essence, betting that your people are smart enough to beat others at your game. As Laurence Capron observed, while that may well be the case, there's also the risk that you have underestimated others or overestimated your abilities to expand into your current market, or another opportunity, using your own resources.

Brands that prefer to take a more open approach in terms of having a larger product set and marketing them on a larger scale are also more likely to bring in partnerships to help them realize their ambitions. The critical decisions for such companies are twofold: finding who to partner with, and finding ways to involve and include those partners in profitable and expandable ventures that don't jeopardize or compromise their core IP.

The organizations with the greatest reserves of goodwill aren't just the big name brands; they're also the brands with whom consumers have the greatest affinity. For example, I have done licensing work for the American Cancer Society. I assessed ACS' capability to create a "seal of approval" program lending their brand to cancer prevention products, such as sunscreen, to help consumers discriminate between brands. This can serve to reduce the proliferation of cancer while contributing funds to ACS to help them find cures for cancer. Other big not-for-profit programs include the following:

- The Sesame Workshop, which is the largest nonprofit brand licensing program, and arguably one of the world's largest programs, with sales in excess of $1.3 billion. Sesame Place celebrated its 35th birthday by hosting a party all-season-long, featuring fun and festive birthday decorations and a fantastic new Neighborhood Birthday Party Parade. *The Sesame Street: Let's Cook!* cookbook, published by Houghton Mifflin Harcourt Press, was covered on *Good Morning America*, *The Tonight Show*, and *Rachael Ray*. The book is now in its fourth printing. *Sesame Street* was a strategic partner for Google Play's launch of its Kids and Family platform. The brand was one of the four selected brands proudly featured at Google's NYC launch event in the summer of 2015.

- Girl Scouts of the USA, the second largest program, had sales in excess of $250 million in 2015 with distribution to top retail partners including Walmart, Target, Albertson's, Kroger, and Safeway. With over 50 million living alumni, the Girl Scouts of the USA's goal is to build products that promote the fun, unique activities, and experiences that are available through Girl Scouting, such as outdoor activities as well as STEM. The year 2017 will be an exciting year for Girl Scouts of the USA as it celebrates the 100th anniversary of the Girl Scout Cookie Sale. As the largest female-run business in the world, the Girl Scout Cookie Program teaches girls five essential skills: goal-setting, decision-making, money management, people skills, and business ethics.

- Similarly, the Boy Scouts of America (BSA) offers licensed properties that emphasize the values and lifestyle of the Boy Scouts. The BSA also has more than 50 million living alumni in the United States. Its goal is to create or develop new licensed products to reconnect with alumni and those with an affinity for the BSA in relevant ways through their daily activities. One of the key licensed properties for retail in 2015 was Pinewood Derby. This property targets youth and skill-building. The BSA has achieved tremendous success in growing the Pinewood Derby program at major craft, hobby, book, and hardware retailers. In 2015, the BSA launched co-branded Ford F-150 SVT Raptor and 2015 Ford Mustang GT Pinewood Derby kits with Revell. Among the newest properties launched is Be Prepared, which is the motto of the BSA. The target audience for Be Prepared licensed products encompasses every age group and product categories wherever readiness and preparedness are important considerations. In the long term, the BSA look to expand into other licensed product categories with emphasis on skill-building, outdoor play, and other active lifestyle opportunities that may fit well with the mission of the organization.

- Founded in 1846, the Smithsonian is the world's largest museum and research complex consisting of 19 museums and galleries, the National Zoological Park, and nine global research facilities. Approximately 28 million people from around the world visited the Smithsonian in 2014, with more than 175 million visits to the Smithsonian websites.

The total number of objects, works of art, and specimens at the Smithsonian is estimated at 138 million. Smithsonian draws inspiration from its world-renowned collections, groundbreaking research, and first-class educational expertise in support of creating dynamic, fun, and meaningful learning experiences through its products with proceeds supporting its stated educational mission for the increase and diffusion of knowledge. Smithsonian's 2015 top retail and licensing programs included the launch of a new eco-product line with master toy licensee NSI for science kits, and the expansion of its fine jewelry program based on the National Gems and Minerals collection to select stores nationwide.

- The U.S. Army licensing program focuses on its values of pride, performance, and personal development to build positive brand awareness and create multiple touch points for Americans to show support for the U.S. Army. In 2015, the program consisted of 280-plus licensees across an impressive breadth of categories including gift and novelty, personal accessories, consumer electronics, headwear, footwear, collectibles, cutlery, fragrance, toys, digital and interactive platforms, tailgating, and cake decoration. The three largest categories in the program were apparel, novelty items, and sporting goods. U.S. Army licensed products are found at every channel of trade in the United States, including mass merchandisers, mid-tier retailers, off-price channels, travel centers, sporting goods stores, toy stores, craft stores, grocery stores, dollar stores, and tourist/museum centers. The program has gained success online with licensees *Cafepress.com*, *Zazzle.com*, and *Amazon.com*, among others. The U.S. Army strengthened its co-brand initiatives with new licensees including Jansport in apparel and accessories and Bridgestone Golf in performance golf balls and golf accessories. In 2016, the U.S. Army program focused on patriotic themed in-store promotions surrounding various holidays such as Veteran's Day, 4th of July, Memorial Day, Flag Day, and Father's Day.[31]

All of these not-for-profit organizations have been able to expand their brands because they stand for ideas and events that people want to associate themselves with closely.

You don't need to own every aspect of a brand in order to have an own-able brand. In fact, every brand is owned in a range of ways, by a range of stakeholders. It's not just proprietary. Consumers also own brands, in the sense that they think of those brands as part of "their" lives. Own-ability is about what your customer feels you own as a brand, why they're excited by it, and why they choose to ascribe that attribute to you and not one of your competitors.

The people within organizations "take ownership" of the brands they work for in the sense that they think of themselves as part of those brands and their success. Sectors own brands, and brands own sectors, because without brands there would be no sensible or efficient way of recognizing and distinguishing between participants. In essence, any stakeholder can lay claim to some level of ownership in a brand, just as I and millions of others did back in 1985 when Coca-Cola decided to change its century-old secret formula and name it New Coke. And, just as importantly, brand ownership can be about what you are prepared not to own, like if you choose to license or open source in order to give others their own sense of belonging.

All of this is pertinent to how a brand looks to grow because expansion requires those who feel they own the brand to agree, either tacitly or explicitly, to changes in brand ownership. Sadly, too many brand expansions lack nuance. They tack a brand onto another brand or they add another asset to a house of brands without thinking through whether the people who support the business really want "more of the same." And while every brand professes to be there for its customers, few, if any, consult their customers

---

31. http://www.licensemag.com/license-global/top-150-global-licensors-2

when they look to change the ownership structure. The general assumption seems to be that the customers will like the change because it involves the brand and/or that they will get used to it.

To reiterate, when a brand chooses to expand beyond its current borders whether geographically, reputationally, or in terms of offering, it must know what aspects of the brand it will carry across to the new sectors, and where it will adapt its core DNA in order to be competitive within that sector. The brand additions must not only feel like they belong to the brand, but the brand itself must seem bigger, deeper, and broader because of the activities that now take place under its name. Simply put, the expanded brand needs to connect its own dots in ways that consumers recognize and enjoy. Successful expansion is about striking the right balance between four elements:

- Involvement — the people who see the brand as part of their lives must feel that they are included, and that they have something to gain from the proposed expansion.

- Leadership — there needs to be a clear sense of where the change takes the brand, in terms of new story and changed experiences.

- Coherence — the expansion needs to make sense — it needs to feel like the continuation of a journey, not just a change in the balance sheet and a press release justification.

- Enhancement — all of the above brings about something that would not have happened, or perhaps even been possible, without reworking the ownership structure.

The own-able quality is often considered in three ways: what companies get, what they own, and what they acquire. It should, of course, be considered in quite a different light altogether: what new things consumers can access, how this impacts their sense of belonging, and what brands can achieve under their banner. Back to my Coca-Cola example with the Olympic pins in Japan: the Japanese people clamoring for Olympic pins accessed memorabilia not everyone else could get, pins that crystallized and symbolized their memory of the Olympic Games. They could connect with other Olympic pin owners as unofficial members of an exclusive unnamed cult of followers who all knew how difficult it was to obtain each prized Olympic pin. And Coca-Cola enjoyed major lagniappe under the banner of the Olympic Games.

Different brands are using different ownership structures and different brand structures to achieve own-ability today. Some are going public, relying on funding from the market to help them achieve critical mass in return for meeting the demands of investors. Others are returning to private ownership, tired of what they see as the short-term expectations of analysts and the markets. Many still feel their best option is to grow using what they own already, or to join forces with others to expand their perceived ownership in the marketplace.

I can't see this slowing down. In fact, I believe own-ability and ownership models will continue to evolve in the next few years as organizations rethink what is theirs and what is shared.

The key responsibility for all brand owners as I see it is that they must be responsive. Every brand is an investment, and should be treated as such. Companies need to be actively managing their brand portfolios to ensure that their brands are as competitive and effective as possible, tightening up how they are structured to defend their position and loosening their structures in order to expand. Most brand portfolios in my experience contain a combination of evergreens, fads, mainstays, and emerging marques, all with different ebbs and flows. Coke, for example, recently changed tack, remodeling its once-separated brands into a consolidated brand because it wanted more direct linkage between products.

Own-ability is also about the return which comes from how you choose to own. The key criteria is return on brand equity (ROBE). Not enough brands have worked through what their brand is worth and the return that they should be getting on that value. In other words, they don't know what their brands contribute and they have not thought through the best structures to achieve the most from them, now and in the years ahead. It's no longer enough to pursue one own-ability strategy. Instead, brands should be evaluating a range of go-to-market strategies and benchmarking them against desired returns, both financially and in terms of customer affinity.

One brand that has had a phenomenal ROBE is CrossFit. Greg Glassman founded CrossFit, Inc. in 2000. By 2005, there were only 13 CrossFit-affiliated gyms, known as "boxes." Over the next nine years, the movement exploded and by 2014 CrossFit-affiliated boxes numbered more than 10,000. Today, CrossFit generates more than $4 billion globally and CrossFit, Inc. has revenue of over $100 million.[32] There are over 13,000 affiliates worldwide, and 50% outside the United States. There are an estimated 2 to 4 million people using CrossFit for their training.[33]

And, while Glassman's tactics may be considered divisive and somewhat unorthodox, one thing that has enabled CrossFit such rapid growth is the simplified certification process. For a mere $1000 for a weekend course to become a Level 1 trainer and a $3000 annual fee, any motivated entrepreneur can gain access to the CrossFit brand. Talk about a shift in the concept of ownership! Glassman's business model and the cult-like addictiveness of the CrossFit brand suggest that the growth of CrossFit has no end in sight.

Today, what you own and how you own it keeps changing. Look at LEGO, and the diverse arrangements they have to bring their products to market, or at how Disney mixes and hybridizes its models to market its properties, or the way that Adobe has completely shifted how it presents its product suite. Sometimes the greatest competitive certainty comes from flexibility.

---

32. http://www.forbes.com/sites/mikeozanian/2015/02/25/how-crossfit-became-a-4-billion-brand/#78d7331d78c1
33. http://www.iclubs.com/more-news/no-sign-of-crossfit-boom-abating.html

Key Takeouts

- Own-able is multi dimensioned. It's not only about structure and properties, but it's also about a crucial sense of belonging. More brands should be looking to sync how they are formed and what they own with the relationships they are looking to build.

- As more models are introduced that challenge assumptions about how business is organized, what companies own, and feel they need to own, will also change. That has challenging implications for how to assess the wealth of brands, and how to judge whether brands are delivering value.

- Current valuation models need to be closely linked to brand equity. Brands tend to be assessed for what they are worth as a whole rather than the difference they generate in markets on a daily basis. It will be exciting when it is finally possible to monitor the changing value of a brand in the same way, and with the same level of sophistication, as we can monitor movements in stock.

- From a brand perspective, in M&A, both parties must thoroughly contemplate and grapple with how they will merge and then strengthen their brand architecture to take advantage of what they now control. Otherwise, there's too much at risk.

- Brand protection, brand valuation, and brand strategy need to stop acting as separate disciplines and work more closely together to align what makes a brand owned and own-able.

- Keeping track of what you are remunerated for also requires tracking where you are most vulnerable to leaving money on the table. Protect what you can afford to protect. If you can't afford to protect something outright, you may want to rethink how you bring it to market.

- To maximize own-ability, start with what you have and structure what you offer to best meet and drive demand in your sector.

Understand what you need to have control of; here are seven searching questions to judge whether you have a highly own-able brand:

1. What structure do you need to deliver your idea to its full potential? How much of that do you need to have a stake in to make your goal a reality?

2. What do you need to own to succeed?

3. What do you expect to own in the next five years, what do you expect to lose or share, and what do you expect to be copied or to become industry standard?

4. Will your ownership model change over the next five years, and how will that affect what's own-able, what's not, and what could be own-able?

5. Where are the revenue streams going? For what will you be remunerated, and for what else will customers be willing to pay going forward?

6. How important is your intellectual property to you? How have you valued that IP? What weaknesses exist in your IP? How and when can competitors copy you?

7. Which is more important in your sector, speed-to-market or ownership of market?

Your Turn

You've come to an exciting place. In the course of this book so far, I've asked you to rate your brand on its ability to extend or expand, its addictive potential, the nature of your story, and the scale at which you are most effective. Now let's do the same thing for own-able. Please think about your answers to the seven questions above, and score your brand below. Base your score on how much you retain control and how you intend to fascinate consumers. There are no right or wrong answers. Some brands will feel that ownership is central to own-ability; others will see ways to codevelop new arrangements. Choose the number that best describes how your brand puts its mark on everything you do. We'll come back and get this number after the next chapter. If you've stuck with me so far, give yourself a pat on the back! You've now grown by a leap year in terms of the knowledge you have of your brand. Next, we're going to put this all together (in Chapter 8).

Own-able Expandability Score Chart.

1	2	3	4	5
We only act within what we know and for what we're known. We're fiercely protective of our IP. We have full ownership of everything we do.	We continue to add new products and IP to our brand through merger and acquisition.	We are open to a limited number of partnerships, joint ventures, and other arrangements that extend our perceived ownership in the marketplace.	We share ownership with other major brands in the marketplace through co-branded projects. We use these projects to redefine how our customers perceive us.	We cultivate an open model where individuals and groups can work with our properties to take them to new and exciting places. Only minimal guidelines are in place.

Is Your Brand Optimized?

Armed with this knowledge, you can begin to see what possibilities might exist to extend or expand your brand.

Congratulations! You have now completed scoring your brand against the five LASSO categories. From these scores I can now help you estimate whether your brand is optimized or not. Armed with this knowledge, you can begin to see what possibilities might exist to extend or expand your brand. As we gain more data points, the LASSO Model[1] will become more robust, and will enable me to help you determine how optimized your brand extension or expansion is, ranging from under-optimized, to slightly under-optimized, to optimized, to slightly over-optimized, to over-optimized. In Chapter 9, I will share with you my 8-Step Licensing Process so you can begin to take the steps required to optimize your brand extension through licensing.

Jeff Lotman, CEO and Founder of Global Icons, an evangelist in the industry sees the possibilities and shares my goal of empowerment. He knows that if every brand owner saw the full value of

---

1. The LASSO Model was co-created by Mark Di Somma and Pete Canalichio.

working with licensing partners to expand and extend their brands he or she would be using it more often. That is where the LASSO Model comes in:

> One of my biggest challenges is getting new clients to understand why connecting brands to customers is so important. New products matter. CMOs worry about losing control. They don't understand the full opportunity. The money [derived from royalties generated] shouldn't matter. There is no way to truly measure the full value a brand licensing program brings. Take for instance sponsorships. For a long time people didn't understand how to measure their Return on Investment (ROI). Thankfully enough people got involved and today, sponsorships make sense and the ROI can be measured. There is no measurement on licensing. In licensing one day you can have no retail presence and the next day you have four feet of shelf space. What is that worth? Or when someone wears your tee shirt that never previously existed. The value is enormous. It would be great if we could all start to agree on how to measure the full value of brand licensing. People don't look at money on PR or advertising, but for some reason people get fixated on it when it comes to licensing.

The LASSO Model is a first attempt to begin "to agree on how to measure the full value of brand licensing." Before calculating your own LASSO score, I want to acquaint you with the methodology used in the Model. I share it so you can fully appreciate the algorithm and its robustness. A full description of this algorithm can be found in the Appendix B.

Overview

The algorithm I built takes into consideration each of the elements of the LASSO scoring framework. This allows users, like you, to self-evaluate their brand according to the guidelines provided in this book and receive recommendations on how optimally the brand is being extended. Using state-of-the-art statistical techniques, the algorithm aims to simulate an expert assessment of brand extension in an automated manner, allowing both consistent and objective brand evaluation.

To develop an algorithm that accurately characterizes complex phenomena, I used the most effective current methods that rely on fitting a statistical model to a verified, known set of training examples, in the process known as supervised learning. For the purpose of developing such an algorithm to characterize brand extension, a "gold-standard" dataset of brand evaluations was generated by an expert panel including me and two other brand specialists. This dataset was used to optimize, train, and evaluate the Model. The resulting algorithm produced by this analysis performs both accurately and repeatedly, providing a robust solution with which users may evaluate their own brands.

Data Collection

The dataset generated by the expert panel consists of both the LASSO scores and a corresponding determination of brand extension for 56 brands. The brands that were evaluated and each expert's determination of brand extension are listed in Table 8.1, with a "True" value indicating that the brand was judged to be under-extended by the corresponding expert. Roughly half of the brands characterized in this dataset were under-extended and the other half were either optimally extended or over extended. Note that this group of brands was selected by the panel to include companies across a diverse range of industries. By including brands of companies both large and small across many industries in this training dataset, the algorithm is able to effectively generalize and characterize a wide spectrum of brands. Indeed, the inclusivity of this

Table 8.1. Expert Classification of Brand Under-Extension for All Brands in Training Dataset.

	Expert 1	Expert 2	Expert 3
Boy Scouts	True	True	True
Entrepreneur	True	True	True
KFC	True	True	True
Rubbermaid	True	True	True
Under Armour	True	True	True
Better Homes & Gardens	True	True	False
Caterpillar	True	True	False
General Electric	True	True	False
Papermate	True	True	NaN
Halo	True	False	True
Lego	True	False	False
Bob The Builder	True	NaN	True
Crockpot	True	NaN	True
Food Network	True	NaN	True
GRACO	True	NaN	True
Go Pro	True	NaN	True
John Deere	True	NaN	True
Little Tykes	True	NaN	True
TCM	True	NaN	True
Wolfgang Puck	True	NaN	True
NFLPA	True	NaN	False
Busted Knuckle	True	NaN	NaN
Girl Scouts	False	True	False

Table 8.1. (*Continued*)

	Expert 1	Expert 2	Expert 3
Angry Birds	False	False	False
Barbie — Mattel	False	False	False
Calvin Klein	False	False	False
Coca-Cola	False	False	False
Ford	False	False	False
Hello Kitty	False	False	False
MLB	False	False	False
Marvel — Superman, Batman, Disney	False	False	False
Mickey Mouse — Disney	False	False	False
Minions	False	False	False
NFL	False	False	False
Pokémon Go	False	False	False
Star Wars	False	False	False
Terminator 2	False	False	False
California Pizza Kitchen	False	False	NaN
Crossfit	False	False	NaN
Chupa Chupps	False	NaN	True
Pink Panther	False	NaN	True
Cars	False	NaN	False
FIFA World Cup	False	NaN	False
Frozen (Movie)	False	NaN	False
Monopoly — Hasbro	False	NaN	False
Nerf-Hasbro	False	NaN	False

Table 8.1. (*Continued*)

	Expert 1	Expert 2	Expert 3
Tommy Hilfiger	False	NaN	False
Chuck E. Cheese	False	NaN	NaN
Adventure Time — Cartoon Network	NaN	NaN	True
Mind Candy (Moshi Monsters!)	NaN	NaN	True
Minecraft	NaN	NaN	True
Moshi Monsters	NaN	NaN	True
Monster High	NaN	NaN	False
My Little Pony — Hasbro	NaN	NaN	False
World of Warriors	NaN	NaN	False

training dataset should enable this algorithm to classify accurately brand extension even for industries not present in this dataset.

To further improve the accuracy and real-world relevance of the algorithm, a subset of 25 of the brands was independently rated by each of the three experts. This overlap allows the model to capture the intrinsic, yet entirely valid, variation in these metrics. In addition, the overlapping set of examples allows a direct comparison of the agreement between predictions made by the algorithm and those made by human experts. See below a process flow chart depicting the steps taken from Data Collection through Model Selection and Training.

Table 8.2 categorizes the brands that were evaluated in the development of the LASSO algorithm by industry. While the entertainment category comprised 24 of the 56 brands evaluated, the brands encompassed 22 distinct industries.

Table 8.2. Evaluated Brands Categorized by Industry.

Industry	Brands (in the Training Set)	Industry	Brands (in the Training Set)
Entertainment	24	Magazine (Home Economics, Interior Design)	1
Consumer Products	10	Electrical	1
Gaming	10	Movies	1
Toys	5	Entertainment (Character)	1
Sports	4	Beverage	1
Machinery	3	Sporting Goods	1
Automotive	3	Electronic Manufacturing	1
Nonprofit	2	Fitness	1
Apparel & Fashion	2	Media	1
Restaurant	2	Consumer Electronics	1
Food	2	Food Production	1

Model Selection

The task of determining whether a brand is extended to an optimal degree or not is best suited to the group of statistical models that aim to classify examples into one category or another, a process known as binary classification. Many such models exist, each with different strengths and weaknesses for various types of

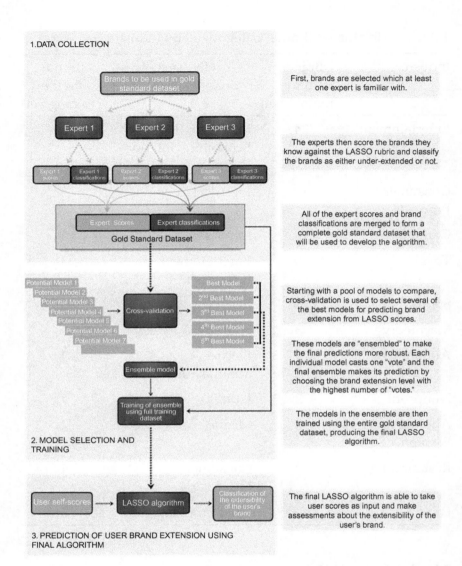

1. DATA COLLECTION

Brands to be used in gold standard dataset

First, brands are selected which at least one expert is familiar with.

Expert 1   Expert 2   Expert 3

The experts then score the brands they know against the LASSO rubric and classify the brands as either under-extended or not.

Expert 1 scores | Expert 1 classifications | Expert 2 scores | Expert 2 classifications | Expert 3 scores | Expert 3 classifications

Expert Scores | Expert classifications

Gold Standard Dataset

All of the expert scores and brand classifications are merged to form a complete gold standard dataset that will be used to develop the algorithm.

Potential Model 1
Potential Model 2
Potential Model 3
Potential Model 4
Potential Model 5
Potential Model 6
Potential Model 7

Cross-validation

Best Model
2nd Best Model
3rd Best Model
4th Best Model
5th Best Model

Starting with a pool of models to compare, cross-validation is used to select several of the best models for predicting brand extension from LASSO scores.

Ensemble model

These models are "ensembled" to make the final predictions more robust. Each individual model casts one "vote" and the final ensemble makes its prediction by choosing the brand extension level with the highest number of "votes."

Training of ensemble using full training dataset

The models in the ensemble are then trained using the entire gold standard dataset, producing the final LASSO algorithm.

2. MODEL SELECTION AND TRAINING

User self-scores → LASSO algorithm → Classification of the extensibility of the user's brand

The final LASSO algorithm is able to take user scores as input and make assessments about the extensibility of the user's brand.

3. PREDICTION OF USER BRAND EXTENSION USING FINAL ALGORITHM

datasets and variables. To identify the best model for the problem of classifying brand extension, several of the most powerful model families from conventional statistics and modern machine learning were evaluated and compared. According to the best practices in statistics, a model cannot be evaluated against the data that it was trained on; an example used to "fit" the model cannot be used to judge the model's performance, or serious biases will invalidate the results. There are many ways to avoid this bias, and all generally involve splitting the entire dataset into both "training" and "testing" subsets. Here, the model being evaluated is fit on the "training" data, and then predictions are made on the "testing" dataset. The accuracy of these predictions is then used to measure the performance of the model. One of the most effective methods for generating these training and testing datasets is a technique known as cross-validation. The main benefit of this technique over other techniques for validating a model lies in the fact that it evaluates the model on every single example in the original dataset. Because of this, a model that classifies some types of brands much better than others will always be penalized to the same extent, while other methods of model evaluation may rate this model higher or lower in a fairly random manner.

Using this cross-validation framework, five models were chosen that showed promise in predicting the expert classification of a particular brand's extension. However, to further enhance the accuracy and reliability of predictions made by this algorithm, one additional step was added. Rather than choosing the single best of the five top-performing models to generate the final predictions, the predictions of all five were combined with a machine learning technique known as ensembling. Essentially, this technique generates individual predictions for each model, and each model then casts a "vote" for its prediction; these votes are then tallied and the prediction given by a majority of the models is used as the final prediction. For example, if three models predict that a brand is under-extended, while the other two predict it is optimally extended, the final "ensembled" model will predict that the brand is under-extended. The power in this technique arises from the fact that the individual models, although performing fairly similarly to each other, make mistakes that are not identical. Because the models do not make exactly the same predictions, the majority consensus will more often be right than any individual model. After applying ensembling to the five best-performing models identified with cross-validation, the algorithm's performance increased significantly to nearly the same level as human experts, as detailed below.

Agreement between Experts

Overall, the panel of brand experts showed a very high level of agreement in their LASSO scoring metrics. The overwhelming majority of scores deviated by at most 1 point in only one of the three experts' scores, suggesting that the LASSO rubric, when properly deployed, is capable of precisely and quantitatively characterizing brands. With regard to the classification of brands as under-extended or not, the expert panel produced a unanimous classification for 19 of the 25 brands, suggesting that it is straightforward to determine brand extensibility in roughly 80% of cases, while one out of every five cases may be more involved and require further consideration. However, it is important to note that the experts surveyed rated brand extension on a more fine-grained, five-point scale (under-optimized, slightly under-optimized, optimized, slightly over-optimized, and over-optimized) that was later down-sampled to a simple under or not-under-extended rubric. This was done due to limitations with the size of the dataset available at the time. Otherwise, this may have resulted in different experts placing brands in the "slightly-under-extended" category with differing frequency due to individual interpretations of this more fine-grained rubric, while this coarser rubric may have resulted in higher unanimity between expert classifications here.

Algorithm Evaluation

The final algorithm, using an ensemble of five well-performing models, was evaluated using two methods. As both methods involve cross-validation, which is difficult to apply to the scores for more than one expert at a time, only the scores and classifications for one expert (Expert 1) were used to generate the model and predictions for this step. For both methods of algorithm evaluation, cross-validation was used to first predict the extendability of each brand in the dataset. The first method aims to assess the absolute capabilities of the algorithm to model this dataset, while the second compares the model's performance with that of the human expert brand specialists.

With such a relatively small set of data, it is difficult to make detailed inferences from these results, but the results do suggest that the algorithm performs respectably, even when compared to expert brand specialists. This is expected, as the algorithm is "trained" on data generated by these very experts. Also, since we believe that it captures the information related to brand extension contained in the LASSO metrics, it follows that a larger volume of expert training data in the future will allow the model to better represent this information and become increasingly robust. Additional enhancements such as including industry information in the model and the previously mentioned fine-grained categories for brand extension are likely to further boost the model's accuracy and precision. In all, however, the algorithm as it currently exists provides a repeatable, widely deployable, and inherently objective method for both expert and amateur owners to evaluate their brand.

Nevertheless, I'm sure you are familiar with the phrase "Garbage in. Garbage out." Keeping this in mind, I want to ensure you are armed with the most accurate scores possible as the effectiveness of the LASSO Model is reliant upon them. Therefore, let's refresh ourselves on the key takeouts from each category described in the earlier chapters: Lateral, Addictive, Storied, Scalable, and Own-able. This will give you an opportunity to adjust your score as necessary.

Lateral

As you consider the Lateral aspect of your brand, having clarity in your mind about what your brand is most linked to — a specific product set or a general idea — and what qualifies your brand to take ownership will enable you to choose those categories that are best suited to your brand. Make sure you also understand the problem consumers are trying to solve and why they would choose your brand to solve it. Understand the limitations of your brand. Are you big enough and well known enough to take on their problem? Do you have staying power? Will the extension be a "no brainer" for consumers, or are you asking them to stretch their minds beyond reason? Finally, is there any downside in this pursuit? Does the extension bring any negative aspects that could hurt your brand's equity or core business? If so, and you choose to proceed, how will you counter it?

Key Takeouts
- A brand will fail to expand successfully if there is a lack of demand, uninspiring supply, the brand itself is not seen as relevant, or the growth plan is badly executed.
- Brand growth is about growing what you already have. Brand extension focuses on building out a brand product portfolio. Brand expansion is about taking the brand into new and unrelated markets.
- Every brand needs an *expansion point*: a pivotal characteristic that gives the brand an emotional basis for growth.
- Where consumers associate a brand closely with a product, the brand is more likely to be successful, looking to extend its product lines within the segment.
- Where a brand is more closely linked with an emotion, it may be easier to expand the brand beyond its initial category.
- Brands should only look to expand into sectors where they will have a specific advantage because of how consumers perceive them.
- If you are going to expand, expand into sectors that have healthy growth potential. There's no point in expanding into a stalling market.

One of the best companies over the past decade at understanding and executing brand expansion has been Newell Brands. They know where their brands are relevant and how to take them into new and unrelated markets. One example of this was with Paper Mate. According to Nat Milburn, then Vice President of External Business Development at Newell Brands (formerly Newell Rubbermaid) and responsible for brand and technology licensing:

> The Paper Mate leadership team understood that licensing allowed the brand to extend into new markets. In the Middle East and Africa there were regulations prohibiting foreign based companies from vertical integration. Therefore, it made more sense for Paper Mate to sell everyday writing components and other components with intellectual property, e.g. inks and tips, into the region by having them assembled by another company. To simplify the process, Paper Mate chose to license their brand to the same company. To expand their brand further we licensed Paper Mate into other stationery categories. In this way, we could increase Paper Mate's total market contribution. This was a market entry strategy that worked exceptionally well for them.

Now that you have had a chance to consider the Lateral category for a second time, does the score you gave your brand in Chapter 3 still make sense? Or, should it be adjusted higher or lower? If you are unsure, I recommend you go back and look at the scoring guidelines at the end of the chapter to aid you.

Addictive

How does expansion play into the overall journey on which you are taking consumers? What part of the journey are you involved in and what parts should be outsourced? What do your current consumers yearn for that your brand can deliver on - escapism, distraction, adventure, or authority? If you expand into specific categories, will consumers see the connections between the various expressions of your brand? How will you engage them and direct them from one activity to another? Is your involvement with the brand tied to a specific time frame or project, or are you targeting a longer horizon? Are you offering your consumers the optimal mix of frequency, intensity, access, and surprise? If so, is it on their terms or yours? How dependent are you on ancillary revenue to meet your growth targets? Can you look to your licensees to build brand loyalty and love in addition to the royalty revenue play? As you ponder these questions, let's look at the key takeouts one more time.

Key Takeouts
- Addictive brands play to people's appetite for "more." Consumers are driven by the thrill of pursuit, the wish to be current and the fear of missing out, the expectation of availability, the strong sense of curiosity we're all born with, and the hyper awareness of the world around us that social media, in particular, has created.

- Addictive brands tend to be consumer-facing and many today have a strong media and social media profile that gives them presence in consumers' lives.

- It's easy to confuse the subject matter with the appeal. *Star Wars* may have been located in space, but its addictive quality for audiences extended far beyond the sci-fi genre.

- Extending or expanding your brand requires taking a holistic approach to managing your branded properties in order to realize their full potential. What more do people want exactly?

- Invest in categories that fit with the brand, but that also align with how and where consumers want to buy.

- Characters can make a brand addictive. However, what adds value and stickiness is authentic storytelling and/or play value.

- Sometimes consumers will hook into properties and ideas that take even the most skilled veterans by surprise. That's the power of serendipity.

- Everything today is about ecosystems. Increasingly, addictiveness is part of the financial model not just the customer relationship model.

Teri Niadna is the Managing Director, Brandgenuity Europe. She oversees the company's London office and is responsible for all its clients across the Middle East and Africa. Prior to assuming this role, she took an opportunity with the NFL to run their international licensing program. In her words, "It was a problem child." Despite having one of the most addictive brands on the planet, the NFL business abroad was "anemic and frustrating." Her job was to reset the business. As Niadna tells it:

> Experience is the core product of the NFL. Many fans want to bring home that perfect souvenir to memorialize their experience. To accomplish this, the NFL sells a lot at events. This involves sales, in tents, in parking lots. We routinely would drive 80,000 fans through a 50 x 20 square meter tent in 5 hours. My job was to ensure the fans experience purchasing NFL merchandise mirrored their experience watching the game. I thought long and hard about that. If experience is the product, how do we ensure quality in all areas? In principle where do we need safeguards and performance standards? What happens if someone is not happy? How do we handle social media? What are the things that matter? Given the narrow window of time for sales, we had to plan carefully. Once the game starts it is too late.

> When I started working at the NFL in January 2010, we had been playing in London for 3 years. When I got there I could not believe how much product

people would buy and what they had to go through to buy it. They were spending £80-£90 pounds a game. However, their experience was a complete nightmare. One of the reasons was that as a policy we were not authorized to sell out of anything. This meant carrying too much stock. With 32 team jerseys and 2 to 3 items for team, the range of products was enormous. There were hundreds of styles and way too many Stock Keeping Units. If the policy remained where could not to sell out of something, I knew we were going to lose a lot of money. There were 40 tills with 40 lines running through our tent. When we opened the gate hundreds ran to the event tent to buy product. With no NFL branded product sold in the marketplace, Game Day was the one day they could buy something. Everyone lined up and waited an hour for merchandise. Our white tent was a sensory deprivation chamber. Between the waiting and no brand engagement, the fans were having a miserable time. I challenged my team to design an experience for the fan where we would get them the merchandise they wanted, allow them to engage the brand and get them finished in the shortest amount of time. The first thing we did was set up a queuing system. We changed from 40 lines to one snaking line where the fans would go to the next open till. A third problem was that unlike in newer stadia, which had large sophisticated shops Wembley stadium had no shops. Instead it had 30-40 kiosks, which were very inefficient. We concluded that we had to build a quick set up shop for the 4-5 hours we were open. With the strength of the NFL brand, we had the revenue potential to justify it. The wait was still too long, but the experience was better. We added video and music. To give fans opportunities to purchase official NFL merchandise away from the game, we found an e-commerce solution through Fanatics.

It worked tremendously and sales grew in both channels. Scalability is a huge challenge when trying to expand an American brand overseas. With 32 teams how do you take the pressure off? We gave the customer a choice to do either buy on Game Day or online.

With a brand as addictive as the NFL, new challenges arise that have to be tackled. Ponder your answers to the questions posed above and how the NFL solved its challenges in Wembley to enhance the consumer experience. Now, reconsider whether the Addictive score you gave your brand in Chapter 4 still makes sense. Should it be adjusted higher or lower? If you are still unsure, take a look at the guidelines at the end of Chapter 4 to guide you.

Storied

How are you expanding how people perceive your brand through storytelling? What role do consumers have in helping to shape and influence that story? Where will you tell your stories in the future and how will you use the channels available to you to broaden the story? How will new partners enhance or change your storytelling? How will their story blend with yours? How have you connected your story to selling your product? How accurately can you measure how and when conversion occurs? Take a look at the key takeouts below as you consider refining your answers to these questions.

Key Takeouts

- Great marketers tell stories that people want to believe. We can argue about how literal they are about that and about the level of loyalty that inspires, but the fact remains that brands cannot simply go to market today with a narrative that's just about features, benefits, and price and be sustainable.

- In order to continually reach buyers, have something interesting to say at all times, and use the platforms available to you to make your brand heard. To do that consistently, there needs to be a central story underpinning what you talk about and how. That doesn't mean you can't sell. It does mean you need to find ways to keep people interested beyond just buying.

- If you're going to build a connective story, then you need to provide people with multiple ways to connect with that story, and you need to provide them with control over the aspects of the narrative that affect them.

- Use short stories to bring people to the brand, like Volvo Trucks did with its Van Damme videos. But don't stop there. Make that story part of a bigger story that brings people to Volvo looking for answers. Tie the strands together.

- Bring in partners that add to the story and help form the wider ecosystem.

- Know your own backstory. Stay true to what you were, and connect that with the story of who you are today. Shuttle back and forth through your history to connect your past with what shapes your brand today. Connect pieces. Bridge gaps. Explain mysteries. That's how you build a true mythology.

- Think long term rather than just campaign to campaign. And, if you're a brand in multiple markets, think anecdotally. Tell stories people relate to, not just those that make you feel comfortable. Link your world with theirs through story.

There are stories, there are stories within stories, and then there are stories *behind* stories, i.e., as the late Paul Harvey used to say, "and now you know the rest of the story." For Clayton Burrous III, Owner and President of Sunbelt Marketing Group, a former Coca-Cola Bottler and 25-year licensee of the Coca-Cola brand:

> You begin to realize the real value of a brand and its story after the 3rd, 4th or 5th [license agreement]

renewal. It's the 3rd, 4th, 5th or even 6th renewal when you become really profitable. The overriding value is continuity. Guarantees don't become an issue any more. Once the licensor knows you are going to perform over time these are less of a concern. The key is to be patient as a licensee. If you chase licenses you are going to get hammered. Be always willing to walk away from a deal. No licensor wants a licensee to fail, but they have their objectives that put a licensee in a bad situation.

Sometimes the story is about how you have delivered excellence over decades as does Sunbelt. Considering this story, the takeouts, and the answers to my questions, does the Storied score you gave your brand in Chapter 5 still make sense? Or, should it be adjusted higher or lower? If needed, go back to the guide provided at the end of the chapter for one more look.

Scalable

Have you ever asked yourself what you want your brand to be worth? Many marketers and business leaders focus on growth, but few ever address this question. It is not only critical as we consider the value of the brand, but it also frames the level of investment required. Moreover, what are the assets you need to own? What IP and protection will you build into your products? How do consumers see you: as a brand that owns ideas, or one that occupies a specific sector? What do they value you for and how elastic is it? What does scale mean for your overall brand presence and value? Where will you take your brand? To how many countries? How many territories in those countries? Why those ones in particular? What is the time horizon you have planned for this expansion? Are your objectives SMART — Specific, Measurable, Achievable, Relevant, and Time-bound? Finally, from where will the resources to achieve this growth come? How will you win? How much will you do yourself and how much will you rely on others to do? Understanding the Scalable key takeouts can help you answer these questions.

Key Takeouts

- Consistent reach is rapidly becoming a historic metric. The years ahead will see a shift not just in how brands scale, but also what they look for from scaling.

- The next era of globalization will need to reconcile not just new markets, but also local and individual relevance, and it will need to do so in ways that make smaller businesses part of the new way that brands build capacity.

- Expect "the world" to increasingly give way to "my world" in terms of where brands need to deliver.

- We will still have, and need, huge brands — but the criteria every marketer should be striving for is critical mass, which is access to the right markets at the right levels of intensity to achieve their business goals.

- Brands will scale in different ways — some will use the leverage of others, some will change who they reach, some will expand what consumers can expect, and some will find new ways and new places to make themselves heard.

- Scalability is not just about growth. Some will choose to expand their profitability by scaling back.

- We'll see more hybridization of character as brands explore how they will grow. Get ready for more monstrous upstarts and more upstart monsters.

- Scale is nothing without a catalyst to drive and maintain it. I like this thought. The biggest challenge brands face, as they look to scale, is their ability, ironically, to stay true to what they are.

One of my favorite examples of a brand that has been able to scale is The Busted Knuckle Garage. It is a relatively unknown brand outside of its core audience, but that is what makes its story that much more compelling. Warren G. Tracy, Head Wrench of The Busted Knuckle Garage, founded the company in the early 2000s. Today he is focused on extending his brand through products and has over 200 Stock Keeping Units in mix. This includes everything from clothing to man-cave stuff like signs, clocks, and thermometers. The Busted Knuckle Garage started with lip balm and hand salve. In the future, Tracy plans to expand into services like car washes, restaurants, themed coffee shops, and the like. Thirty-six independent garages carry Busted Knuckle products. The Busted Knuckle Garage products help garage owners connect with their customers in a unique and differentiated way.

Tracy's story dates back to 1988 when he was a student at Arizona State University. Sitting in a classroom one day, he was inspired by the story of Cherokee brands and found it fascinating. This became the genesis of The Busted Knuckle Garage, a brand that could appeal to guys that loved cars, garages, and grease. Tracy reflects on his success thus far:

> We partner with companies that can leverage all of what we do. They can take my brand idea and make it a brand reality. This has been my desire all along. It was my end goal. Licensing has enabled me to transition from a business development advocate to a full-blown licensing company leader. I now generate the artwork and product ideas that represent The Busted Knuckle brand and the consumer who appreciates that lifestyle.

> Licensing takes a small company with a big idea to big companies looking for new product lines. In my 16 years running The Busted Knuckle Garage, I have discovered that a lot of large companies don't have time to create product lines or in-house brands. One of our newest licensees is Ace Branded Products out of Milwaukee. They have had Harley-Davidson since 1947, Ford, Jack Daniels and recently The Busted Knuckle Garage. They had been working for 2 years on a tool line. They didn't know what to do with it or what to call it until they met me. The Busted Knuckle Garage was an answer for them.

Knowing the plan you will invoke to achieve growth and scalability as Tracy did with The Busted Knuckle Garage will make all the difference. With this in mind, does the Scalable score you gave your brand in Chapter 6 still make sense? Or, should it be adjusted higher or lower? Use the guide at the end of the chapter to help you decide.

Own-able

Have you considered what structure you need to deliver your idea to its full potential or how much of that structure you need to own to make it a reality? Just how important is your IP to you? How have you valued that IP? Where are you vulnerable to leaving money on the table? What do you actually need to own to succeed? What do you expect to own in the next five years? Ten years? What do you expect to lose or share, and what do you expect to be copied or to become industry standard? Will your ownership model change over the next five years? How will that impact what's own-able, what isn't, and what could be? Where are the revenue streams going? For what will you be compensated, and for what else will customers be willing to pay going forward? Finally, what is more important in your sector, speed to market or ownership of market? The Own-able key takeouts below may help you define or refine your answers.

Key Takeouts
- Own-able is multi dimensioned. It's about structure and properties, but it's also about a crucial sense of belonging. More brands should be looking to sync how they are formed and what they own with the relationships they are looking to build.

- As more models are introduced that challenge assumptions about how business is organized, what companies own, and feel they need to own, will also change. That has challenging implications for how to assess the wealth of brands, and how to judge whether brands are delivering value.

- Current valuation models need to be closely linked to brand equity. Brands tend to be assessed for what they are worth as a whole rather than the difference they generate in markets on a daily basis. It will be exciting when it is finally possible to monitor the changing value of a brand in the same way, and with the same level of sophistication, as we can monitor movements in stock.

- From a brand perspective, in mergers and acquisitions, both parties must thoroughly contemplate and grapple with how they will merge and then strengthen their brand architecture to take advantage of what they now control. Otherwise, there's too much at risk.

- Brand protection, brand valuation, and brand strategy need to stop acting as separate disciplines and work more closely together to align what makes a brand owned and own-able.

- Keeping track of what you are remunerated for also requires tracking where you are most vulnerable to leaving money on the table. Protect what you can afford to protect. If you can't afford to protect something outright, you may want to rethink how you bring it to the market.

- To maximize own-ability, start with what you have and structure what you offer to best meet and drive demand in your sector.

A great example of this new way of thinking about ownership comes from a story about the Graco brand. Graco baby products is a leading baby products manufacturer of infant car seats, strollers, and playards. Several market forces combined with Graco's already high market penetration made expanding into new product categories a critical element of its growth strategy. According to Nat Milburn, then Vice President of External Business Development at Newell Brands (formerly Newell Rubbermaid) and responsible for brand and technology licensing, the Graco leadership team was looking for ways to get consumers to engage with the brand earlier than they normally would.

The consumer journey for baby products begins in earnest when a mother first learns she is pregnant. However, Graco's core product categories (e.g., infant car seats, strollers, and playards) are not used until after the baby arrives. Our consumer research showed that setting up the baby's nursery is a new family's first major milestone in preparing for baby's arrival. One consumer comment that reflected the sentiment of many was, "Seeing a room of our home transformed into the baby's nursery helped [my husband and me] experience the excitement of our pregnancy in a way the fuzzy ultrasound images posted on our refrigerator never did." The Graco brand team needed to grow sales beyond its core categories and this category was an excellent fit with its core brand attributes and meaning.

Graco lacked manufacturing and sourcing capabilities in wood based products. Their design and supply chain strength was in plastics. The Graco sourcing team said they could find the products and do it themselves, but our licensing business case was more compelling in almost every way. Unfortunately, almost two years prior to the corporate licensing function being created, the Graco division had licensed a manufacturer for cribs that I insisted we terminate upon the creation of our corporate licensing function. The royalties for the product were over a million dollars annually, but the licensed manufacturer refused to agree to our new contract provisions that established a best-in-class quality assurance protocol. One of our team's Guiding Principles for licensing brand assets was "Brands before Revenue," meaning we would always serve to protect consumers and the brand first, and then worry about the revenue a licensing deal could or would no longer bring. The termination of the legacy crib deal was an example of that principle in action: Our largest customer was not happy they would no longer be able to sell the product and losing a million dollars of royalty profit wasn't easy for the Graco business either. However, we and the brand knew it was the right decision to make if the licensee wouldn't allow us to be more involved in ensuring product quality. 30-days after we terminated the rogue licensee for their refusal to allow us to inspect more fully their quality processes, the CPSC did a recall on the manufacturer's cribs, including those with Disney and Graco brands. Some consumers suffered serious harm in the Graco branded crib produced by the rogue licensee.

With this legacy in furniture licensing, the cards were stacked against licensing as a viable model for reentering the category via licensing. However, as a result of the quality assurance processes and standards we had set and the business case for licensing in the category, Graco senior leadership elected to re-enter the category via licensing the brand to top furniture and textiles manufacturers. We developed a high-end line with a leading furniture manufacturer, which we sold at Baby's R Us. This led to licenses for Graco-branded decorative bedding and nursery décor that was also successful. Graco branded gliders and nursery furniture were also popular at Target. We licensed the cribs category to a manufacturer whose brands were Italian higher-end designs. All licensees accepted our higher quality assurance and contract compliance requirements and performed very well. The result was higher quality products, enabling the Graco brand to delight consumers during an important part of the consumer journey toward parenthood. The business also enjoyed a greater than 30% growth in royalties over the period when a lower quality licensee sold the brand in higher volumes, showing "Brands before Revenue" was a winning principle for us.

In the Graco example, we see how insights drove process, which in turn drove structure. Ultimately, this left them with a better partner and a stronger brand. As you contemplate the take-outs, and the answers to the questions posed in this section, does the Own-able score you gave your brand in Chapter 7 still make sense? Or, should it be adjusted higher or lower? If you have any uncertainty, go back to the guide at the end of the chapter for help.

One of the people who intrinsically understands the LASSO parameters and their implication on a brand is Peter Weedfald. Weedfald is Senior Vice President at Sharp Electronics and a former executive at Samsung and Circuit City. Before Sharp he founded GEN1 Ventures, which held a 5-year contract with GE Licensing inside GE Corporation. GE Licensing held licenses with 20 to 50 different manufacturers and included everything from diabetic products to electronics to power generation. At GEN1, Weedfald had the ear of GE's Chief Executive Officer.

> Products make brands, not the other way around. Products have to be outstanding. On the other hand, brands must have emotional capital. If we can add the emotional capital to the product through the brand, we can drive gross margin. Brand Licensing's goal, therefore, is to defer the cost of time-based competition — meaning all the costs involved — without losing the benefit of product differentiation. The way for businesses to compete is to enlist a super brand through licensing to improve the power, value, density, and profitability of the retailer, consumers, their P&L. The shortcut and smart way to do this is to find a brand that allows you to conscript consumers and retailers. It's the push and pull. Brands help both. The brand ensures viability of the P&L.

The characteristics of a successful license are the additional choices consumers can make and that brands get great products at a low cost. Moreover, those who believe in a brand do not require proof of performance. Conversely, if you do not have consumers that believe in your brand, no proof is possible. A brand is the refuge of the ignorant. Once the brand has a rhythm there is no stopping it. Let's take Apple as an example. They are so strong because:

1. They have a great brand to license, which enables them to get the product to market faster with a shorter and less expensive investment period.

2. Retailers recognize the product. This means less inventory risk and a better opportunity of sell through.

3. The brand and its product provide a rational channel strategy. When you don't have a brand, you can't rationale the channel strategy because there is no brand power that retailer's respect.

4. It gives them a competitive advantage on the shelf and offers product discipline in the marketplace.

5. The analyst community listens when a kinetic assiduous brand makes a move.

6. The wide arm of the licensor helps the licensee providing them a huge benefit.

I couldn't have said it better. Great brands understand this and utilize their strengths to reach new heights. With your revised scores in hand and an understanding of the methodology behind the LASSO Model, let's find out whether your brand today is under-optimized or doing well. To obtain your score you will need access to the Internet. Open your browser and type in www. PeteCanalichio.com/LASSO. Now input your scores for each category. There is also a place to input your industry sector in the areas of character, collegiate, corporate brands, entertainment, fashion, and sport. If you don't know your sector or it is not listed, don't worry. Leave this space blank. While losing a small amount of accuracy, the model will still provide you with a reasonable determination. As we build the database of inputs, we will build in additional industry sectors to enhance the Model's accuracy.

If the LASSO Model, based on your input, said your brand is "Optimized," then you have my hearty congratulations! There is nothing more for you to do at present beyond what you are currently doing. However, be sure to reevaluate your brand's score on an annual basis to determine if there have been any changes that could result in a different score. If, however, your LASSO score came back as "Under-Optimized," then you are in the position to extend and/or expand your brand into a new set of categories. Chapter 9 will help you determine what those categories should be and whether they should be extended internally or externally. If you are either limited by capability or capacity, you may be a candidate for licensing your brand. Turn the page to find out!

Making the Decision to License

9

Only the strongest brands, the ones possessing the highest levels of brand loyalty, are candidates to be licensed.

What is Licensing?

Licensing means nothing more than the renting or leasing of an intangible asset.

A company owns tangible assets and intangible assets. Tangible assets are physical assets such as factory machines, buildings, computers, furniture, etc. Intangible assets include a company's brand such as Caterpillar, a character owned by a company such as Donald Duck, its employees' skills, or ideas. An arrangement to license a brand requires a licensing agreement. A licensing agreement authorizes a company, which markets a product or service, a licensee, to lease or rent a brand from a brand owner who operates a licensing program, a licensor.

Earlier, I listed several examples of brand owners who have successfully licensed their brands. Some licensing examples are rather obvious like Better Homes and Gardens décor, NFL apparel, Kathy Ireland makeup, *Star Wars* figurines, Mind Candy trading cards, Coca-Cola lapel pins, or NASCAR replica diecast cars. However, many examples are not so obvious. How about

Rubbermaid branded closet storage, Mr. Clean cleaning buckets, or Entrepreneur business coaching? While the list of examples is as broad and varied as the mind can ponder, there is one thing in common among all successful brand licensing programs. Each has a brand that is well known and loved among its target market. And, while the consumers may not have demanded the product or service before it was created, they were certainly glad to discover it after the fact.

What Makes a Brand License-able?

I have often been asked, "Can you help me license my brand?" While relatively benign, this question actually tells us a lot about the inquirer. Before replying, "yes," I will always ask, "What is the name of your brand?" and then wait for the answer. If I don't recognize the brand name or it is not in the top three of unaided[1] responses for a particular category, the likelihood is that I probably cannot help the brand owner, at least not yet.

Only the strongest brands, the ones possessing the highest levels of brand loyalty, are candidates to be licensed. If one considers that the company paying the brand owner for the rights to license the brand must also pay for the development of the product or service plus the product or service itself, any ongoing innovation, testing, marketing, and the royalties due to the brand owner, the brand under consideration better be one that consumers or end users not only insistent upon, but also advocate. While the idea of collecting royalties and having someone else pick up the tab for bringing the officially licensed merchandise to market probably sounds compelling to our prospective client, it

---

1. Brand recognition or awareness is usually referenced as *aided*, when a consumer recognizes a brand after he or she is asked its given name, and *unaided*, when consumers mention a particular brand when asked if they know any brands in a particular category. Unaided awareness is seen as a higher level of brand recognition.

has less than a snowball's chance in hell of happening unless the target market first loves the brand.

If the brand in question happens to be a relatively new one, I usually use this opportunity as a teaching moment. I talk with the owner about the hierarchy of a brand, and how brands are like friendships. I explain that whenever I first meet someone, I try to learn his or her name. Many times after being introduced to that person, despite my best efforts, I immediately forget the person's name! No matter how often and how embarrassing this has become, I have not gotten that much better at remembering. I have even tried tools like using mnemonics to improve my name recollection with little success. If the person I have just met has the name Jack Powell, and Jack has a muscular build, I might come up with the phrase "Jack the Powerful." While this might help me remember the last name, it still requires I remember the first name, Jack. And even if I remember Jack, I still might not remember the mnemonic stands for Powell. It can be so frustrating. The same holds true for consumers when they try to remember new brands. That is why companies develop marketing strategies and create advertising campaigns to reach their target market; they know that it takes multiple encounters to build awareness and name recognition.

The hierarchy of branding begins with awareness. If I don't know the brand, my experience stops before it has the chance to start. For this reason, companies use a variety of tools including advertising, sampling, public relations, and experiential marketing to reach their target and create a memorable impression. The key is to expose the consumer to the brand and then to get them try it. If the company has done a good job of targeting the right market segment and identifying the consumer's needs then they will be in a strong position to address those needs. When this happens, the consumer may have a good experience; she may begin to build a preference for the brand.

Let us go back to our example about Jack Powell. Say I meet Jack through Bill, a mutual friend. Through Bill's introduction, which I trust, I get an opportunity to learn a little about Jack. This costs me a small investment of my time so there is little at risk.

If our first meeting goes well, I may suggest we meet for coffee. If from our coffee meeting, I learn that Jack and I have a lot in common — let's say we went to the same university and enjoy playing tennis — we likely will want to meet again. In brand terminology, I am beginning to build a preference for Jack.

Over time, my preference may develop into a friendship and I will begin to trust Jack. If Jack can be consistently relied upon to follow through with his commitments, I will become loyal to Jack. Like any good friendship, I will want to spend additional time with Jack doing things we both like. Let's say we both have enjoyed playing tennis and are getting quite competitive. While I enjoy playing tennis with other friends, I may begin to prefer to play with Jack and do so whenever possible. In brand terminology, I have become loyal to Jack.

Later, we discover that we both love to travel. We begin making trips together and build lasting memories. Eventually my friendship with Jack develops to the point where I consider Jack like a brother. One day in autumn, I tell Jack that I would like for us to make a trip to Antarctica together. Jack agrees and we begin planning to go the following summer when the weather is optimal. A month before the trip, Jack breaks his leg and cannot travel. He knows how much I want to go and suggests I go with our mutual friend, Bill. However, I cannot imagine making the trip without Jack and politely decline his offer. In brand terminology, I have become brand-insistent. There can be no other choice for the trip but Jack.

Jack is truly touched by my commitment to him. This solidifies our friendship even further. His leg heals and we make the trip together the following summer. We have an experience like none other, full of challenges and encounters that require team effort to overcome. After completing the trip Jack and I have built a bond that will span the test of time. I tell everyone just how great a friend Jack is to me, and wax of his tremendous skills, character, and attributes. In brand terminology, I have become Jack's advocate; I want others to become Jack's friend so they can enjoy his friendship like I do.

What Sort of Brand Should It Be?

If we think of brands in the same way as friendships, we can begin to see why consumers become so committed to certain brands. Like good friends, those brands are reliable; our quality of experiences is enhanced because of the brand's attributes. We learn we can trust those brands to be there where and when we need them. In fact, we discover that the experience with a particular brand is better than the experiences we have had with other brands. Soon we come to expect the brand to offer us more choices of products or services. It is at this point where we have granted the brand permission to extend into new categories. Moreover, we *want* the brand's owners to create new products and services so we can enjoy them in more places and on more occasions. When this occurs, the brand owner must not only decide when and where to extend, but how. The brand owners can choose either to make or to source the product or service in the new chosen category themselves, or they can extend via a third party. If they choose to use a third party, they can either acquire a company that makes the product or provides the service, or they can license their brand to a company which can deliver the product or service at a level consumers expect.

In 2009 Darran Garnham joined Mind Candy. At that time Mind Candy was a small startup with nine employees. Mind Candy is a British entertainment company, formed in 2004 by UK Internet entrepreneur Michael Acton Smith.[2] Its first online game was Perplex City.[3] In 2007, the company began development on Moshi Monsters,[4] a virtual world and online game aimed at children aged between 6 and 12, which allows users to adopt their own pet monster, socialize, and play educational

---

2. https://en.wikipedia.org/wiki/Michael_Acton_Smith
3. https://en.wikipedia.org/wiki/Perplex_City; https://en.wikipedia.org/wiki/Mind_Candy#cite_note-guardian1-1
4. https://en.wikipedia.org/wiki/Moshi_Monsters

puzzles.[5] With a million users playing Moshi Monsters, Moshi Monsters has been likened to a Facebook for kids[6] and as of 2012 had over 75 million users.[7] Darran recalls how he literally launched a brand from Moshi Monsters' digital fan base. "We set up a small brand and licensing division. This included a licensing and retail team and a small entertainment team." In 2011, Moshi Monsters launched a range of physical products including toys, books, membership cards, trading cards, Top Trumps,[8] and Plush Toys.[9,10] The program continued to grow and, by March 2012, Mind Candy confirmed a major partnership deal with Sony Music.[11] The deal followed the launch of Mind Candy's own music label, Moshi Monsters Music. As of 2015, over $100 million in Mind Candy merchandise has been sold.

The Critical Success Factors for Licensing

Reading the story above, you can appreciate the reasons why Mind Candy would wish to license the Moshi Monster brand, but how about for the company that secures the license? After all, the costs and risks are many. For the companies securing the license, Moshi Monsters offered immediate credibility and recognition, enabling them as licensees to enter new markets while enhancing sales of their core products. Toys, trading cards, and publishing have been the three core pillars for the brand. This brought great success to Mercury Inpress, makers of coloring and activity books, Topps for their Moshi trading cards, and Random House Penguins.

---

5. https://en.wikipedia.org/wiki/Mind_Candy#cite_note-thisislondon1-2
6. https://en.wikipedia.org/wiki/Mind_Candy#cite_note-3
7. https://en.wikipedia.org/wiki/Mind_Candy#cite_note-4
8. https://en.wikipedia.org/wiki/Top_Trumps
9. https://en.wikipedia.org/wiki/Mind_Candy#cite_note-thisislondon1-2
10. https://en.wikipedia.org/wiki/Mind_Candy#cite_note-5
11. https://en.wikipedia.org/wiki/Sony_Music; https://en.wikipedia.org/wiki/Mind_Candy#cite_note-6

Licensees also gain authenticity and legitimacy from the brand. Consider the video game manufacturer who has developed an amazing soccer game. When they can acquire a license with FIFA World Cup, they gain immediate access to the sport's most popular marks in the world's most popular sport. For FIFA, the video game manufacturer and licensee is EA Sports. According to the video game manufacturer,

> FIFA, has always been the highlight of the year for the company in terms of sales; the soccer franchise accounted for 27% of the company's net revenues and 23% of the company's gross profits in 2013. With technological advancements, improved graphics, detailed visuals and new digital content features, the demand for FIFA has increased exponentially over the last five years. The number of FIFA units sold has almost doubled from 6.4 million in 2010 to 12.45 million in 2013.[12]

Of course only the best companies can obtain the rights to a license as big as the FIFA brand. To put the acquisition of a FIFA license in perspective, it is important to understand the truly global appeal of the FIFA brand and what FIFA expects from those charged to manage its IP. According to Mark Matheny, Founder of Licensing Matters Global, who with several business partners acquired a master license from FIFA in early 2006 for the 2010 FIFA World Cup quadrennial:

> FIFA required that our Master Licensing Agreement's minimum financial guarantee be paid using cash, or secured by a Letter of Credit and/or Bank Guarantee. FIFA uses guarantees of this type to finance their operational costs related to its Competitions, such as World Cup and all their other World Championships, for which we acquired a worldwide license. This license

---

12. *Forbes*, October 6, 2014.

included the copyrights, the trademark and the word-mark for FIFA back to the time of its founding, 1904. We had rights to create merchandise for clothing, sporting goods, collectables, souvenirs and a host of other categories. We created a FIFA football retail concept, which would include the products of the trademark, and copyrights we acquired plus those of other companies such as adidas, creating a unique and authentic football themed shopping experience. Our other strategy was to take an event based business — where 70% of the licensing revenue typically came from host nation — and make it a global platform. Considering the size of the Minimum Guarantee, which was very significant, we had to activate many countries to make the program financially successful. We hired a merchandising team to develop a detailed digital toolkit that covered everything. The toolkit was sent to manufacturing partners to replicate the designs on products in a way to adjust to seasonality — northern and southern hemispheres and local tastes. With FIFA we created a Official Event Retailer concept too. By becoming an Official Event Retailer you were allowed to bring people in-store to buy official licensed products and other products marketed by other companies within FIFA's partnership network, such as Electronic Arts FIFA game, Panini football cards and even football themed Coca-Cola licensed merchandise. Moreover, we gave the consumer a chance to win an all expense paid trip to go to the FIFA World Cup in South Africa. We ended up activating the rights in over 60 countries with official retailers all over the world — from the UK to US, and from Indonesia to Brazil. Walmart was a partner in 14 countries. By incorporating the retailer into the program we stripped out the time required to manage a licensee network. We ended up placing official licensed FIFA product in 5000 store locations with 1 million square feet of retail selling space.

Similarly, a maker of automotive parts or accessories, like Proform, will license car brands such as Ford or General Motors for the sole purpose of establishing in the consumers' mind that its products will work seamlessly with each brand of vehicle.

A manufacturer who acquires a major license often gains the licensor's preferred pricing on items such as raw materials, shipping, or creatives. In addition, they gain access to the licensor's style guide, which provides them with most of the imagery and artwork they need to design their products. Depending on the licensee's business, these savings can go a long way to offset the cost of the license, which can be significant. When I was at Rubbermaid, many of the licensees made products with resin made from oil. As one of the world's biggest purchasers of resin, Rubbermaid bought resin at the world's best prices, and in turn, offered their licensees a significant savings they could not otherwise obtain.

Brand licensing offers licensees access into new distribution channels. Consider the scenario where a manufacturer whose products sell under a brand in mass merchandise outlets; with the right license, the manufacturer could begin to market a more upscale, high quality line of their products in specialty stores or department stores that would not typically carry the lower end products. Consider Graco, which sells strollers, pack 'n plays, and cribs. They also sell car seats to stores like Sears, JCPenney, and Kmart. Graco might consider entering the upscale channel for their car seats via licensing. They could approach Bugaboo, a maker of high-end strollers, about extending their brand into car seats. If Bugaboo agrees to license their brand, Graco would begin selling car seats into upscale stores like Neiman Marcus and Jacadi. Bugaboo satisfies a pent-up desire from its consumers to buy Bugaboo-branded car seats and Graco gets access to a new channel.

Licensing offers licensees the ability to enter new regions. A doormat manufacturer based in Germany and selling its product in Europe may be able to enter the U.S. market by licensing a major household brand like Better Homes and Gardens. The Better Homes and Gardens brand may agree to license their brand if the manufacturer has superior quality and a presence with a global retailer such a Walmart.

Through licensing, manufacturers and service providers gain access to intangibles such as the licensor's subject-matter expertise. This could include areas where they may not be proficient such as marketing, supply chain management, and customs. In addition, the acquiring company can benefit from the licensor's databases and libraries gaining access to market research, manufacturing, product design, and even customer lists. As true partners, licensors and licensees can identify where each other's strengths exist and tap into them. For example, Entrepreneur Media, Inc. (EMI) has extended a license with Professional Education Institute (PEI) for business coaching. PEI has deep expertise in coaching entrepreneurs and small business owners on how to build business plans, write marketing plans, and acquire customers. They understand that an optimal way to grow their customer base is to leverage EMI's database of readers. On a monthly basis, more than 10 million readers come to entrepreneur.com for advice. PEI and EMI work together seamlessly to create and publish compelling content on entrepreneur.com. Inside the content, EMI posts advertisements directing readers to Entrepreneur Coaching where they can get additional help on the topic discussed. For the reader the advertisement for Entrepreneur Coaching is not seen as an interruption to their train of thought as they consider the implications of the article, but rather a welcome and perhaps unexpected value added. The net effect is that the reader appreciates EMI for offering the coaching service even if they choose not to use it, PEI gains incremental customers who are ideally suited for their services, and EMI "brand love" grows while driving royalty revenue to the EMI bottom line.

For some companies, acquiring one license often will open the doors to other licenses. For others, gaining access to an important known brand can add instant value to their organization, which may be an important consideration when the owners are contemplating selling the company. Manufacturers and sourcing companies often consider these benefits when making a decision to acquire a license.

The Brand Licensing Process

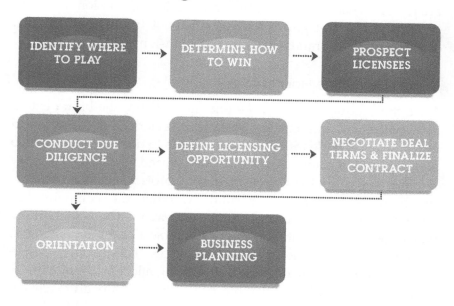

Step 1: Identify Where to Play

As explained in the previous sections, when consumers become delighted by a particular brand experience, they begin to bond emotionally with the brand. They become brand loyalists and advocates, buying the brand more often and recommending it to others. This behavior builds the brand's reputation. Consumers will often purchase a brand for the first time because of its reputation. The brand, therefore, adds value and certainty to an otherwise unknown product.

The stronger a brand's reputation, the higher the value of the brand and the greater revenue it will drive for its owner. Prospective licensees want to license brands with the strongest reputation, as these are the brands consumers demand and retailers prefer most. The stronger the brand, the higher likelihood retailers will buy the licensed products and that consumers will subsequently purchase them. Brand loyalists and advocates look to their preferred brands to deliver more and better products year after year. When this occurs, the brand gains permission to extend or expand into categories that complement its original offering. This is known as brand extension or expansion.

Step 2: Determine How to Win

Once the product category, the one that satisfies the brand extension objectives and creates positive associations for the brand owner, has been identified, the next step is to determine how to go about executing the extension. Any brand extension activity requires substantial resources. Before a project to extend begins, the brand owner must determine whether the company has enough resources to complete the endeavor. There is nothing worse for management than starting a project and then having to terminate midway due to lack of resources. This happens sometimes when resources are frozen after being allocated. While undesirable, that scenario is tolerable. However, to start an extension with insufficient resources is unacceptable. How should the brand owner determine the best way to go about entering the product category that has been selected? A first step would be to mobilize key departments within the organization to conduct their own due diligence.

When contemplating entering a new product category, the first step is to determine whether the company has the competency to design, produce, and market the product with internal resources.[13] One way to accomplish this is to ask the operations team to evaluate the competency of manufacturing or sourcing the product, and the finance team to conduct a cost/benefit analysis of manufacturing versus sourcing the product. If the analysis affirms the company's ability to produce the product, the next step is to determine whether there is sufficient budget and capability to market the product. Are there adequate resources to invest in product

---

13. When we refer to internal resources, we are referring to either the company's manufacturing capability to produce the product or its ability to source the product competitively from one of its third-party suppliers.

development, advertising, and promotional activities? Do relationships exist with distributors and retail channels through which the product will be sold? Is there sufficient presence in enough geographic locations to make the brand extension viable?

Even if a company can produce or source a product, price it competitively, and earn a healthy profit margin, the company may lack the resources or the capability to market the product effectively. This can impact the decision of whether to manufacture the product internally. If at the end of the analysis, it's determined that the company has the capability to design, produce, and market the product, it should go ahead and proceed with product development. However, if a company does not possess the capability to produce the product internally, it should look at other available options.

One way to extend the brand into the new category is to acquire a company, which can manufacture, market, and sell the product using its own resources. This option is often harder than it seems. For one thing, a company would need the available cash or have access to it, to fund such a transaction. Also, acquiring new businesses is a time-consuming proposition. First, potential target companies must be identified. Next, due diligence must be completed before negotiating an acquisition price. Once acquired, the company must be integrated within the existing company structure. Because of the lengthy process, critical time can be lost in launching the product. Even if a company decides to go with this option and the timing fits, it still may not have the marketing budget or the capability to move forward.

Another way to extend the brand externally is to license the brand to a manufacturer of the product in the same category. As mentioned in previous sections, there are several advantages to licensing a brand. To begin with, the manufacturer, or licensee, possesses the capability to not only manufacture the product but also market it, having done so for unbranded items or lesser-known brands. They also possess the necessary relationships with distributors and retailers to make a success of the program. Adversely, the brand owner forgoes some control when she chooses to license the brand. However, entering a new market via licensing has lower investment risk.

Step 3: Prospect Licensees

Once a product category that qualifies for brand extension has been identified, and brand licensing is the preferred method to achieve this extension, it is time to scout for prospective licensees within the selected product category.

Before short-listing the licensees, it is important to put together a basic checklist of parameters in which to evaluate the licensees. These parameters, to be defined by the brand owner, include:

- Size and financial strength
- Market share in the product category
- Current or previous licenses held
- Awards received
- Consumer perception

Once the checklist has been developed, the next step is to identify companies that manufacture the selected product category. These can be found relatively easily with research. The most common sources of information are trade directories, trade magazines, trade shows, and research companies like Hoovers, Dun and Bradstreet, Frost & Sullivan, and Vault Reports. Another way for the licensor to identify prospective licensees is to get out of the office and conduct a market tour. Through "store walks" the licensing specialist can physically see what products are on the shelf. The manufacturers may be using their own brand or a licensed brand. Licensed products are required to have legal language on the packaging, which will reveal the manufacturer. Once a comprehensive list of prospects is identified, these candidates should then be evaluated based on the parameters listed above. This will provide the licensor with a pool of qualified companies to investigate further.

Step 4: Conduct Due Diligence

This is the stage when the brand owner begins rigorously qualifying the prospective licensees to determine whether they will progress to the next phase. The due diligence stage involves conducting an evaluation of the business from a financial, legal, and risk management perspective. The more comprehensive the evaluation, the less likely the licensee selected will have unforeseen issues going forward.

A good first step in this process is to develop a Licensing Application that requests detailed information on all aspects of the prospective licensee's company. The information gathered from the application will serve to substantiate whatever secondary research has been collected. A Licensing Application should typically include an assessment of the company's strategic reasoning, financial strength, marketing acumen, and operational capability. In addition, it should include a forecast of the licensed product sales. If the size of the projection is not sufficient to justify the investment, then additional efforts to secure this company as a licensee may be in vain.

Step 5: Define Licensing Opportunity

After completing the due diligence process, the licensor should ideally be left with two to three qualified prospects. Now it's time to assess the size and scope of the actual licensed product program. This requires the licensor to work with the candidate licensees to understand their strengths and determine whether the licensing opportunity is viable.

Outstanding candidate licensees will immerse themselves in the licensor's brand, gaining a full understanding of the brand's positioning and architecture. With this knowledge, the candidate licensee should propose the look and feel of the licensed products, and incorporate the brand attributes into the design of their products. Licensees will pay particular attention to the details such as placement of the logo on the product and how it is affixed, and the material from which it is constructed. An astute licensee will request that the licensor provide them with the brand's style guide so they have the required information to create concepts that will represent the brand accurately.

Step 6: Negotiate Deal Terms and Finalize Contract

The scope of the licensing opportunity should have been established by the conservative sales estimates developed in the previous step. It is now time to determine the core deal terms. These parameters define the structure of the contract, including the *term* of the contract, where the licensed products will be sold, what royalty rate will be paid, and what trademarks will be used. Because the value of these terms will be unique to every licensing contract, they must be negotiated between the licensor and prospective licensee.

While each party inherently wants to arrive at the most favorable terms for their side, the best set of deal terms are those that allow both parties to achieve a successful long-term licensing program. Successful licensors keep the end in mind and practice win-win negotiating strategies. Similarly, smart licensees will have identified several choices of brands from which to acquire a license and will set limits on what deal terms they will accept, regardless of the brand. In these instances both parties can shake hands on a set of terms they know will allow them both to be successful.

Step 7: Orientation

The execution of the contract signifies the beginning of the relationship. It is therefore important for the licensee to get as familiar as possible with the licensor and the licensing program. It is the licensor's responsibility to make sure that they provide the licensee with all the information they need to be successful. Well-run licensing programs include a formal orientation session shortly after the contract is signed. The orientation provides an opportunity for key members from the licensor and licensee's companies to meet, get to know each other, and review expectations and contractual requirements.

Attendees from the licensor's side should include, at minimum, members from the licensing group, the brand group, product development, and sales. The licensee should send the general manager, and if possible, product development, account management, and sales and marketing representatives. The licensor normally provides an overview of the brand architecture, brand positioning, and category positioning. The licensor also takes the licensee through the product approval processes, time lines, and key terms in the licensing agreement. The orientation session also includes a review of all testing and auditing protocols. The licensee typically provides an overview of the staff and resources dedicated to the licensing program. If known, the licensee should review the product forecast and marketing plans and provide concepts for review. For *Sesame Street*, the orientation process is extremely important as Will DePippo, Assistant Director, International Licensing at Sesame Workshop alludes:

> One of the most important considerations when orienting a new licensee is to make sure they understand what the expectations are. If they are new to licensing, there's a lot of education that needs to happen so that the licensee understands what they're getting into.

> For a company new to licensing, you have to make it especially clear what's allowed and what's not. In our case, we make it clear that our character images can be on approved products, but the characters themselves can't be used as spokespersons or be seen as promoting the products. Also, as a non-profit, with the exception of our educational content, we rely on our licensees to take the lead on marketing when it comes to general merchandise categories. Sesame has a big megaphone, but we use it to support our mission of helping kids grow smarter, stronger, and kinder — not to promote licensed merchandise.

So, it's not a situation where you get the license, and then you can just run with it and do whatever you want. On the contrary, it's a partnership. It's a back-and-forth. So when we start out with a new licensee, we make sure it's crystal clear that absolutely everything needs to be submitted for review and approval, as we need to ensure that everything is on brand and appropriate for our target. It's a collaborative process.

When we started working with LaFood, our food licensee in Europe (from 2013-2016) another consideration was that all of the products needed to pass Sesame Workshop's nutritional guidelines.

Being an educational nonprofit organization, we put the interest of kids first, so it's important to Sesame Workshop that everyday food items picturing the Sesame characters meet our nutritional criteria. Because we have very strict guidelines on nutritional profile and ingredients, we scheduled a conference call after the contract with our licensee, LaFood, was finalized, to talk through our guidelines to make sure we were all on the same page.

And these initial conversations can be very helpful. From the very beginning the [retail] partner wanted to introduce a whole range of fruit spreads, assorted jams and jellies in different flavors. But the licensee wanted to use added sugar. During one of our orientation calls, we invited our nutrition adviser to join the call, and we were able to persuade the licensee to use only 100% fruit for their spreads — meaning the various jams and jellies were sweetened by the natural fruit juices only, with no sugar added. We all felt really proud of the end result, because the Sesame products that ended up on supermarket shelves were truly best-in-class. In recognition of the high quality of the food range that our licensee,

LaFood, launched, the Sesame Street food range won the 2015 International LIMA Licensing Award for Best Character License — Hard Goods.

Normally the licensor will deliver a brand licensing style guide to the licensee at orientation. The style guide helps direct the licensee on how to use the brand logo and style elements when creating products, packaging, and marketing collateral. If the licensor does not have a brand licensing style guide, it is highly recommended that they develop one to avoid wasting the licensee's resources and frustrating them when their concepts get disapproved. Finally, the orientation session is used to walk the new licensee through the approval process as *Sesame* did with LaFood in the example above. The licensee must be familiar with the approval process if they wish to get their products approved quickly and avoid frustrating the licensor.

Step 8: Business Planning

Once the licensor has signed a contract and made sure the licensee has a good understanding of the brand, it is important to give the licensee the right tools to be successful. Monitoring the licensee's business and ensuring that they set achievable targets empowers the licensee to maximize the license.

The licensee should begin with developing a one-year business plan. The business plan begins with a firm understanding of the licensor's brand and category positioning statements. Key targets taken from the licensing contract should also be cited in the business plan.

These include minimum sales, minimum guarantees, and royalty rate.

The business plan should also contain a clear understanding of the product development and commercialization time line, the Stock Keeping Units (SKUs) they plan to sell including any new products that they plan to develop, and the key retailers where the licensee plans to sell their licensed product over the next year. The sales plan should be built by month, by retailer, and if applicable, by region. Projected royalties should be calculated based on the sales projections and reviewed against minimum royalties to assess the robustness of the plan.

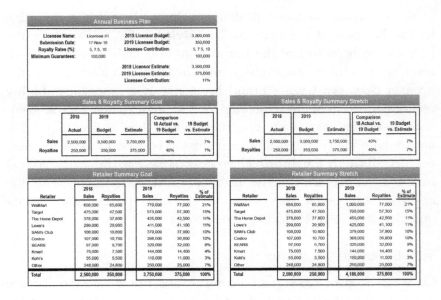

The Brand Scorecard

Now that we know how brand owners use licensing to expand their business and what steps are involved to ensure a best-in-class, built-to-last program, we need to understand what brands are *actually* license-able? For a brand to be license-able:

- It must have high top-of-mind brand awareness when a category is mentioned, which means consumers must name it when asked which brands are best in its class.

- The brand must command consumer loyalty and is therefore something that customers do not want to be without.

- Consumers must understand the brand and embrace what it stands for.

- It achieves superior business results in its margin, sales growth, and expandability.[14]

Below is a scorecard that can help brand owners determine the license-ability of their brand. The scoring is not intended to be scientifically rigorous, but rather to give the brand owner a sense for the relative strength of the brand with its target so as to ascertain the license-ability of the brand. When answering the questions below, each brand steward should make an educated guess at the answer and assign an appropriate score.

CRITERIA	SCORE	SCORING GUIDE
High top-of-mind awareness with target audience?		For brands with an unaided top 3 ranking, assign a score of 10 points; top 6, 7 points; top 10, 5 points. If aided, 3 points.
Considered best in class by consumers?		If yes, assign a score 10. If no, score 0.
Consumers do not want to be without the brand?		If the brand has a significant number of Advocates, assign a score of 10; Brand Insisters, 8; Loyalists, 6; Consumers who Prefer, 4; Samplers of the brand, 2.
Consumers understand and embrace the brand?		Based on brand measurement with consumers: If high, assign a score of 10; If medium, score 7; If low, score 5.
Consumers ask for additional products or services?		Consumers post on social media or write to company asking for additional products. If yes, score 10; If no, score 0.
Organization achieves superior results?		If the company hit financial targets last 12 quarters, score 10; 8 quarters, 7; 4 quarters, 5.
Total Score		Above 40, the brand can be considered license-able. Maximum score: 60 points

A company with a score above 40 implies the brand is a leader in at least four categories.

Let's evaluate a couple of well-known brands. If we take Apple, the NFL, or SpongeBob, the scores for each would be arguably above 50; these are clearly license-able brands and the success of

---

14. Mark Ketchum, CEO Newell Brands (formerly Newell Rubbermaid), 2008.

their existing licensing programs affirms this fact. How about a new brand? The likelihood is that the score would be much lower, well below 40. An exception might be an overnight brand sensation like Uber. However, even in this example, consumers may not be ready for the brand to extend beyond Uber's core business. What other products or services might consumers want Uber to provide? Over time the answer to this question will become clearer and at that point the brand owners can decide if they want to extend their brand. Of course, it is always the companies on the threshold of success that are the hardest to decide a course of action. Therefore, brand owners should be brutally honest when asking and answering the questions above. The true litmus test of license-ability is whether *any* company has *any* interest in securing a license in *any* category from the brand owner. If no product or service provider has expressed an interest in licensing the brand, then the brand is not yet license-able.

Knowing When to License

In Step 2, How to Win, of the 8-Step Brand Licensing Process, I articulated the selection process for choosing whether to license versus manufacture or acquire. While this evaluation can be a helpful tool, it does not address the root question: *Should* you license? Choosing to license is a foundational question that gets at the essence or personality of an organization. It requires the willingness for the owners of the brand to relinquish some of their control. For many organizations licensing is "off the table." Senior executives have heard or read about the horror stories of licensing programs that have gone awry and they want nothing to do with it. They would never trust another company with their brand. Others simply do not believe that any other organization should represent their brand even if the prospective licensee could provide the assurances needed that the products or services created would meet or exceed any particular brand standard. For these companies, licensing is not an option because it would never gain the internal support needed to be successful. Sadly, this conclusion and justification means a significant amount of missed opportunity for these brands and their stewards. And while the company may suffer from lack of growth, consumers are the ones who will really suffer because they will never get the chance to interact with the brands they love in products or services they desire to have.

With proper structures and processes in place, brand licensing programs operate efficiently and effectively. This has been demonstrated by the size of the licensing industry[15] and the hundreds of successful programs in the marketplace today. One best-in-class example is Proctor & Gamble (P&G). P&G has dozens of billion dollar brands that must grow to meet the company's business objectives and shareholder expectation. P&G knows that despite being 31st of the Fortune 500 companies in 2014, they do not have all the resources to maximize their brands' growth opportunities and to create shareholder value. For this reason, no option for growth is off the table. This includes franchising, licensing, mergers and acquisitions, and even co-opetition.[16] Using these proven alternatives for growth does not mean P&G has lowered its standards. In fact, in many ways their rigorous licensing processes and standards may be even higher with third parties than those used internally. All licensed products must pass multiple checks to ensure they are ready to go to market. This includes brand standards and product checks at the concept phase, the prototype phase, and at final production. Moreover, the products must undergo performance and safety checks to ensure they meet government, industry, and P&G standards. Any third-party manufacturer must also

---

15. In 2016, global retail sales of licensed merchandise, according to LIMA, grew to $262.9 billion, a 4.4% increase over the $251.9 billion reported for the prior year. The revenues from licensed products outpaced the 2.9% growth rate that was observed for overall retail sales worldwide (2017 LIMA Global Study).

16. Cooperation between competing companies. Businesses (http://www.investopedia.com/terms/b/business.asp) that engage in both competition and cooperation are said to be in co-opetition. Certain businesses gain an advantage by using a judicious mixture of cooperation with suppliers, customers, and firms (http://www.investopedia.com/terms/f/firm.asp) producing complementary or related products (http://www.investopedia.com/terms/c/coopetition.asp#ixzz3wDqU62B1)

pass audits and inspections to ensure that standards are met for the operational effectiveness of their equipment and the safe and effective practice of their employees. This includes the protection against the use of child or slave labor. Ultimately this means that consumers get great P&G-branded products regardless of whether P&G or another company makes them.

For other companies the idea of licensing is an attractive one. They understand the benefits and are willing to entrust others with their brand. However, just because they have a brand or brands strong enough to license does not mean they should unless they are prepared to make the proper investment. Establishing a successful and ongoing licensing program requires a significant amount of resources. These resources are used to establish an infrastructure needed to manage the program. When a brand owner decides to license he has two options moving forward. He can either manage the licensing program internally or use an agent. Some of the benefits of keeping a program in-house include:

- Employees are trained in deal negotiation and licensing management.

- The organization builds a repository for all licenses.

- The company creates a "licensing" knowledge asset.

- The program is less costly to run over the long-term.

If a company chooses a licensing agent, some of its benefits will include:

- *Less upfront investment.* This means fewer internal full-time equivalent positions, variable versus fixed costs, which are driven by the revenue generated and a success-based commission structure.

- *Easier and faster ramp up.* An agency can provide a turnkey solution and get products to market in 6–12 months versus 24–36 months if executed internally. Finally, it allows the company to keep focused on their core business.

- *Proof of concept established.* This further mitigates risk and helps to validate brand preference.

If the licensor chooses to manage its program in-house, a typical licensing program requires a team of individuals working together to ensure the program is managed properly. An example of a typical organization chart is depicted on the next page.

Selecting Categories for Licensing

When I was at Newell Brands (formerly Newell Rubbermaid) running Rubbermaid's global licensing business, I would work with the company's business units to determine the categories in which to extend the Rubbermaid brand. While Newell Brands (formerly Newell Rubbermaid) used brand extension research to identify categories for extension, suggested categories also came from Rubbermaid consumers who shared their ideas for extension with the company.

At Newell Brands (formerly Newell Rubbermaid), I would follow a four-step category selection process:

1. *Determine Brand Criteria* – Obtain a clear understanding of the Brand's positioning, promise, and strategy to ensure a fruitful extension.

2. *Develop a Universe of Categories* – Alternative categories provide an opportunity to expose the brand to new audiences. However, the categories identified have to be seen as viable by the brand owner and its consumers.

3. *Apply Filters to Produce a Qualified List* – Ensure brand positioning and key equities are aligned to ensure a relevant connection in the consumer's mind. Consider negative associations from a brand and category perspective.

4. *Prioritize Categories for Optimal Impact* – Prioritize the category characteristics and brand objectives to identify the most opportunistic and strategically relevant categories.

Example of In-House Licensing Organizational Chart.

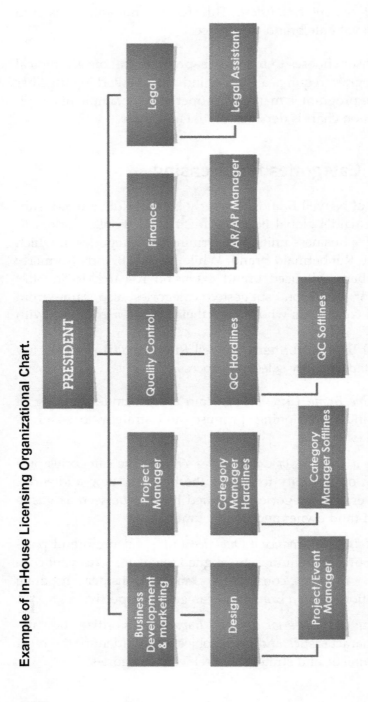

Once I knew what categories were optimal for extension, I then need to confer with colleagues to determine what the best option was to go to market. If the category was one in which Rubbermaid had a core competency, Rubbermaid would normally manufacture or source the product themselves. If they did not possess the competency, then they either acquired a company or licensed the brand to a company which was successfully selling the product in the marketplace.

The Role and Importance of a Licensing Agency

For a company that does not have internal subject-matter expertise in brand licensing and would prefer to use an agency instead of building a team internally, it is important to understand the role of the brand owner and the role of the agency. There are a number of responsibilities the brand owner must execute. The department that oversees the licensing agency, which typically sits inside the External Business Development department or the Marketing department, must:

- Develop a licensing plan to support business strategy
- Manage the licensing agency
- Manage the approval process — over time this process can be delegated to the licensing agency.

The agency's primary roles are to:

- Identify potential licensing candidates
- Conduct due diligence to vet each candidate
- Negotiate the licensing deal terms and contract
- Ensure contract compliance by the licensees
- Manage financial forecasts to ensure the licensee remains on track

- Collect the royalties and ensure they are paid correctly and promptly — some brand owners choose to take on this responsibility.

Finally, the business unit of the brand owner must:

- Provide the brand platform from which to build the licensing program
- Recommend product categories that are aligned with the brand's position and equities
- Develop the brand strategy and business plan
- Approve all licensing deals to ensure there is internal alignment
- Provide legal and risk management support to ensure the right candidates are approved to become licensees
- Approve all licensee product development and packaging
- Approve marketing materials and program collateral
- Track brand and consumer metrics.

It should be noted that the business unit should already be following these steps for their core business. As such, these are not substantive additional burdens on the organization.

If the decision to create a brand licensing program is through a licensing agency, it is critical that the brand owners choose the right agency. The first criteria in a search for a brand licensing partner is to be sure the agency understands branding and brand extension theory. This requirement will ensure the agency possesses the competency to drive the category selection process. Choosing the right categories will ensure they reinforce the brand's position and equities. Conversely, without a deep understanding of brand strategy and positioning, the agency may select extensions that could damage the brand's equity. There are dozens of cases where agencies were either not aware of the adverse impact of a poor extension or more concerned with earning their fees, and therefore, they disregarded the brand dilution caused by the extension.

Second, brand owners must be sure the agency knows how to find best-in-class vendors to commercialize products that will deliver the brand's promise. As James Collins states in *Good to Great*, "Get the right people on the bus, the wrong people off the bus, and the right people in the right seats." If the agency gets these two things right, the rest tends to take care of itself. By selecting categories that deliver against the brand position, every licensed product purchased will reinforce that position in the mind of the consumer, thus strengthening their brand loyalty and allegiance. By having best-in-class vendors as licensees, the execution will be top-notch, which means the program will grow faster and more successfully, delivering value to the brand and all stakeholders.

I also recommend that the agency possess a rigorous brand licensing process to eliminate guess work, and a robust standardized contract to protect the company and the brand in case anything goes wrong, which may likely occur at some point. Finally, the agency must have expert negotiators who know how to extract the maximum value from the license for the brand owner. This includes negotiating the optimal royalty rate, minimum guaranteed royalty, and minimum net sales, while not demanding too much from the licensee. The fastest way to blow up a licensing contract is to agree terms that the licensee cannot possibly achieve even if they agreed to them!

Most agencies require a substantial upfront fee to get a licensing program up and running and then a percentage of the royalties collected. The agency typically manages the collection process on behalf of the brand owner. Some agents are open to receiving a retainer in lieu of an upfront fee to mitigate the licensor's costs and the adverse impact a large upfront payment can have on their cash flow. A small percentage of agencies will offer transition management services to the brand owner to ensure the program does not get derailed when the licensor decides to take management of the licensing program in-house. When this occurs, future royalties on new deals will go to the licensor after the transition management fees are paid.

Whether a Program is Being Managed Successfully

Most brand owners are happy when their brand licensing programs grow over time. Growth could come through additional licensees, greater numbers of approved licensed products, higher sales of licensed product, increased royalty rates, or a combination of the above. On the surface a program growing year over year would seem to be run effectively. Often, however, these programs are not optimized and could even be at risk. For example, when I first joined Newell Brands (formerly Newell Rubbermaid), the Rubbermaid program I was responsible for had previously been managed by a licensing agency. Upon inspection, I found that a few of the licensees in the Rubbermaid portfolio accounted for most of the royalty revenue. The old 80/20 rule applied. Twenty percent of the licensees were bringing in 80% of the revenue. I realized if Rubbermaid were to lose those top-performing licensees through bankruptcy as occurred for many companies in the 2009 recession, it would cost them the majority of their licensed sales and royalties. I also discovered that some of our licensees gained the majority of their sales from only one or two retailers. I knew if those retailers chose another supplier, as they often do, Rubbermaid would lose a large amount of its licensed sales and royalties. I also saw that a handful of Rubbermaid's licensees had most of their revenue tied up in one or two SKUs. If those SKUs were to get dropped, the revenue for these licensees would drop disproportionately impacting Rubbermaid's royalties. As a result I made a concerted effort to gain more balance and optimization in the Rubbermaid portfolio while adding best-in-class licensees to fill categories of strategic importance. This meant pushing each of the licensees to commercialize all of their approved retail channels and to develop new innovative Rubbermaid licensed products that would be attractive to retailers and consumers diversifying their product portfolios. Over time, this helped Rubbermaid to not only grow its revenue base, but to do so optimally.

Lessons and Advice

Will DePippo, Assistant Director, International Licensing at Sesame Workshop has three lessons and pieces of advice to share, from his experience helping to extend and expand the *Sesame Street* brand via licensing:

1. Play to your brands strengths.

   At *Sesame Street* we help kids grow smarter, stronger, and kinder. One-third of our revenue comes from extending our brand through licensing. One way we have done this is by licensing our characters into the food category. There, we try to make a distinction between everyday and 'sometimes foods' more suitable for occasions like birthdays and celebrations. One of our strengths is that we have multiple characters. Our licensee, Brand and Vision, which creates fruit and vegetable purees for toddlers, is able to use a different character for each flavor. In the Netherlands, we launched an anniversary campaign with our co-production partner, NTR, the Netherlands public broadcaster. NTR commissioned an artist to do a rendition of Van Gogh painting, *The Bedroom* where the artist painted the *Sesame Street* Muppet characters into the painting. The painting then drew kids into the Van Gogh Museum to see the painting while producing tremendous publicity for *Sesame* as well.

2. Be careful with a company that is new to licensing, from a licensor perspective. According to DePippo,

   Sometimes we have been so excited about a new license we glossed over the licensee's lack of experience and understanding of what they are getting into. Some companies think the license is enough. They don't think they need to market or promote the product, which is absolutely critical. There was a company that signed on to do licensed accessories. They didn't do a good job forecasting or putting a business plan together. Their product development took over a year. They lost a lot of time getting to market and developed too many SKUs [Stock Keeping Units] instead of starting with Elmo and Cookie Monster, the most popular characters. Here the licensee was not going to earn their minimum guarantee. Experienced ones know this will be a risk. With new licensees this can be a hard lesson for them.

3. Be on guard for licensees to break the rules. DePippo elaborates,

Licensees will be granted specific territory rights and then sell outside the country. We had a licensee do this and we found out. The breach led to penalties. It was a mess. We have one situation right now with a licensee who misled us on the structure of their business. They were sub-licensing and didn't make us aware of it. We had entrusted them with assets, and were worried we might not get them back. Ultimately, they did not cure the breach so we had to terminate the agreement and get a new partner. In the past we have perhaps been too trusting on occasion. One of my mentors' mottos is "trust, but verify." And that's my motto too, now.

How a License Can Work to a Brand's Competitive Advantage

Companies extend their brands via licensing for a variety of reasons. Licensing enables companies with brands that have high preference to unlock their brands' latent value and satisfy pent-up demand. Through licensing, brand owners have the ability to enter new categories practically overnight, gaining them immediate brand presence on store shelves and often in the media.

By licensing their brands, companies are able to satisfy consumer needs in categories that are not core to their business. When Apple launched the iPod a number of years ago, they revolutionized the way in which people listen to their music. The iPod was so successful that its quick acceptance created an immediate need for accessories such as armbands, adapters, and auto chargers. Apple could have chosen to manufacture and distribute these accessories themselves. Instead, Apple decided that these accessories were not core to their business expertise and therefore chose to satisfy the need through sourcing and licensing. By licensing the iPod brand, Apple enabled a tremendous number of companies to produce all kinds of terrific products to make the iPod more user-friendly and to enhance the listening experience. Examples of licensed products for the iPod include the Bose Sound System with iPod docking station, the Nike + running shoe, auto adaptor kits, armbands, and many other products. All these accessories are sold by licensees.

Some licensors see licensing as an opportunity to "test" the viability of a new category without having to make a major investment in new manufacturing processes, machinery, or facilities. In a well-run licensing program, the brand owner maintains control over the brand image and how it's portrayed via the approval processes and other contractual structures, positioning itself to reap the benefit of additional revenue from royalties, and additional brand exposure through product displayed through new channels and incremental shelf space. For example, Rubbermaid gained additional revenue and brand presence by licensing kitty litter containers that are sold in the mass channel in stores like Walmart, which are core to Rubbermaid, and in specialty pet shops such as Petsmart and Petco, which are core to United Pet Group, the licensee.

How can a brand owner determine a brand's extendibility and identify in what new product categories it can sell? It takes understanding the brand's vision, architecture, positioning, and the value that the brand provides. Before brand owners extend their brands into categories in which they intend to license, they should conduct market research. This would include reviewing secondary research, holding focus groups, conducting interviews, and performing field surveys to clearly understand what consumers believe about and expect from the brand. Once this is obtained, brand owners will be able to identify suitable categories in which to extend. Each category should then be evaluated on the prominence of brand associations, favorability of associations inferred by the extension, and uniqueness of association from the new category.

Once the list of possible extensions has been trimmed, brand owners should then conduct an industry and competitive analysis of the category. Specifically, research should include the size of the market, current competitors, industry growth rate, and competitive nature. This analysis will enable the brand owner to determine whether it makes sense to even enter the category. Techniques to use include a Strengths — Weaknesses — Opportunities — Threats (SWOT) analysis or a Porter's Five Forces analysis. These methods are helpful in evaluating a business or a project from a strategic point of view. They involve specifying the objective of the venture, identifying the external and internal factors that are favorable or unfavorable to achieving that objective, and to determining the attractiveness of the venture.

Expectations of Licensors, Licensees, and Agents

For many new to brand licensing, there can be a tremendous amount of angst about entering a licensing agreement. Brand owners and licensees want to know:

- What does the other party expect from the partnership?
- How demanding will meeting the deal terms be on our organization?
- How can we ensure the agreement enables us to achieve our goals?

For the most part, licensors (brand owners) want their licensees to focus on manufacturing, marketing, and commercializing approved products as quickly as possible. Licensees (manufacturers), on the other hand, desire carte blanche rights to use the licensor's brand as they see fit with minimal disruption and meddling. This lack of alignment can often lead to frustration, loss of time, and money.

The likelihood of a successful outcome can be directly tied to the level of understanding each party has to goals and expectations of the other party. Here are some of the expectations shared by licensors and licensees regarding each other and their agents who support them.

Expectations of Licensors

Licensors expect that the licensee will be committed to investing in the category they license. This means they will work hard to understand the essence of the brand and develop their licensed product in a way that captures that essence. In other words, the licensed products should connect with the consumer both functionally and emotionally. If the licensee does this, the products they develop will be approved without delay or difficulty. This takes time and money. While both parties want to commercialize the category as soon as possible, the licensor will expect the licensee to start with building the brand into the product first. This includes:

- Brand enhancement in the licensed category — the licensee should develop products that reinforce the brand's consumer promise.

- Functional benefit brand connection — the licensee should understand the functional benefits (e.g., speed, durability, intuitiveness) and design the product with these attributes.

- Emotional brand connection — the licensee should understand the emotional benefits (e.g., trust, control, happiness) and design the product to develop these over time.

- Award winning product — the licensee should strive to market innovative products that get recognized by organizations such as the International Licensing and Merchandisers Association annually. While the awards offer bragging rights to the licensees and licensors, they typically underscore the commercial success the licensed products have enjoyed.

The licensor expects the licensee to be familiar with the contract and to meet the obligations of the contract. That is why it is important for the licensee to ensure all staff in the licensee's organization who are working on the license be familiar with the contractual obligations. At minimum this means the staff will ensure:

- The brand is protected.
- The brand treatment is in compliance with Visual Identification System.
- The manufacturing process meets social compliance, e.g., there is no child or slave labor.
- The product meets quality compliance, e.g., there are no heavy metals used.
- The product passes audit compliance for approved product only.
- The product is approved at each stage. Typically this follows a three-step process: concept, prototype, and final production.
- There are no sales of unapproved product or approved product within unauthorized channels or regions.
- The royalties are accurately reported and paid on time.
- There is accurate accounting on all sales of the licensed product.

With an approved product in hand, the licensor will expect the licensee to commercialize their products expeditiously in each authorized channel. This includes:

- The product is on shelf in all authorized channels — typically a channel is deemed to be commercialized if there is licensed product in two of the top five retailers in the channel.

- The marketing support for the licensed product is engaged — the licensee should dedicate a marketing budget to the sale of the product in the category in line with their other internal product lines.

- Minimum sales targets are achieved by channel — in total the sale of licensed product within a channel meets or exceeds the minimum sales targets outlined in the licensing agreement.

Finally, the licensor will expect the licensee to meet or exceed the projected sales targets in the category. These typically are twice as much as the contractually obligated minimum sales targets highlighted about. This will manifest itself in award-winning products that meet or exceed annual sales and royalty targets.

Expectations of Licensees

Licensees typically expect that the license they have acquired will provide them with sales growth, and rightfully so. This sales growth may be in the form of growth within existing channels or the opportunity to enter a new channel or new market. To accomplish this objective, licensees expect that the brand they are licensing has high awareness and brand preference, will open new and more doors, and will help them meet or exceed their business objectives.

Moreover, licensees expect that the licensor or their agents will run a simple, straightforward licensing program that will not tax their organization administratively. Finally, licensees expect that the licensor will approach the licensing relationship with a win-win or partnership attitude that will allow them to move quickly and take advantage of opportunities that present themselves. Because licensing contracts obligate the licensee to specified sales targets and royalties, the licensee's goal will be to meet these requirements as soon as possible. Licensees are looking for the following:

- Minimal administrative requirements — Licensees typically have lean organizations. Too many administrative burdens such as weekly, monthly, or quarterly meetings or reports can severely hamper their resources.

- Straightforward and timely product approvals — Conflict can arise when a licensee is unable to take advantage of an opportunity because their product does not get approved in a timely fashion.

- No contractual "gotchas" — Many licensees do not have in-house attorneys or staff dedicated to contract negotiation. As such, they may perceive wording in a contract to be limiting or punitive. Therefore, it is important for the licensor to point out any areas where the licensee may not be clear regarding their obligations.

- Sales support — Licensees will look to the licensor for support in helping to drive sales. This can come in the form of introductions to new customers, presentation materials, research data, and joint calls.

- Brand support — Licensees expects the licensor to support their brand and to provide them with market research that will help them in marketing the licensor's branded product.

- Marketing support — Licensees will expect the licensor to support the brand with marketing budgets and while the licensor will look to the licensee to support the category, the licensee should be aware of how much advertising and promotional dollars the licensor will dedicate to the overall brand.

Agents and Consultants

Licensors often retain licensing agents to manage their licensing programs. These agents assume duties for their clients such as contract negotiations or the product approval processes. In return, the agent receives a certain percentage of all royalty revenues. For the licensor the advantage of retaining a licensing agent involves the agent's expertise and network of contacts. The licensor also weighs the cost of the agent against the cost and time involved in building up an internal licensing department to handle the business.

Manufacturers, on the other hand, may retain a licensing consultant whose duties are equivalent to those of the licensing agent. The licensing consultant supports manufacturers who are largely involved in licensing, but who do not have in-house staff to handle the business. It is the consultant's responsibility to represent manufacturers in their licensing activities, including the evaluation of license-able properties, the availability of these properties, and the development and implementation of licensing strategies. The terms under which licensing consultants are paid vary extensively, but typically are based on commissions derived from the sale of the respective licensed product.

Different Kinds of Licensing Arrangements

While a traditional license usually involves the licensee paying the licensor a percentage of their net sales on a quarterly basis, there are a myriad of ways a license can be structured, as many as the mind can imagine. Charles Klein, a partner at Davidoff Hutcher & Citron LLP, shared a story that illustrates this point. One of his clients was a designer of a line of luxury accessories. His line was doing well. Eventually he was approached by an old-line accessories company and joined forces. Klein's client was hired by the acquiring company and retained one-third ownership in the new entity. Soon the business took off. Later, the old-line accessories company realized they failed to purchase his client's trademark, putting the business at risk. The company approached Klein's client about getting rights to the trademark. Klein discussed the options with his client. They agreed it would be advantageous to all parties if the company were rewarded in growing the accessories' business, for despite being a one-third owner in the company, Klein's client had not received dividends and had no prospects to do so.

Klein recommended that his client give up his equity in exchange for a licensing relationship that would pay him royalties.

To make it profitable for the old-line accessories company, the royalties would only become payable after a "break-even point." This protected the company while giving Klein's client substantial upside if the business grew. Klein recommended to his client that they give his employer, and now new licensee, a long-term 12-year contract. This made it attractive for the company to invest in the accessory line. Ultimately, they worked out a royalty that was set below market value.

During the next 10 years, his client's income increased six fold as the new license structure ensured Klein's client received royalties on the revenue earned by the company versus hoping that the majority shareholders would issue a dividend under the previous ownership structure. In addition, Klein added a provision that stipulated if there were a sale or if the company's president no longer was running the company, his client could terminate the license. Eventually this provision was triggered and his client was able to transfer the license to another operator. While it took a long time to put the license in place, it created a win-win for both licensor and licensee as both parties were rewarded handsomely.

How to Find an Agency

Finding the right agency can be a bit like finding a needle in a haystack. There are organizations like LIMA, the International Licensor and Merchandisers Association, and LES, the Licensing Executives Society, that have a number of agents listed in their database. There are also trade publications such as the *Licensing Journal*, *Licensing Letter*, *License Global!*, and *Total Licensing* that feature articles and advertisements by licensing agents. Social media platforms such as LinkedIn offer a number of resources dedicated to the licensing industry. I started a LinkedIn Group called Brand Licensing Expert back in 2010. Groups like Brand Licensing Expert have hundreds to thousands of members, many of which are licensing agents or who know agents and are happy to share what they know. Finally there are a series of trade shows sponsored by LIMA, LES, and others across the globe that are attended by licensing agents. These shows take place in cities including Las Vegas, London, Hong Kong, Mumbai, and Tokyo.

While these are helpful resources for finding licensing agents, choosing the right agent is challenging. Unfortunately, not many agents are set up to help new and growing underfunded brand owners. Conversely, there are few structured pathways to get into the brand expansion and licensing industry if you wanted to go that route.

Like many people that have ended up in licensing those of us who have been in the business a couple decades got into it by happenstance. I fell into licensing while working at The Coca-Cola Company on the activation of the Atlanta 1996 Olympic Games. The Director of Worldwide Licensing had success with co-branded merchandise and offered me the job of leading the Event Merchandising Group.[17] Mark Matheny, founder of the Licensing Matters Group, has a similar story. After graduate school he was a lobbyist at the Alliance of Motion Producers, a trade organization that negotiates labor agreements and represents its clients on various film production business initiatives, such as tax credits, and filming permits. Most of the members were headquartered in California. There he met some folks from Warner Bros (WB), and several years later after a career change that led to a stint launching personal care products in the US and abroad, Matheny got a call from WB. They were starting a group called Warner Bros. Consumer Products — International (WBCP) and asked him to join.

According to Matheny,

> It was 1989 and even then the licensing industry was still in its infancy. Because licensing was grossly underdeveloped this made the opportunity more exciting, and I was intrigued with the idea running an asset-light virtual consumer products company. The prospect of

---

17. For more on my story of how I got into licensing, see Chapter 1 or go to petecanalichio.com.

marketing a broad range of products worldwide without the usual inventory risk associated with such a move and working with an entertainment company with tremendous storytelling capabilities sealed the deal for me. At the time, US based licensing companies were staffed mainly by executives having little real merchandising, retail, consumer products experience, or international experience, so I believed I could really make a difference, and joined WBCP to jumpstart its international licensing business. To put things into clearer view, at the time I joined WBCP its annual gross royalty revenue was in the low/mid USD eight (8) figures with WBCP's International area accounting for barely over three (3) percent of the total. I ended up staying at WBCP for 15 years until 2004, and at the time I left International was well over half of WBCP's total revenues and the business had grown twenty (20) times. Although at the beginning, WBCP's support of international was modest; after we started winning significant business the company dedicated adequate resources to drive business growth.

Skills and Knowledge You'll Need to Drive Licensing Revenue

Licensors who want to extend a recognized brand and licensees with the capacity to bring it to market share one unfortunate commonality — an alarming lack of centralized information. Ultimately, that lack of access is apt to derail their efforts, squander opportunities, and rack up needless losses.

That's why I've set up a suite of information products that will help you avoid pitfalls and point you toward success. They include dozens of case studies, market intel, useful insights, first-class tools, custom templates, and step-by-step coaching covering the full range of licensing programs.

For Licensors

Brands who want to extend into categories that are not core to their business should check out my free and paid library of multimedia information guides at http://bit.ly/2C6Zmbs.

For Licensees

Companies who want to enter new markets through licensing a recognized brand should browse through my state-of-the-art collection of tools and guides at http://bit.ly/2AHDl71.

Now that you have a framework from which to decide whether to expand your brand and a process from which to do so, let's take a look back over the past century and see how the licensing industry got to where it is today. Knowing how the great brands and characters of today got their origins may help you become a better brand steward. You might even be surprised to learn how they ended up where they are today.

License to Operate — The Future of the Licensed Brand

10

As brand owners follow the LASSO Model and consider each element —
Lateral, Addictive, Storied, Scalable, and Own-able — they will be forced
to consider whether their brand is capable of extending into a new cate-
gory and, if so, exactly how to do so.

While no one really knows when brand licensing began, it is
believed that its origin can best be traced to the Middle Ages
when it was reported that the Roman Catholic Popes would grant
licenses to local tax collectors, who in turn paid "royalties" to the
Vatican, for the right to be associated with the Church. It is
believed that this practice continued for centuries and set the basis
for what would become Modern Day brand licensing.[1]

The practice of granting rights in exchange for the payment of
"royalties" is believed to have continued in the 18th century when
two British ladies of nobility were reported to have authorized a

---

1. Chapter 1, "The History of Licensing," believed to be written by Gregory Battersby, is a
major source for this chapter.

cosmetics' manufacturer to use their names on its products in exchange for a percentage of the revenues derived from its sales.

Modern merchandising is believed to have formally begun in the 1870s, supposedly when Adolphus Busch allowed manufacturers to produce and sell a wine key that included a small blade, foil cutter, and a basic corkscrew with the name "Busch" presumably in exchange for some form of compensation.

Early into the 20th century, licensing became more prevalent. In 1903, Beatrix Potter is believed to have designed a soft toy based on the character Peter Rabbit which had appeared in a book she had originally written and self-published in 1901. Potter would eventually enter into an agreement in 1902 with the British publisher, Frederick Warne & Co. who published a color version of the work that same year. It is believed that this makes "Peter Rabbit" the oldest licensed character.

In 1904, *New York Herald* cartoonist Richard Outcault, who had created the "Buster Brown" characters as part of a comic strip that debuted in 1902, licensed the rights to the character for use by more than 20 licensees, including for use on a shoe that was introduced at the 1904 World's Fair. That same year, the Brown Shoe Company purchased the licensing rights to Buster Brown for reportedly $200.

While many people know the Peter Rabbit and Buster Brown brands because of licensing, one of the biggest brands that came out of the early 20th century was the Teddy Bear. The bear affectionately gained its name when President Teddy Roosevelt, who was a big game hunter, told his guide to put down an injured bear rather than shoot it for sport. The story of Roosevelt's benevolence quickly spread after a political cartoonist ran it in several newspapers. The story goes that a shopkeeper, named Morris Michtom, took a pair of stuffed bears that had been made by his wife and asked the former President for permission to call them Teddy Bears. The store would ultimately become the Ideal Novelty and Toy Company. The name "Teddy Bear" eventually caught on and, in later years, was licensed to toy companies for a royalty that was used to establish a network of National Parks. What a history for the teddy bear!

From those humble beginnings arose brand expansion programs for the Girl Scouts with its famous cookies teaming up with Raggedy Ann and Andy books and in collaboration with a Little Orphan Annie radio show. In 1926, A.A. Milne created the Winnie the Pooh character. In 1930, Stephen Slesinger purchased the U.S. and Canadian merchandising rights to the character as well as television, recording, and other rights. Pooh quickly became the main character in a number of books and brandished a sundry of other products. Slesinger was one of the pioneers of modern licensing and within a year Pooh was a $50 million business! Slesinger licensed the Pooh and friends characters for more than 30 years, creating a plethora of Pooh dolls, records, board games, and puzzles, as well as broadcast and motion picture films.

In 1961, the Walt Disney Company acquired the rights to Pooh from Slesinger to produce articles of merchandise based on the character. Today, Winnie the Pooh is a global icon, known in virtually every country in the world. Literally, thousands of different Pooh products have been manufactured under license from Disney generating billions of dollars in revenue!

Possibly the most famous licensed character of all time, Mickey Mouse, was created on November 28, 1928 by Walt Disney and Ub Iwerks. Mickey gained notoriety with the release of the *Steamboat Willie* cartoon. Shortly thereafter, Disney began licensing the rights to the then Steamboat Mickey to Waldburger, Tanner in Switzerland for Mickey and Minnie handkerchiefs. In 1934, at the height of the Depression, General Foods, the makers of Post Toasties, paid $1 million for the right to put Mickey Mouse cut outs on the back of cereal boxes. While the Mickey Mouse licensing program that was developed certainly benefitted Disney, it had a very positive impact on its licensees as well. It is reported that its watch licensee, Ingersoll Waterbury, was able to stave off bankruptcy on the strength of its Mickey Mouse license. In one day, Macy's New York sold a record 11,000 timepieces. The Mickey brand can be seen today extended across hundreds of categories, on thousands of products, around the world.

The *Looney Tunes* animated cartoon series by Warner Bros. began its run in movie theaters in 1930 and continued until the late 1960s and would produce such highly recognizable and heavily licensed characters as Bugs Bunny, Daffy Duck, Porky Pig, Elmer Fudd, Sylvester, Tweety, Wile E. Coyote, Road Runner, Foghorn Leghorn, Yosemite Sam, Pepe Le Pew, and Speedy Gonzales. The Looney Tunes property would ultimately become one of the most successful licensing programs of all time and serve as the cornerstone for the creation of the Licensing Corporation of America, which was unquestionably the most powerful licensing agency through the late 1980s handling not only the Warner Bros. properties but also most of the major sports leagues before the leagues decided to create their own in-house properties divisions. Today more than $6 billion of licensed Warner Bros. products are sold on a worldwide basis.

In 1932, Jerry Siegel and Joe Shuster created the fictional super-hero Superman and, in 1938, sold the character rights to Detective Comics, Inc. (now DC Comics) in 1938. The character, with its distinctive red, blue, and yellow costume, cape, and large "S" on his chest, was one of the early superhero characters and ultimately launched an entire superhero market for comic books and related licensed products as well as related characters like Supergirl and Superboy. In 1940, the character was featured for the first time in the Macy's Thanksgiving Parade. The earliest Superman licensed product appears to have been marketed in 1939 as a button signifying membership in the Superman Club of America. By 1942, sales of Superman comic books surpassed 1.5 million copies and during World War II, the U.S. Department of the Navy mandated the inclusion of Superman comic books as part of the supplies provided to U.S. Marines in Midway. During the 1940s, licensed Superman merchandise included jigsaw puzzles, paper dolls, bubble gum, trading cards, and wooden or metal figures. Its popularity as a licensed property continues today, fueled in part by the release of blockbuster motion pictures by Warner Bros. based on the character.

DC Comics, created in 1934 (as National Allied Publications), would ultimately become one of the largest and most successful publishers in the comic book market, developing and popularizing such characters as Superman, Batman, Wonder Woman, Green Lantern, Captain Marvel, and Catwoman. It is now the publishing division of DC Entertainment Inc., a subsidiary company of Warner Bros. Entertainment.

Its major competitor, Marvel Comics, which would ultimately become a major force in modern licensing, was formed in 1939 by Martin Goodman as Timely Publications. Since then, it has created some of the most licensable characters in the business, including Spider-Man, Iron Man, the X-Men, Wolverine, the Hulk, Fantastic Four, Captain America, and Ghost Rider. Its first publication, titled Marvel Comics #1, was published in October 1939, and introduced the superhero, the Human Torch, and the anti-hero, Namor, The Submariner. The company would expand greatly over the years and develop strong entertainment and licensing arms. Marvel characters have been adapted to many other media, including television and motion pictures, which led to the creation of its own production company, Marvel Studios, to produce entertainment products using licensed Marvel material. Their projects include a number of television series, both live-action and animated, based on the characters. The company was acquired by Disney in 2009 for $4 billion and currently generates more than $3 billion in retail sales of licensed product annually.

The decades of the 1940s and 1950s saw the birth of such brands as Archie, Thomas the Tank Engine, Howdy Doodie, NASCAR, Peanuts, Playboy, James Bond 007, Kermit the Frog, the Los Angeles Rams, Elvis Presley, the Smurfs, Paddington Bear, and Barbie and Hanna Barbera Cartoons including the *Flintstones*, *Scooby-Doo*, *Yogi Bear Show*, *Jetsons*, *Huckleberry Hound Show*, and *Top Cat*. With the invention of the television, millions of Americans could enjoy watching their favorite characters in the comfort of their homes. This drove consumer demand and the sales of licensed merchandise dramatically. As a result of this familiarity and the evolution of brand engagement, almost all of these brands continue to thrive today.

The 1960s brought an evolution of brand extension and expansion as the rock band, Beatles, and the National Football League gained prominence. Due to the immense popularity of the Beatles, American teenagers would spend $50 million in 1964 alone for Beatles products. One licensee, the Reliance Manufacturing Company paid $100,000 for a license and sold over a million Beatles T-shirts in three days. Remco Toys ramped up for 100,000 Beatles dolls but was faced with orders for an additional 500,000. The Lowell Toy Corporation was selling Beatles wigs at the rate of 35,000 per day. All told, their licensing company, Seltaeb (Beatles spelled backwards), granted licenses for 150 different products on an international basis with products ranging from dolls, scarves, mugs, wigs, T-shirts, bubble gum, licorice, cans of "Beatles Breath," badges, and posters.

NFL Properties, a subsidiary of the National Football League, was formed in 1963 as the first licensing division of any of the professional sports leagues. Controlling the licensing rights for all of the NFL teams and associated properties such as the Super Bowl, it would become one of the most dominating sports licensing divisions in the world with sales of licensed NFL products topping $3 billion at retail today. The other sports leagues would follow. Major League Baseball Properties (MLBP) was formed in 1966, and NBA Properties was formed in 1967.

Hasbro introduced G.I. Joe in 1964 in the middle of the Vietnam War, as the Adventures of G.I. Joe. Looking to downplay the war theme, Hasbro would relaunch the product in 1970 and call it simply G.I. Joe under a nonmilitary theme. G.I. Joe launched the "action figure" category. While the G.I. Joe characters are not superheroes, per se, they all have special skills in martial arts, weapons, and explosives. The characters have been used and licensed extensively by Hasbro and have evolved into motion pictures and video games.

Anpanman, a fictional character created by Takashi Yanase and one of the most popular animated children's cartoon series in Japan, was inspired by a soldier struggling to survive in World War II. Anpanman was introduced as a series of books in 1968 and became a television series in Japan in 1988. By 2006, more than 50 million Anpanman books were sold in Japan and Anpanman became the most popular fictional character in Japan for the under 12-year-old market. Anpanman has been heavily merchandised, appearing on licensed products, including apparel, video games, toys, and snack foods.

One of the longest running children's television shows of all time, *Sesame Street*, premiered in 1969. Produced by Sesame Workshop, *Sesame Street* was founded by Joan Ganz Cooney and Lloyd Morrisett Jr. As a pioneer of contemporary educational television, combining both education and entertainment, *Sesame Street* was the first preschool educational television program to base its contents and production values on laboratory and formative research. Sesame Workshop has developed and licensed such characters as Oscar The Grouch, Big Bird, Bert, Ernie, and, likely the most famous, Elmo. In 1970, Sesame Workshop (known then as Children's Television Workshop) created a licensing department to oversee the development of "non-broadcast" materials, which published the *Sesame Street Magazine* in its first year. In 1971, its licensee, Western Publishing, introduced a line of books based on the characters. To date, more than 600 individual titles have been produced with various licensees. Of course, where *Sesame Street* had its biggest impact on licensing was the toy line, initially by Tyco Toys, and subsequently by Mattel and then Hasbro. And while those lines continue to be strong for *Sesame Street*, the brand has ventured into a number of new arenas. According to Will DePippo, Assistant Director, International Licensing at Sesame Workshop, this venturing has enabled it to extend the Sesame universe tremendously. Below are three examples:

> In Asia we work with Universal Studios Japan. There, we created a themed hotel room concept. We completely renovated and themed the room at the hotel to keep the magic and fun of the Universal Studios theme park going. To enhance the experience we decked out the lobby and the hallway leading to the rooms. This is a great partnership with Universal and has enabled us to make the Sesame Street experience truly special.

Another example of extending the experience was with TomTom to create Sesame Street GPS voices. The actors who represent Bert and Ernie tag-teamed on this opportunity and recorded the script. It was cool to watch them read from a 30 page script to make the driving experience for our fans that much more enjoyable. While the revenue is important, the brand exposure was the most significant. Here we got to use a partner to reach a group of fans on an occasion and in a way we would never reach them otherwise.

The third example is when we did a branded television advertisement campaign in 2016. If the theme is true to a character we will occasionally allow the character to appear in commercials. Each opportunity is approved on a case by case basis. In this particular instance we worked with Federópticos, based out of Spain. They were launching a new line of progressive lenses for seeing close-up and far away. Our partner in Spain, LABSTORE Y&R, realized the target audience grew up with Sesame Street and likely would remember the "near and far" theme where Grover put his face right up on the camera to give the audience an understanding of the word, "near" and then walked away to express the word, "far." To ensure the campaign depicted Grover accurately, we got a Sesame Street writer involved. We knew that Grover is the expert in near and far, and Federópticos was the expert in progressive lens. Fat Blue (aka Mr. Johnson) was Grover's sidekick for the ad campaign. Together they paired up and were featured not only on the ads but also on Point of Sale (POS) in store and in the optometrist's office with an eye chart showing Grover pointing directions in lieu of letters.[2]

---

2. Interview with Will DePippo, Assistant Director, International Licensing at Sesame Workshop, April 20, 2017.

The Federópticos license was nominated for an International Licensing Award at the 2017 Licensing Expo in Las Vegas. Not only was this a new revenue stream for *Sesame Street*, it produced huge brand awareness with 37.9 million impressions and received 12.4 million unique visits in its first year in the country of Spain. Moreover, Federópticos' sales went up 26%, all the while introducing humor into a relatively humorless space, the optometrist's office. No wonder *Sesame Street* remains one of the strongest entertainment brands today, with reported sales of merchandise in excess of $1.5 billion.

The decade of the 1970s brought a number of fashion brands including Ralph Lauren, and design firms such as Pierre Cardin, Calvin Klein, Gloria Vanderbilt, Tommy Hilfiger, and Chanel. In 1972, Ralph Lauren would introduce a short-sleeved, mesh shirt with the Polo logo on it. The shirt gained fame when it appeared in the motion picture, *The Great Gatsby*. The Ralph Lauren Empire grew to more than $5 billion by 2009 and is one of the most recognizable labels in the world. It spawned the fashion, or designer, licensing industry.

Hello Kitty, the fictional character originally based on Japanese pop culture featuring a female white bobtail cat with a red bow, was designed by Yuko Shimizu and first introduced in Japan by Sanrio in 1975 as a vinyl coin purse. A year later, it found its way into the United States. It proved to be an immensely popular licensing property and more than $1 billion of licensed Hello Kitty products are sold annually, ranging from dolls to stickers, greeting cards, apparel, accessories, school supplies, dishes, and home appliances. There are two Hello Kitty-branded theme parks in Japan, Harmonyland and Sanrio Puroland.

I asked Tim Kilpin, former Mattel and Disney executive, what he thought made the Hello Kitty brand so popular and successful. Kilpin remarked:

> Hello Kitty has gone through its ebbs and its flows. There are certain categories where you might think it would work, but it doesn't. For example, in the toy category people have tried multiple times to make it work,

but it never does. My supposition is that it doesn't represent a play pattern. There is no story to latch onto; there is nothing about the character that people care to understand. There is no way to "play it out." What it is, is a social expression brand. It is a brand through which you can express your own feelings, whether they are happiness or sorrow or thanks or condolences. It is a safe character to express your feelings. People have identified with it for that reason and it is cute. There is a collectability component to it, with multiple characters surrounding it. However, there is no story to hold it together. It is very much a social expression brand. It is a difficult brand to extend. It works well in certain categories. It has an ongoing interest with a certain audience, but I'm not sure it will ever grow much. Connection to it is through collectability, social expression, and cuteness. I don't know if there is deep attachment that goes along with it.

I then challenged Kilpin to describe what he would do with the Hello Kitty brand if he were put in charge — would he create a story behind the character and build it up like he has done at Disney and Mattel?

I would do consumer work to understand who the brand is talking to today. Is there a new audience coming to the brand? Are there underlying attributes to the brand and the characters that are extendable? I would have to answer that from a consumer lens first. We might just find consumers tell us that "It is what it is. Don't try to make it what it is not." Until I did the consumer work, I would be wary of saying I could convert this from a $300 million brand to a billion dollar brand. People have tried but it hasn't worked. There is something underlying about the brand's attributes that have to be addressed.

Muriel Fahrion created the original design for the character, Strawberry Shortcake, in 1977 while working as a greeting cards illustrator for American Greetings. The characters each had a dessert-themed name with matching clothing as well as a companion pet. Each of the characters had similarly scented hair and they lived in a world called Strawberryland. When American Greetings presented the concept to Bernie Loomis at General Mills, a licensing legend was born. The character was so popular that American Greetings even created its own licensing division, called Those Characters from Cleveland. Throughout the 1980s the character was licensed for virtually every type of children's product, including albums, clothing, and video games. There were even several television specials featuring the character. While its popularity faded by the end of the 1980s, it was reintroduced with a different look in 2002 and, once again, became quite popular, particularly on toys, DVDs, and video games.

Character and Entertainment licensing reached a new level in the late 1970s when 20th Century Fox released *Star Wars* on May 25, 1977. It was the first of six blockbuster motion pictures from its creator, George Lucas, with the last motion picture being released in 2005. In 2012, The Walt Disney Company acquired Lucasfilm for $4.06 billion and announced three new *Star Wars* films; the first film of that trilogy, *Star Wars: The Force Awakens*, was released in 2015. The success of the Star Wars brand was a tipping point for the licensing industry. It was the first of many multiplatform megahits and paved the way for other platforms including Batman, Transformers, and Frozen.

Total box office revenues for the original six *Star Wars* motion pictures exceeded $5 billion, which put the series in third place for total revenue makers, behind the *James Bond* and *Harry Potter* movies. While the motion pictures were hits, the merchandising associated with them paved a new path for merchandising, as virtually every conceivable Star Wars product that could be produced, was produced. Pevers knew if he could land a strong toy company, the rest would take care of itself. Kenner Products came out with a line of Star Wars toys and action figures that served as a fuse for the meteoric sale of Star Wars merchandise. We will see later in the chapter that this same formula would serve Licensing Executive Holly Stein Shulman well 20 years later, when she was head of global licensing at HIT Entertainment and launched the Bob the Builder brand in the U.S. market.

In the late 1980s, Major League Baseball under Peter Ueberroth's reign as commissioner would assume and consolidate control for retail product rights from their outside agent, Time Warner.

According to Rick White, Founder and CEO of Major League Baseball Properties (MLBP), "Peter agreed with me that MLB should run the business, not an outside agent." White explains, "We took a $200 million retail business and grew it to $2 billion in 5 years. Correspondingly, royalties grew from less than $2 million annually to over $150 million. This explosive growth came from hard work, a greater focus on opportunities, and a fair amount of creativity." Under a previous nonexclusive arrangement with an outside agent, the Milwaukee Brewers, in one of the league's smallest markets, were selling the most branded merchandise of any team. Licensing a broad assortment of products, the Brewers were generating about $200,000 in royalties per year. Comparatively, the New York Yankees were generating $20,000. "I told Ueberroth that within three years every club could get to the Brewers level." White elaborates,

> We ultimately got every team to agree with our exclusive plan, except the Yankees, Red Sox and Reds. Finally, at the 11th hour we got all the teams consolidated into MLBP. This required that we grandfather some rights, as a couple clubs had literally given their team marks for merchandise to local suppliers. In the case of the Red Sox, we had to grandfather Fenway Park to a local supplier called 47 Brands, which is still selling Fenway merchandise today. For the most part their merchandise was limited to gifts, novelties, and wearables.

White decided to follow the NFL licensing program that started in the 1960s and it became evident in short order that he had made the right move. "At the time there was no such thing as Authentic Products," quipped White. "There were no retro-inspired products. No Fan Festivals. No charitable licensing going on to support the Negro Leagues. We pioneered every one of these things." White then conducted a series of brand audits to understand the brand characteristics of each of the clubs. Further, MLBP looked for insights that might help them better understand the needs of the consumer. They met and spoke with the fans where they shopped. Through this equivalent of "pitching and catching," White's team discovered pent-up assets they could leverage and bundle.

The beginning of collegiate licensing came into a somewhat bizarre twist when, in 1982, a court decided in a case between the University of Pittsburgh and Champion Products, Inc.[3] that Champion's production of non-licensed Pitt clothing did *not* constitute trademark infringement. However, this case led the parties to sit down and collectively agree to work together. At the time of the decision, Champion was selling more than $100 million of articles of apparel bearing the logos of as many as 10,000 different educational institutions. Although the decision could have given Champion the right to continue on an unlicensed basis, more reasonable minds prevailed and Champion (and later hundreds of other manufacturers) made the decision to recognize that these schools and colleges had valid trademark rights, and accepted licenses to use these collegiate marks on their products, creating the first officially licensed collegiate merchandise.

In 1981, Bill Battle, a former football coach from Alabama, signed legendary coach Paul "Bear" Bryant to a licensing agreement. In the process of developing a licensing program for Coach Bryant, Battle discovered that The University of Alabama did not have a licensing program. Armed with this knowledge, Bill Battle formed the Collegiate Licensing Company (CLC) and Alabama soon signed on as CLC's first university client. Eight other schools quickly followed, and an industry was born. Today CLC

---

3. 686 F.2d 1040, 3rd Cir. 1982.

represents nearly 200 of the nation's top colleges, universities, bowl games, athletic conferences, the Heisman Trophy, and the NCAA. The collegiate partners that entrust CLC to protect, promote, and grow their brands comprise nearly 80% of the $4.6 billion retail market for collegiate licensed merchandise. In 2007, global sports, fashion, and media leader, IMG Worldwide, bought CLC and operated the business as an affiliate unit of IMG College.[4]

In the 1980s, other "evergreen" properties that rose to prominence included Martha Stewart, Teenage Mutant Ninja Turtles, and Barney. Several corporate brands also saw significant growth in their licensing programs including Coca-Cola, Harley Davidson, Pepsi, Coors, and John Deere. The 1990s saw the growth of a number of character programs that were launched from either feature films or television shows, including *Goosebumps*, *Mighty Morphin Power Rangers*, *Pokémon*, *South Park*, *Teletubbies*, *Dora the Explorer*, and *SpongeBob*. Each of these properties has gone on to sell dozens of products, generating hundreds of millions of dollars of product in the retail market across multiple countries.

One of the true legends of merchandising, Harry Potter, was introduced in June 1997. This was the first of what would become seven fantasy novels written by J.K. Rowling titled *Harry Potter and the Philosopher's Stone*, which describe the exploits of a young wizard, Harry Potter, and his friends at the Hogwarts School of Witchcraft and Wizardry. Over the next 11 years, more than 400 million copies of these books would be sold in 67 different languages, with many setting all-time sales records for books. The books and related movies and merchandising have made Rowling perhaps the only billionaire author. The motion picture versions of the books by Warner Bros. have each achieved blockbuster status and are among the highest grossing films of all time. As one would expect, merchandising has been extensive, particularly in

---

4. https://www.clc.com/About-CLC.aspx

the toy, game, video, and costume areas. A Wizarding World of Harry Potter theme park was recently opened in Orlando, Florida.

In the late 1990s, there was no children's television entertainment property like *Bob the Builder* in the U.S. market. There were highly successful preschool brands like Teletubbies, but the style of animation for *Bob the Builder* was very different. "The series was animated using the stop-motion style characters that actually looked like toys," remarked Holly Stein Shulman, who led global merchandise licensing for HIT Entertainment, a small UK-based company at the time which owned the brand. "It was a sweet little property that had all the right ingredients to be successful as a television show for preschoolers and could inspire great toys." In June 1999, Holly went to the Licensing Expo, which was hosted at the Javitz Center in New York City to introduce *Bob the Builder* to the U.S. market. As remarked by Stein Shulman:

> All we had available to promote the property was a single image sell sheet, and placed in an ad with the same image in an industry trade publication. All of the leading manufacturers in multiple categories wanted to meet with me because the look of the property was so special and they wanted to know more.

Later that year, HIT Entertainment finalized the licensor for the broadcast rights to Nickelodeon and Nick Jr. "As soon as HIT announced the deal with Nick, senior executives of Hasbro and Mattel were pursuing us to license the property to them," conveyed Stein Shulman. "I had a tough decision to make." Both were great companies that could catapult the brand and ensure its success. Ultimately, Stein Shulman was presented the strategy and vision for the brand from both toy companies. She knew the right choice could the *Bob the Builder* to achieve great success across multiple categories.

Hasbro's vision was to create a "preschool world" across multiple toy categories which could enable them to get a better footing in the U.S. preschool market at the time. "Mattel was more interested in the anthropomorphic style of the vehicles as a way to adjunct their Hot Wheels or Matchbox brands, rather than to integrate the property into their Fisher Price preschool brand portfolio," shared Stein Shulman. "There was a lot of competition between Hasbro and Mattel for the toy rights, which was an interesting and exciting position for HIT to be in, particularly since they were new to the U.S. region at this juncture," Stein Shulman explained. "Financially the offers were pretty comparable, but the strategic vision from Hasbro to create a larger footprint for property across multiple preschool products and categories helped guide our decision," Stein Shulman recalled.

And, of course, a little extra effort on Hasbro's part to build the relationship and show their commitment to HIT Entertainment and *Bob the Builder* certainly was a factor in swaying the decision. "I'm sure most licensing industry executives would agree with my position that building and nurturing relationships in this business are critical to successful partnerships. Some of the best friends I have to this day are those I've met through working in licensing." Stein Shulman continues:

> Hasbro really went above and beyond the norm to exhibit their desire and commitment to me, to HIT and to *Bob the Builder*. While we were in the middle of trying to decide which toy partner to choose, I received frequent calls directly from Alan Hassenfeld, Hasbro's CEO at that time, from wherever he was in the world. He would repeatedly ensure me how dedicated Hasbro was to making the brand a success — that they would treat it like their own brand, and that they were in it for the long haul, and of course that Hasbro would be the best toy partner. Getting direct calls on a regular basis from such an industry icon was a thrill!

Stein Shulman recalls that perhaps one of the things that cinched HIT's decision happened when she and several other HIT U.K. senior executives attended the International Toy Fair in New York City in 2000.

We arrived to the Hasbro New York offices for a tour of their showroom, and our Hasbro contact asked us if we had time to meet with Alan. What my U.K. colleagues didn't know was how rare of request that was — of course we knew Alan was in the building, but his time was so valuable and was mostly spent in meetings with much more important people. It was a rarity for any company in our position to be invited to meet with Hasbro's CEO.

Holly recalls many visits to the Hasbro offices during Toy Fairs over the years from the time she was just starting out as a young executive and dreaming that one day she'd be invited to a meeting at the top of the illusive staircase where the executive offices were located to meet with Mr. Hassenfeld. "When we walked into Alan's office, there he was fully dressed as Bob the Builder — overalls, tool belt, hard hat and all!" On a more tactical note, the "preschool world" of product that Hasbro presented far outdistanced the narrower scope program put forward by Mattel. "It was the right decision to go with Hasbro," recalls Stein Shulman. The toy program was hugely successful and catapulted the *Bob the Builder* franchise across multiple licensed categories and products for years to come.

How Far Licensing Has Come

According to the Licensing Industry and Merchandisers' Association (LIMA), global retail sales of licensed merchandise and services in 2016 reached $262.9 billion, generating $14.1 billion in royalty revenue for the owners of the trademarks.[5] This compares to approximately $168.0 billion in global retail sales and $8.4 billion in royalty revenue in 1998. That equates to a compound annual growth rate of 2.29% over the 16-year period, which is aligned with the average inflation rate (2.36%) for the same period.[6] I believe

---

5. 2017 LIMA Annual Global Licensing Industry Survey, www.licensing.org
6. http://www.usinflationcalculator.com/, using the United States as a proxy.

that while the licensing industry today is clearly massive, there is tremendous opportunity for much greater and richer growth. As more and more people in positions of authority become aware of brand expansion and extension opportunities through licensing, and begin to consider a holistic plan for the growth of those brands, many more branded products and services will make their way into the market. This, in turn, will delight consumers who have a love affair with their favorite brands.

How does this come to life? Well you may recall my Bulgari story back in Chapter 3. There, Bulgari Creative Director Silvio Ursini challenged all brand owners with his statement that a brand should only venture into a market when it has "something distinctive to say." Chief Executive Jean-Christophe Babin took Ursini's statement a step further by saying that "to follow your competitors into a sector out of fear, or just to keep up, would be disastrous." In this vein, Bulgari has made what many might consider a unexpected leap by venturing into the hotel business.[7] However, I imagine that Babin would argue this is the perfect place for the Bulgari brand to expand.

For my wife and me, engaging with the Bulgari brand on the remote island of Bali at such a special time in our lives was not only surprising, it was unforgettable. Bulgari understood that by extending into resorts they could contribute to their mission of "making the lady more unique, more special." When brands truly understand their consumers, they create opportunities for special experiences like this to happen.

When the International Licensing and Merchandisers Association (LIMA) conducts its annual survey, it breaks the licensed properties into five major categories. They are Character & Entertainment, Corporate Trademarks, Sports, Fashion, and Collegiate. If we examine the top licensing property type, Character and Entertainment, we will see that it encapsulates the LASSO structure and that may answer why the property type continues to dominate the industry

---

7. http://www.bbc.com/news/business-35857946

with a 45.0% share of the licensed retail market.[8] The licensing programs and platforms are *Lateral*. They stretch and pry themselves into our homes and lives intersecting with us on occasions that complement our activities and just make sense. They are *Addictive*. We have fallen in love with these characters and cannot imagine a world without them. They are rich in Stories dating back decades and sometimes, centuries. We can relate personally to the characters because often we have grown up with them. We look to them as role models as they have overcome struggles similar to our own. The programs are also truly *Scalable* and have expanded to dozens and sometimes hundreds of product lines in our towns, throughout our countries, and all around the globe. Finally, they are *Own-able*. The characters no longer belong to the companies from which they have been created, but rather are owned by their rabid fans that must be consulted before those placed in charge of their keeping do anything.

This domination in share of this property type has held steady since the survey began in 1998, and for a very good reason. The brand owners in this category understand what is important to their consumers and how to create unique experiences that delight them and keep them coming back. Let me share a couple examples that bring this to life.

Today the entertainment world and film industry have changed dramatically. According to Tim Kilpin, Executive Vice President of Mattel from 2011 to 2015, and former Disney toy business executive in the early 2000s, "Disney is the largest consumer products licensor in the world, far and away beyond the number 2 licensor. Across so many categories and properties, Disney sets the pace." For Disney, the consumer products business, which oversees all licensing is an important pillar in their overall growth strategy. It is their mechanism for how brands like Mickey and Pooh come to life beyond the entertainment. And while other studios recently have embraced licensing, consumer products for them have traditionally been an ancillary business. For those other studios, the

---

8. LIMA Global Study 2017, www.licensing.org

feature film or television series was core and any consumer products licensing revenue was considered gravy. For this reason, Disney factors in all revenue-producing facets of their business — licensed merchandise, on demand, product placement, theme parks — when acquiring a new property such as Lucasfilm or Marvel Entertainment.

Since the buyout of Marvel in 2009, Disney has generated over $8.5 billion in global box office receipts with surprises like *Guardians of the Galaxy* grossing $774 million.[9] According to data released by *The Licensing Letter*, Spider-Man leads the pack of brands with global retail sales in 2013 of $1.3 billion, and *The Avengers* brought in $325 million that same year. Globally, *Star Wars: Episode VII — The Force Awakens* has generated $1.8 billion (as of January 18, 2016) since it opened in North America throughout the month of December 2015.[10] Though the movie is expected to earn big bucks at the box office, the real moneymaker for Disney is *Star Wars* merchandise. Analysts predicted *Star Wars* merchandise would generate some $3 billion in sales in 2015, and $5 billion over the next 12 months.[11] Hasbro Inc. reported strong revenue during the holiday period, helped by a surge in demand for lightsabers, action figures, and other toys tied to *Star Wars*.

Hasbro's deep lineup of toys related to the blockbuster film led them to a 35% sales increase in their boys segment, helping overall revenue rise of 13% to $1.47 billion. Chief Executive Brian Goldner said the company's overall *Star Wars* business for the year was "very similar" to the nearly $500 million the company made in 2005 when the last installment of the movie hit theaters. And in 2016 the company forecasted *Star Wars* sales to be around that level again.[12]

9. http://www.newsarama.com/24999-disney-s-4-billion-marvel-buy-was-it-worth-it.html
10. http://www.forbes.com/sites/lisachanson/2016/01/21/culture-wars-star-wars-under-performs-in-china-and-the-differences-emerge/#257407b47805
11. http://www.forbes.com/sites/natalierobehmed/2015/12/16/how-disneys-star-wars-merchandise-is-set-to-make-billions/#3a1d2f7541a4
12. Ziobro, P., & Hufford, A. (2016). "Star Wars" is the force behind strong Hasbro sales. *The Wall Street Journal*, February 8.

Corporate Trademark Licensing

The Corporate Trademarks property segment from the 2017 LIMA Global Study also turned out to be very sizable at 20.8% of total retail revenues. Fashion was the next largest licensed property type at 12% of the market, while Sports Properties registered at a 10% share. These compare with Corporate at 16.8%, Fashion at 16.8%, and Sports Properties at 12.3% back in 2000. The increase of more than 3% in Corporate Trademarks indicates how Fortune 500 and other companies are taking advantage of brand expansion and extension opportunities to grow their business. And while Fashion and Sports Properties have grown substantially since 2000, they have lost share by 4.8% and 2.3%, respectively.

Global Retail Sales of Licensed Merchandise, By Property Type, 2016

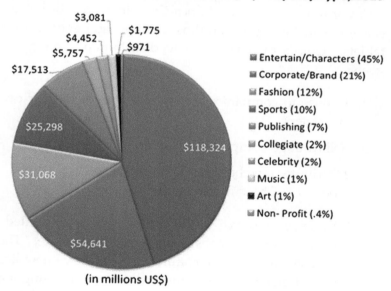

- Entertain/Characters (45%)
- Corporate/Brand (21%)
- Fashion (12%)
- Sports (10%)
- Publishing (7%)
- Collegiate (2%)
- Celebrity (2%)
- Music (1%)
- Art (1%)
- Non- Profit (.4%)

(in millions US$)

Source: LIMA Annual Global Licensing Survey, 2017 Edition. Retrieved from https://www.licensing.org/research/licensing-survey/

Let's go on a little journey back in time to the mid-1990s. Back then, Tom McGuire was the Vice President of Marketing and Executive Assistant to Sergio Zyman, Chief Marketing Officer of The Coca-Cola Company. At the time, Tom was charged with managing several disparate parts of the marketing department including Archives, The Everything Coca-Cola company stores located in Atlanta and Las Vegas which sold Coke merchandise, a museum in Atlanta called the World of Coke, Worldwide Licensing, and Promotional Merchandise. Tom's primary job was to integrate each of these businesses. Having access to the Archives Department enabled Coke to lead the production and sale of merchandise that connected with the Coke brand and its rich history. Collectively, the businesses under Tom's tutelage were self-sustaining, generating about $40 million in total revenue, 70% of which came through licensing.

According to McGuire, "Coca-Cola licensed a broad variety of categories including toys, radios, clothing, soft goods, pencils, and tablets." Coke's merchandise and distribution strategy had three goals:

1. License to companies that would market to their own retail customers.

2. Sell through company-owned stores.

3. Distribute merchandise through a catalog owned by the Coca-Cola Chattanooga bottler.

    "We gave guidance to the licensees and distributed to our customers and consumers," recalls McGuire. "There was a senior executive committee to approve new licensees and merchandise. It ensured that the licensing managers, who were charged to get new licensees, stayed focused. At times they would stray from strategy in an attempt to hit their royalty revenue targets and the committee played an integral role to ensure that did not happen."

For McGuire "licensing revenue was the icing." The licensing platform was one of the few ways the consumers could touch and feel the brand beyond the beverage. The brand offers an experience, an attitude, a feeling, and a badge. The Coca-Cola branded products enabled the consumer to buy into the brand.

> "Let's face it," continued McGuire, "it's hard to buy a Pepsi, when you are wearing a Coke tee shirt." Licensing in the late 1990s offered Coca-Cola all kinds of "other" non-financial benefits. "It provided incremental advertising to the brand and served as an important part of a 360 degree marketing plan," McGuire continued. "I just don't know why you would not use licensing if you have a brand at a stage that could support it. Licensed merchandise is purchased by the consumer; they are literally buying the brand."

Today, licensing continues to serve as an important part of a 360 degree marketing plan for Coca-Cola, but the focus is narrower. Coke has limited the number of categories and SKUs to those more aligned with their brand goals. In addition, they have restricted the number of channels for their products. Coke is less interested today in selling through the mass-market channel, which drove a significant part of their revenue in the past, unless it can extend the brand experience and connect with consumers.

As part of a larger initiative within the company to promote healthy, active lifestyles, The Coca-Cola Company became a founding member of the Healthy Weight Commitment Foundation, which aims to reduce 1.5 trillion calories in the U.S. marketplace by 2015. As part of this movement, Coca-Cola's licensing division has been ramping up its consumer products and partnerships to support health and wellness.

> "In order for The Coca-Cola Company to succeed as a business, it is critical that the communities we operate in are sustainable," says Kate Dwyer, group director of

worldwide licensing in The Coca-Cola Company. "Accordingly, we have focused time, energy and resources against encouraging consumers to live active, healthy lifestyles. We believe in the importance of energy balance: balancing the calories that go in with the calories that go out. We believe that this can be achieved through fun, engaging activities such as swimming, skiing, and cycling. We have developed an extensive range of Coca-Cola licensed products that support our direction."[13]

About the same time, The Coca-Cola Company and musical artist and producer will.i.am partnered to create Ekocycle, an initiative to brand recycled products and encourage sustainability among young consumers. The company said it would donate its portion of licensing profits from the Ekocycle brand initiative to support additional recycling and community improvement organizations. In support of this effort, Coca-Cola made a minimum $1 million financial commitment to the Ekocycle brand initiative over the next five years (2012–2017).[14]

This more integrated approach has contributed to the success of Coca-Cola retail licensing. Since 2009, Coke licensing has sustained double-digit annual sales growth with sales of $1.3 billion reported in 2013. More than 500 million Coca-Cola brand products are now purchased annually. "The licensing business has nearly tripled in that time," says Dwyer. "Strong partnerships and geographic expansion have been the strongest contributors to that growth."

In 2009, North America and Western Europe were the biggest generators of retail licensing revenue for the company, but strong growth in Latin America and Asia has been boosting sales ever since. "Putting time, attention and resources into

---

13. http://www.licensemag.com/license-global/always-coca-cola, June 1, 2013.
14. http://www.environmentalleader.com/2012/08/01/coca-cola-will-i-am-launch-eko-cycle-brand-to-promote-recycling/#ixzz44rphW4J9

those areas has paid off," Dwyer says. Today, international markets account for 70% of the licensing business.[15]

As brands continue to proliferate, and vie for consumer attention and share of wallet, maintaining a point of relevance will become increasingly more difficult. Feeling the squeeze, many marketers may drift from their brand pillars onto the proverbial rocks of Sirenum scopuli just as Jason of Argo of Greek mythology almost did when he heard the call of the Sirens.[16] The lure of a quick success through brand licensing could become too compelling, offering those floundering marketers a treacherous path to brand relevance at the cost of brand clarity, consistency, and promise. Marketers have to find their own Orpheus to steer them back to safety. The LASSO Model is that Orpheus.[17]

Anthony Shaut is the Director of Royalty Audits at Spielman Koenigsberg & Parker, LLP. He leads royalty audits conducted on behalf of clients within the fashion, sports, entertainment, and confectionary industries. Shaut says:

> "Sometimes smaller brands under tremendous pressure to succeed go after 'any' licensing partner that comes along. They don't know enough or don't have enough resources to draft an adequate agreement. They have a mentality of 'let's get the business going (*at any cost*[18]).' This showcases the lack of preparation in the beginning when they should have it and, oftentimes, the situation is only going to get worse." Shaut adds, "So many times the structure of the licensing business is completely disconnected from the licensing agreement. In their minds,

---

15. https://www.linkedin.com/pulse/20140707142105-35455432-apparel-and-accessories-account-for-65-of-coca-cola-s-licensing-business
16. The Sirens lived on three small, rocky islands called *Sirenum scopuli* and sang beautiful songs that enticed sailors to come to them, which resulted in the crashing of their ship into the islands, https://en.wikipedia.org/wiki/Jason
17. When Orpheus heard their voices, he drew his *lyre* and played music that was more beautiful and louder, drowning out the Sirens' bewitching songs, https://en.wikipedia.org/wiki/Jason
18. Author's emphasis.

licensees don't think they have many restrictions other than territory and channels." This further puts brands at risk, which don't manage their programs well.

As brand owners follow the LASSO Model and consider each element — Lateral, Addictive, Storied, Scalable, and Own-able — they will be forced to consider whether their brand is capable of extending into a new category and, if so, exactly how to do so.

According to Christine Cool, Area Licensing Manager of Perfetti Van Melle:

> Today's landscape, especially in lifestyle, is very crowded. Many people are selling properties and more companies are becoming aware of licensing as a tool, driving more competition. Perfetti Van Melle was a true pioneer. Today there are many others. This causes the market to get overcrowded. As a result, agreements are getting shorter. Partners want to renew more frequently. Licensing managers need to be on the ball to have new partners lined up to launch your product if an existing licensee drops off driving tremendous pressure on brands. We want to create new design materials and retailer programs to stay ahead of our competitors. The way we work around this is by giving licensees visual assets to create differential products and ideas for experiences at retail and combination with the candy to improve the experience. This offers new ways to market. Sometimes we develop our own display inspirations. We help our licensing partners visualize what's possible by seeing what we do with our candy.

One major trend over the past 16 years since the LIMA survey started has been online retail sales. From a base of approximately 3% overall sales online in 1998, e-commerce sales of licensed products versus brick and mortar retail has demonstrated rapid growth.[19] Online sales in China, as a result of developing broadband connections throughout the country and the strength of Alibaba,[20] accounted for 33% of retail sales of licensed goods, the highest in the world by a wide margin. According to LIMA, China could be a microcosm as to how the rest of the developing world could quickly adopt e-commerce platforms over traditional brick and mortar retail product distribution models. LIMA also suggested that India, because of the efficiency advantages of the e-distribution model, could follow in China's footsteps.

One major insight emerging from the LIMA analysis is that digital technology is clearly changing the way in which consumers play and entertain themselves. Certain licensed products are now predominantly purchased and distributed through electronic means and are starting to become a much more significant share of the overall licensed product market. The tablet, smartphone, and other mobile devices, such as the Kindle Starfire, have changed the way consumers watch entertainment programming. Disney's consumer and interactive products divisions have combined; this merger underscores the blurring of the lines in children's entertainment and play categories. The Video Games/Software/Apps, Publishing and Music/Video categories, distributed mostly digitally now, when taken together, comprise over 12% of licensed product share.

Interestingly, as these digital segments continue to grow, they are making licensed products much more accessible to the rest of the world due to their ease of distribution in broadband connected countries. As a result of this phenomenon, North America's share (58%) of licensed product sales in LIMA's study came in lower than many have previously thought, with additional share being spread to places like Europe (24%), Latin America (4%), and the Middle East/Africa (2%). Furthermore, LIMA anticipates share in the Asia-Pacific region (12%), given its huge population, will

---

19. http://www.forbes.com/1998/12/04/feat.html, online sales.
20. A Chinese *e-commerce* company that provides *consumer-to-consumer, business-to-consumer,* and *business-to-business* sales services via *web portals.*

accelerate significantly over time as these countries continue to develop economically and broadband connections become more widespread. LIMA believes increased broadband connectivity will allow not only for more digital consumption, but also for more online ordering of licensed products from websites like Alibaba and Amazon's international sites.

While many cited the overwhelming success of Disney's licensing of *Frozen* in 2014, it was viewed as both a blessing and a curse. On the positive side, it "brought the understanding back to retailers that they can sell a character license throughout the store." On the negative side for some, *Frozen* was viewed as "freezing out" other attractive licenses as retailers were too overwhelmed in their support of the *Frozen* property at the expense of placing other licensed goods on the shelf.

Conclusion

The worldwide licensing industry is becoming increasingly global with much of its new opportunity outside of the more saturated North American market. While economies are finally starting to rebound after the recession of 2008–2009, leading to strong growth trends in the licensing industry, the risks associated with a *black swan*[21] occurrence such as terrorist attacks, the disintegration of the European Union after Brexit, and the continued collapse of the oil industry could cause an implosion of the world market affecting the licensing industry in a significantly adverse way. Nontraditional retail channels and online commerce are, and will be, key sources of growth going forward. Direct-to-Retail license agreements, where retailers work directly with brand owners and cut out the licensee, continue to be an important mechanism to

---

21. The *black swan theory* or *theory of black swan events* developed by Nassim Nicholas Taleb is a *metaphor* that describes an event that comes as a surprise, has a major effect, and is often inappropriately rationalized after the fact with the benefit of *hindsight*. The term is based on an ancient saying which presumed black swans did not exist, but the saying was rewritten after black swans were discovered in the wild.

break into retail, because they enable brands to offer retailers something unique in a declining brick and mortar shelf space environment, and for new brands a chance to gain a foothold into the retail market. Notwithstanding, Direct-to-Retail license agreements could have an adverse impact on licensing overall as many companies with innovative products and services are blocked from participating.

As physical shelf space contracts, online shelf space is multiplying at a very rapid pace. The impact of digital product distribution is impacting the way we live, consume, and entertain ourselves, and that is serving to accelerate the globalization of our industry. Worldwide online retail spending is expected to grow rapidly over the next few years. The web will account for 7.4% of total retail spending in 2016 (about $1.88 trillion), which will grow further to 8.8% by 2018, and 12.4% by 2019, up from 5.9% in 2014.[22] And finally, online e-commerce is turning into *the* key distribution channel for licensed goods in developing markets as broadband infrastructure is being put in place ahead of traditional brick and mortar retail locations.

Brands that desire to stay relevant must dedicate themselves to building ever-growing and increasingly interactive universes for their consumers, fans, and loyalists to dwell. Those that refuse will lose relevance quickly and will cease to exist. One way to maintain relevance is to adopt and embrace the concept of pooling resources from all entities — suppliers, licensees, retailers, and enthusiasts — that see the value in the brand and want to be a part of the brand's growth and success. For those willing to change, the "go solo" approach of the Twentieth Century is no longer sustainable and will lead to an inevitable decline.

With consumer demand accelerating, change clearly is the one constant in this world of brand extension and expansion. From all indications, the pace of change will continue to accelerate. For

---

22. Read more at http://www.business2community.com/infographics/future-online-retail-shopping-bright-statistics-trends-01458175#tr2zgkSyGtPTJOov.99

those brands dedicated to embracing change, the future looks bright.

Moreover, as the McKinsey article explains, and contrary to what many brand owners believe, more brands don't necessarily mean greater market share or even greater market reach. Instead, it can often add up to greater confusion, more dilution, more cost, and lower returns from each brand.

Epilogue

11

On March 2–3, 2017 many of the world's greatest leaders in the retail, sports, fashion, consumer products, and entertainment industries gathered in New York City for the second annual NYC Licensing Summit. Unlike the Licensing Expos held in Las Vegas, London, Hong Kong, Tokyo, and elsewhere around the world, this summit brought together thought leaders and key decision-makers from top licensees, retailers, agents, and licensors from around the globe specifically to discuss those issues confronting the viability, sustainability, and thrive-ability of the brand licensing industry. On this occasion, there was much to discuss, both publically in the brightly lit banquet hall of the Marriott Marquis where the Summit was held, and more privately in the hotel's less-illuminated nooks and alcoves. There was true concern in the air, and those leaders who were asked to speak did not mince words about the impact of consumers and technology.

The consensus rested on a seismic shift taking place in the consumer landscape. Many argued that millennials were now more significant in dollar spend than boomers and, in case anyone hadn't noticed, millennials vote with their wallets in vastly different ways. Digitally savvy millennials are spending incredible amounts of time online conducting research. Once they have it, they share it across a plethora of digital mediums. Often, their goal is pure discovery, i.e., to find out what's trending. For this, millennials frequently rely on their "go to" influencers — friends, well-established bloggers, and celebrities. Combined, these trend-makers have had a powerful sway on millennials' purchase decisions. Many of these purchases are now taking place via their mobile phones. Impressionable, socially conscious millennials prefer brands that not only fulfill their immediate wants and desires, but also choose to give back, like Starbucks and Tom's. The challenge for brands today is staying relevant long enough to earn millennials' loyalty and being nimble enough to keep it.

The rapid change in technology has had a powerful impact on the rate of change in the retail landscape. To put this in perspective, 81% of adults in the United States own a smartphone today. Their appetite for online access via their smartphones has become insatiable, more than doubling from 1:15 to 2:32 per day (Q4 2016 vs. 2015). Mobile sales on Black Friday in 2016 increased 34% versus 2015 and comprised 31% (including tablets) of overall sales for the day.[1] With this shift to e-commerce, a.k.a., "Give me what I want, when I want it," the retail landscape has become littered with the tombstones of former retail giants. Circuit City, The Limited, Service Merchandise, Sports Authority, Western Auto, to name a few, are all gone. With more and more people buying online everyday, those that have found a way to stay solvent today will continue to face formidable headwinds and an uncertain future. If this devastation can happen with e-commerce in its infancy (comprising 8.3% of total sales in 2016), one can only surmise the adverse impact there will be when it reaches 23% by 2020.[2] Despite these harrowing retail statistics, the Off Price channel has continued to perform well and is expected to grow in 2017 at a 9% Compounded Annual Growth Rate (CAGR); this doesn't paint a pretty picture for traditional retail. Consumers have a "see now, buy now," mentality, making "Fast Fashion" the norm for brands wishing to keep up. With the world at their fingertips, consumers have become the experts in virtually everything and are constantly on the hunt for their next best deal.

---

1. *Source*: Nielsen Total Audience Report extracted from presentation by Cole Gahagan, CCO Fanatics, Keynote Presentation, 2017 Licensing Expo, Las Vegas, NV.
2. US Census Bureau News, https://www.census.gov/retail/mrts/www/data/pdf/ec_current.pdf

One of the most outspoken speakers at the Summit was Yehuda Shmidman. He joined Sequential Brands Group as CEO and as a member of the Board of Directors in 2012. Since that time, Sequential has grown from less than $100 million in retail sales to becoming one of the largest pure-play brand management companies in the world with a portfolio of powerful consumer brands in the fashion, home, and active categories, generating $4 billion annually in global retail sales.[3] According to Shmidman:

"Retail [in the United States] is getting crushed. Bankruptcies are up in 2017. There is lots of negativity. The worst may be the *mall* itself. Traffic [there] was off 5–6% in November 2016 and 10% in December." Countering this dark forecast Shmidman retorted, "We are seeing low unemployment and an increase in wages. With gas prices continuing to remain low and retail sales up 3%–4%, consumers are experiencing an amazing time. We will look back at this year [2017] and view it as equivalent to the 2008 crisis, this time for retail. It will get figured out like the banking industry did. There will be a few losers like Lehman Brothers and Bear Sterns, but winners will get through." Shmidman continued, "What are the root causes, so we can see who will win? First off, retail per square feet is too high in the United States. There are too many stores. Retail space in the U.S. is eight times Australia! Second, there is a radical shift to e-commerce. Sales were $400 billion in 2016. The rate of e-commerce increase is incredibly fast at a 10-12% growth rate. These two things [help us to] make sense of what is happening. The consumer has [too] many choices and stores have to recoil in this new crazy world.

---

3. NYC Summit: The Business of Brand Licensing Mobile App.

If we look at the fate of the book industry we can begin to picture what is happening and will happen in the apparel industry. Digital sales of books, post the book crisis, are at 50% of overall sales. Today apparel comprises 15% online of overall sales and likely will grow higher. We have more store-closings coming. Books tell us a lot. The winners are Amazon and Barnes & Noble, but not Borders. The other winner is the author. You can access your customer far easier and distribution is broader. When we are all out of this mess, the winners will be Alibaba and Amazon and Walmart AND the brands. We know in the brand space, the data is consistent. People choose brands every time, all things being equal."

Ken Wyse, President of Global Licensing and PR for PVH Corp, the world's third-ranked licensor with more than $9 billion in sales of fashion merchandise for brands including Calvin Klein, Tommy Hilfiger, IZOD, Van Heusen, and Arrow, echoed Shmidman's comments.[4] "We must consolidate and continue to be the #1 tenant. We've maintained this position by upgrading the product and getting it to the consumer more quickly." In his 30 years with PVH, Wyse has watched Amazon become their second-biggest account. Remarkably this is concerning to Wyse not because of Amazon's buyer influence, which continues to grow higher and higher, but rather "because of the foreign exchange devaluation of the currency versus the dollar in recent years."

Dave Jones, another industry leader who addressed those gathered, exclaimed, "For brands to survive and thrive, it comes down to owning and controlling the process through the product's entire life cycle." Since 2015, Jones as Executive Vice President and Chief Financial Officer at Iconix has led the financial and technology functions for the company. As the world's fourth-largest licensor, Iconix generated $13 billion in retail sales of licensed merchandise

---

4. NYC Summit: The Business of Brand Licensing Mobile App.

worldwide in 2015 with more than 30 brands across fashion, home, and entertainment including Mossimo, Candie's, and Umbro.[5] To achieve this scale, Iconix has more than 50 direct-to-retail licenses and more than 1700 total licenses.[6] "The worst thing in the world is to have a brand go to retail and then become a commodity." To preclude this, Jones argues that brands must control the landing sites and let their partners handle the transactions. They must create more experiences for the consumer. As an illustration of this thinking, Iconix recently created the Danskin Half Marathon to reposition Danskin as an athletic brand that transcends the dance category. Similarly, Iconix has helped to move Snoopy and the Peanuts characters into the adult apparel category. According to Jones, a woman from Japan loved Snoopy so much she ordered and bought a custom-made Snoopy suit. She travels the world in the suit. This type of brand advocacy is priceless. Ken Wyse reinforced Jones' point when he avowed, "Although we love licensing, we like to own the business more. We license categories where we don't have expertise. Where it makes sense we bring the categories back in house." Under Wyse's leadership, PVH has been able to reduce its time to market by a remarkable 2–4 months.

More and more brands have engaged in partnering arrangements with celebrities who serve as brand ambassadors. They look for up-and-coming actors that have an extensive following on social media *and* have expressed a passion for a certain brand. According to Jones, who has witnessed Iconix' foray into this arena, "We give them creative control, but not ownership. The creative control is what excites [the celebrity]. These 'ambassadors' love to be involved with a hand on the design." Once these celebrity-influenced lines hit the market, Iconix supports their brick and mortar customers (the retailers) through an e-commerce presence. Having a strong affinity with the consumer ensures Iconix can keep its product on the shelf even if a retailer chooses

---

5. License Global's Annual Top 150 Global Licensors.
6. NYC Summit: The Business of Brand Licensing Mobile App.

to drop the line. Clubs, Off Price, Discount, and Dollar channels, where consumers tend to search for brands that deliver value, have proven to be a mainstay for them.

In his remarks, Robert W. D'Loren, Chairman and CEO of Xcel Brands, stressed that retail was in the middle of "winds of change" akin to Moore's Law.[7] D'Loren emphasized, "As an industry we have to innovate our way out of this [difficulty] by controlling our margin and by shifting our perspective from a retailer to a consumer view." For Xcel, which owns Isaac Mizrahi, Judith Ripka, and Highline Collective, this means considering themselves differently than they once did. "We are a media company that does fashion, and not a fashion company that does media." D'Loren, who has been an entrepreneur, innovator, and pioneer of consumer products, media, and entertainment industries for the past 35 years, was hired by Xcel to provoke thought about change and innovation. Since the company's founding in 2011, D'Loren has spearheaded its unique ubiquitous channel strategy, connecting the channels of e-commerce, TV, brick and mortar, and social media to re imagine shopping, entertainment, and social as one universe.[8] "We have to solve for 'Fast Production' in every sector. Consumer behavior has changed. It has become a disruptive voice that is driving 'Fast Fashion.' This means 52 Seasons, one every week, for Xcel. We got to go from 'Sketch' to Store in 6 weeks." To accomplish this, Xcel invests in data science, supply chain, and delivering 360 degrees of service. Ninety of its 125 employees at Xcel are designers. "We give the customer what they want, when they want it. We have to be authentic. The customer knows everything today." D'Loren knows Xcel must collaborate fairly to win. They give the product to their retailers at first cost and then work on a revenue share. This ensures everyone wins when the product lines are successful.

---

7. Moore's Law is a computing term, which originated around 1970; the simplified version of this law states that processor speeds, or overall processing power for computers, will double every two years; http://www.mooreslaw.org/
8. NYC Summit: The Business of Brand Licensing Mobile App.

Focusing on the consumer experience means not only giving them more choices more often, but also making the brand more accessible. "As a brand you have to evolve your distribution to where the consumer is right now," proposed Shmidman. "Consumers have a great affinity for the Martha Stewart brand. Today she is on PBS, VH1, and Facebook Live. Stewart is where she needs to be to keep the brand relevant." Taking advantage of this broad appeal, Sequential Brands launched Martha & Marley Spoon, an online business, which delivers pre-portioned seasonal ingredients and delicious recipes directly to the consumers' door.

> It is a pure-play digital solution that is growing double-digit month to month. If we are going to grow, we have to focus on building distribution angles that compliment what we are doing in brick and mortar. The consumer is still two-thirds of the economy. We [understand that and] are best positioned to be one of the winners coming out of the mess.

> Ninety-seven percent of groceries are still bought in grocery store. In the home and housewares category, purchases today are already 15% online. If we consider what has happened to book sales, this figure could grow to 50%. The implications of that kind of shift are staggering. This implies the industry has to move faster. To do so requires a greater level of logistics, as these online purchases must find a way to consumers' homes. Brands have to ensure the content is relevant, the shipping (including perishables) is airtight and the quality of the product is exceptional. To achieve this, great brands are partnering with great licensees to drive the content and the products. It all relies on the brand experience.

As the American market undergoes rapid change and the retail industry continues to consolidate, global brands are looking to China for a much-needed growth. According to Shmidman, Alibaba, China's largest online retailer, hit half a trillion dollars in gross merchant volume in just 13 years. In comparison, Walmart took 54 years to achieve this same number. This suggests incredible opportunity in China. Jamie Stevens, Executive Vice President of Worldwide Consumer Products at Sony Pictures Entertainment, reinforced Shmidman's remarks saying:

> China is the world's largest e-Commerce marketplace. Alibaba is twice as large as Amazon. Singles Day, China's [version of] Black Friday, which takes place on November 11 recorded $17.8 billion in 2016.[9] This is twice as large as Black Friday and Cyber Monday, combined.

Under Steven's direction, Sony Pictures Entertainment's Global Consumer Products and Licensing team led efforts to expand and capitalize on product and licensing opportunities from the studio's film franchises *Hotel Transylvania*, *Smurfs*, *Ghostbusters*, *The Emoji Movie*, and *Peter Rabbit*. Stevens understands the implications of China's enormous appetite for entertainment. Stevens says, "China brings big opportunities and challenges. Eighty percent of wealthy Chinese consumers are under 45 years old. They are natural born consumers." To satisfy this enormous demand, China is building 300 new malls per year. The Chinese see malls as places to socialize and offer family entertainment. Many malls contain theme parks and movie theaters, helping the Chinese overcome air pollution, which limits their time outdoors. She goes on:

> Movies are huge in China with a greater attendance than in the USA and more than half the box office revenue [$6.58 billion versus $11.35 billion in US].

> China boasted 668 million Internet users in 2015, and while there is no Facebook, Twitter, Snapchat or Instagram, there is ZQQ, which has 496 million users

---

9. The number 1 represents each individual in China making 11/11 a uniquely special day.

and WeChat with 535 million users. Combined they are bigger than all social media in the United States. By 2030, there will be 70 million tweens [ages 9-12] in China and 86 million teenagers [ages 13-19].

With a reputation as one of the motion picture industry's leaders in developing and executing strategic, creative, and profitable product and licensing programs, Stevens offered one more brain-numbing thought: "There are 30 Tier 2 cities in China each with 3 to 15 million in population. Altogether, they ship 54% of US imports."

Most entertainment brands today are looking to Virtual Reality (VR) and Augmented Reality (AR) to enhance the consumers' experience. According to Lisa Silverman Meyers, Senior Vice President of Operations and Business Planning at Nickelodeon Viacom Consumer Products, "Millennials are interested in experiences and then sharing them. We are investing in resorts [with both VR and AR] to fulfill this need." Silverman Meyers leads oversight of NVCP's international recreation business, i.e. theme parks, hotels, live shows, etc., and the consumer products content division including publishing, home video, and video games. Meyers summed it up this way: "We have to have a deep level of 'fan-dom.' Content is really important as it lends itself well to an immersive experience. You have to be working with spectacular partnerships that have a passion for the brand and understand the brand completely. The pitch and catch between the licensor and the partner make all the difference."

Jill Tully, Vice President of Brand Licensing at A + E Networks, which includes the History Channel, Lifetime, and A&E, stated it this way, "Our goal is to create best in class content for our audience and partners." With 335 million houses globally, A + E Networks are using experiential and live events to drive fan engagement and 360 degree brand development. As an example, A + E launched "Bring it! Live," based on the hit Lifetime series and the first-ever "Alien Con" event inspired by the History Channel's "Ancient Aliens." The tour traveled to 31 cities and had a 90% sell-through. In its second year, A + E plan to increase the tour to 40 cities. "There's nothing like live!" exclaimed Tully. "At Alien Con we expected 5,000 and got 15,000. As a result we underestimated sales of our [event] merchandise souvenirs and were sold out by [the second day]." For A + E, Alien Con turned into a social media event, garnering over 1.3 million Facebook followers.

Amy Kule who leads the development of Macy's world-famous holiday traditions including the Macy's Thanksgiving Day Parade and Macy's Fourth of July Fireworks built on the theme used by Silverman Meyers and Tully. "We focus on spectacle and celebration. Our 4th of July celebration in NYC is the largest in the country with 3.5 million watching. The Thanksgiving Parade is watched by 60 million on TV and 3 million along the parade route. It is a piece of pure entertainment. At Macy's events [the consumer] can't buy anything! Our events create a 'halo effect' which drives good will and ultimately purchase."

Pete Yoder, Vice President of Cartoon Network Consumer Products, oversees all of the home entertainment, licensing and consumer products initiatives for Cartoon Network (CN) and Adult Swim brands in the United States and Canada. According to Yoder, "Kids are platform agnostic. They consume in dozens of ways." For CN, their approach must be multi-platform and experiential. "We have highly engaged fans. Nothing is passive. Our fans are the network with 400 million online." CN apps, including Ben 10 and Adventure Time, give a voice to the fans. They have 150 million followers on Facebook and another 100 million on YouTube. These multisensory platforms give fans what they want. In keeping with a multi-platform approach, CN recently launched their theme parks in Thailand and Dubai. Each features all of CN brands giving fans one more way to engage. Equally important to CN are their smaller events emphasizing fan engagement.

Major League Gaming (MLG) Activision Blizzard is the world's leader in eSports boasting 500 million monthly active users. The platform routinely draws 10,000 fans into arenas across the United States to watch online gaming competitions. The result is MLG TV and the creation of Global Gaming superstars. According to Mike Sepso, Senior Vice President who launched Activision Blizzard Media Networks with Steve Bornstein, the Network is devoted to creating the best eSports experiences for fans across games, platforms, and geographies. "Big players are becoming stars in their own right," added Sepso. Game developers and league organization must work well together. With the tremendous success of their live events, MLG Activision Blizzard is designing games just to be watched, in addition to being played. "We even use predictive modeling to enhance the fan watching experience," added Sepso. With 100 live events a year, MLG Activision Blizzard boasts over 45 million hours of consumed content making them the biggest publisher on the planet. "We are stunned by the growth," asserts Sepso. "We borrow a lot from traditional sports, so we are not totally reinventing the wheel." That has proven to be a smart decision as Activision Blizzard has begun attracting attention from both the NBA and NFL.

Carlos Saavedra is the Senior Director of Culture Marketing & Innovation at PepsiCo North America and founder of Creator,[10] a lab at PepsiCo, that collaborates with creators. Saavedra's comments were exceptionally telling for corporate brands, which must begin to view themselves having to compete for consumers with other brands across all industries. "Licensing needs to be a part of your marketing. It allows for storytelling and enables PepsiCo to reach millennials who value experiences over 'things.' Lastly, licensing drives innovation and enables PepsiCo to go beyond bottles and cans to build lifestyle brands."

I could go on with more stories, vignettes, and learning points, but the dialogue would never end. Throughout the process of writing this book, I have learned so much from more than 40 of the many industry titans responsible for greater than 60 unique brands in 22 different industries. Not only have they contributed integral knowledge and understanding to its content, the stories they have shared left me in awe of their amazing accomplishments and helped me illustrate each of the many points I strove to make along the way. Without them, the book

---

10. Creator's mission is to explore the edges of culture and co-create innovative experiences across the cultural landscape. Taken from NYC Licensing Summit online app.

would have been little more than a long list of to-dos and not to-dos. Moreover, their insights helped to make the book so much more robust than it would have been, and helped to establish a truly best-in-class set of standards for anyone venturing into the brand licensing industry. In closing, let me share this: If you own a brand, you should put your consumers in the center of its universe. Engage with them in continuously new and exciting ways. Let them enter and exit your brand's universe whenever they want from wherever they want. Ask for their opinions and listen to each of them when they answers. Borrow ideas from other industries to enhance their experiences. Use every resource available to help you achieve this. Never stop reinventing and refreshing your brand. If you do all these things, your consumers will grow to love your brand (even more) for how it enhances their lives and makes them feel. This is the true ticket to enduring success.

Final Thoughts

Hopefully over the course of this book I have made a sufficiently compelling argument for why the LASSO Model has merit. For more details on the statistical robustness of the Model, see the Appendix B.

For the branding and brand licensing expert, the LASSO Model and 8-Step Process give you immediate and actionable steps to take brands to the next level. As a professional, you should be able to accurately score yourselves using the Model and find the framework's accompanying rigorous set of questions to be full-bodied, systematic and orderly, practical and heuristic.

For the layperson out there, I hope I have encouraged you to dream of either building your own brand or lassoing someone else's. You can, by applying honest answers to the LASSO framework, use the LASSO Model to roughly assess your brand, and then come to a brand licensing expert to professionally help you assess and direct your next steps in an adventuresome and exciting partnership. Let this be your first step in achieving your dream.

For the skeptic, consider this: The LASSO Model was developed to provide you with a rough measure of whether your brand is over- or under-extended. Sometimes there is value in going through the exercise even if you aren't confident you will gain the desired results you set out to achieve. An example of this can be found by watching a TEDx talk I gave in 2017 titled *Achieve Your Dreams through Visualization*.

> With each dream, I would picture what I wanted, and I would visualize myself in that place. The visualization gave me the clarity I needed along with the ambition and courage to risk possible failure. As the saying goes, "You can't make a basket if you never take the shot." I knew that sometimes I would miss the shot and while my spirits would be dampened, I would be better off for my efforts.

Like in the visualization example above, think in terms of a binary answer, 1 or 0. However, if you think the Model needs more data points to provide you with feedback you feel could immediately apply, you can still use the LASSO framework to run your brand through the most robust collection of questions available to date. These questions, when answered honestly and accurately, will provide immediate value to your business. In other words, you will "be better off for your efforts."

I hope you feel motivated to share your data in the LASSO Model. It's secure, and your data will remain anonymous to others. Each set of data points added will enhance the robustness and accuracy of the Model. Over time this means the scores coming from the Model will be more consistent and more predictable.[11] But what's in it for you today? Well, as my gift to

---

11. See the Appendix B for the methodology of the LASSO Model, which addresses this and other pertinent questions.

you for inputting your data, I will give you a downloadable PDF from www.PeteCanalichio.com/LASSO with all the questions of the LASSO framework to use again and again as you work hard to make your brands more lucrative, memorable, and salient every year.

Appendix

LASSO Evaluation, Questions and Scoring Kit

Chapter 3

Look before you leap; here are seven searching questions to answer before you decide where to extend or expand:

1. What exactly is the problem that you're solving for buyers? And why would consumers look to you to solve it?

2. Is your brand closely linked to a specific product set or to a more general idea? If it's the latter, what qualifies your brand to take ownership of that broader idea?

3. Are you big enough and well known enough to extend or expand? What makes you more than a "fad" in the minds of those who buy into you?

4. What do consumers want more of from your brand, if anything? Will the association make sense to them? Will it change their world for the better?

5. How does your brand fit into the lives of your core consumers? What latitude will they give the brand to take up more space in their lives?

6. Do the dynamics of the sector(s) you are looking to expand into warrant your presence?

7. How will you counter the downsides of being more widely available?

Your Turn

Professor Kevin Keller's book *Strategic Brand Management: Building, Measuring and Managing Brand Equity* includes a very good Brand Extendibility Scorecard. I was so taken with his idea that I've adapted it for the LASSO Model using a spider web evaluation tool. We'll build one for your brand over the course of the book.

Were you able to select a Lateral score that best matches your brand? Good! Jot it down in the margin for easy reference. Once you're ready, turn to the next section and get ready to evaluate your brand from an Addictive perspective, the second element of the LASSO Model.

Chapter 4

Keep them coming back; here are seven searching questions to judge whether you have a highly addictive brand:

1. What more does the brand deliver that people want — escapism, distraction, adventure, authority?

2. Will consumers see the connections between the various expressions of your brand? How will you direct them from one activity to another?

3. Do you understand the overall playbook? On what journey are you taking consumers? With what part of that journey are you involved?

Lateral Expandability Score Chart.

1	2	3	4	5
We will only ever stay in the one category.	We could extend our brand to include new or evolving opportunities, but still within our core category.	We could extend our brand into a number of related categories.	Our brand has enough latitude to expand into a new and unrelated category with strong growth characteristics. We have the Opportunity, Fit and Leverage to do that successfully.	Our customers align with our brand on emotive much more than product lines. As long as we stay consistent with that emotion, we can take the brand into a range of different and unrelated sectors.

4. How long do you want to keep customers buying? Is your involvement with the brand tied to a specific time frame or project, or is it longer?

5. Does your program have the best mix of frequency, intensity, access, and surprise?

6. What's your exploration bonus?

If you are the brand owner, is your core business inherently profitable? How dependent are you on ancillary revenue to hit your growth targets? And therefore, how big does your licensee community need to be?

Your Turn

In the previous chapter, we asked you to rate your brand's ability to extend or expand. Now let's do the same thing for Addictiveness. Please think about your answers to the seven questions we just asked and score your brand on its addictive potential. Once again, there are no right or wrong answers. Some brands will feel that they are not addictive and have no interest in becoming addictive. Others will see opportunities to make a lot more frequently recurring income. Choose the number that best describes your brand's potential to keep buyers coming back for more. We'll come back and get this number later (see next page).

Were you able to select an Addictive score that matches your brand? If so, great job! Let's keep the momentum going. Now that you're assessed how Lateral and Addictive your brand is, when you're ready, turn to the next section and get ready to evaluate your brand from a Storied perspective, the third element of the LASSO Model.

Addictive Expandability Score Chart.

1	2	3	4	5
There are only limited opportunities to interact with our brand. We tend to work on an "as-required" basis.	We need to find new ways to involve our customers more within our core category. We need to give them more reasons to come back to us.	We could be more inventive in how we involve people with our brand. We need to forge stronger links between what we continue to give them and what we ask them to continue to pay for.	Our brand is compelling enough to expand into whole new areas and to take our audiences with us. We'll change our revenue model by continuing to surprise and delight via what they can access.	Our "core business" is just the starting point for a highly inclusive, engaging journey with our customers that spans all sorts of touchpoints. That journey is where we generate the real money.

Chapter 5

Inviting people in; here are six searching questions to assess the state of your story:

1. What do people most want to know about that pertains to what you do? If you work in a high-interest sector, how will you compete for attention? If you have a low-interest brand, what can you do, say, stand for, or talk about that will get people leaning toward you?

2. How are you expanding how people perceive your brand through storytelling?

3. Where will you tell your stories, and how will you use the channels to shuttle between the immediate and your wider world?

4. What role do customers have in helping to shape and influence your story?

5. How will new partners change your storytelling? How will their stories blend with yours?

6. How have you connected your storying to your selling? How accurately can you measure how and when conversion occurs? Which of your storylines are most profitable?

Your Turn

Is your brand building its story into a rich mythology? Please score your brand on how powerfully you think your brand is framed in the minds of consumers below. Once again, there are no right or wrong answers. Some brands will feel that storytelling is just part of how they explain themselves; others will see it as a way to continually redefine and refresh everything they represent. Choose the number that best describes how your brand connects and explains its actions and viewpoints. We'll come back and get this number shortly.

Storied Expandability Score Chart.

1	2	3	4	5
We don't have a continuous story. It's campaign- or product-focused. The stories we do tell make our products more accessible but we have not extended beyond that yet.	We're starting to extend our story through content marketing into various channels. We're engaging with our customers to help us do that.	We have a sense of our wider story, and we are working with partners to connect everything we have in ways that will make sense for our customers. We'd like to involve them more further down the line.	We have a purpose that drives us as a company. Our portfolio of brands reports to that ambition, but right now they do that as separate brands. Each brand has a fiercely strong tribe of customers.	Our brand is a multilayer, multichannel, multi-partner universe held together by principles that make it consistent and that enable us to work together to build out what we stand for and to shuttle stories back and forth across a range of time frames. Everything we do takes place within this context.

What is the Storied score that matches your brand? Mull it over and then decide. You've come a long way! I hope you have been diligent and honest in evaluating your brand in the LASSO Model along the Lateral, Addiction, and Storied attributes. When you're ready, turn to the next section and get ready to evaluate your brand from a Scalable perspective, the fourth element of the LASSO Model. You're almost there!

Chapter 6

A framework for scale; here are six questions on size and scope:

1. **How much do you want the brand to be worth?** — It's surprising how seldom this question gets asked by marketers and those building brands, and yet it's critical because it not only defines the value of the brand for the business, but also frames the level of investment that the business is prepared to make in the brand. You can define brand worth in a range of ways of course — by revenue, by margin, by percentage of total market share, or by book value. The important thing is that you have a number that defines success which forms the basis for what you bankroll.

2. **What are your critical assets?** — What are the key ideas that you need to own, and therefore be able to defend, if you are to achieve your plans? What IP and protection will you build into your products, for example, that enables them to be less susceptible to counterfeiting? What allowance have you made for including the contributions of others in your new product development, and how will you define what you simply incorporate versus that for which you decide to charge? How will you value those owned assets in terms of the returns you expect from them, and will that contribution be transparent to decision makers so that they can judge asset effectiveness?

3. **Over how many sectors can and should your brand stretch?** — It's important to have an overview of the potential stretch of the brand. How do consumers see you as a brand that owns an idea, or one that occupies a specific sector? What do they value you for, and how elastic is that? In other words, what mandate do you have to extend or expand, or do you even have one? With traditional licensing deals for example, so many brands think about expanding on an offer-by-offer basis rather than consciously planning where the next brand interaction sector might be from the "big picture" down. My experience and research shows that successful brands know how they will expand, where and with whom, and have supporting research for doing so. They also need to be aware of the contribution to overall worth that they wish to derive from within each sector. In other words, they need to consider not just the financial returns but also what expansion might mean for overall brand presence and value. They need to be able to strategize top-down and bottom-up. Critically, they should define "trip points" in terms of reach and revenue in their strategy that decide when they should consider casting their net wider or deeper.

4. **Across how many countries can your brand travel?** — If your brand is ranged across multiple countries or regions, are you doing this to grow the brand you have, or as part of a broader expansion strategy? Entrepreneur Media, Inc. has taken an approach of extending its core business, its publishing, via licensing and joint venture to countries outside the United States including India, Mexico, the Philippines, and South Africa. By gaining a presence in these regions, it enables Entrepreneur to offer additional products and services to its consumers in those markets. As Bill Shaw, Entrepreneur's President said,

> The way we look at it, advertising is our main revenue stream but licensing allows us to diversify and

create a monthly annuity so we're not so reliant on media which can be very unstable. Licensing also offers a way we can extend our brand so more people can see it.

It's vital that you plot where you will expand market participation and in what order. This should be led by market appetite, but you should also factor in potential market size, uptake rates, the success paths of others in each market, the levels of competition in the sectors you are looking to expand into, and of course whether you will be able to achieve benchmarked levels of margin as you go.

5. **Over what period of time can you afford to grow?** — It's important to know the time frames within which you want to achieve growth. Are you using SMART — Specific, Measureable, Achievable, Relevant, Time-oriented — objectives to achieve your goals? Again, while that may seem obvious, a lot of brands don't think through the implications of those specifics in terms of forward-planning, resourcing and, particularly, runways. The key determinant here will be market demand. How quickly will you need to expand in order to fulfill consumer interest, and what dependencies will you put around extending into a particular market?

6. **What resources are available to you?** — Where will the growth come from? After determining where to play, you need to determine how you will win. This requires you to take a look at your internal capabilities and priorities. What part of the expansion can you do and have the capacity to do? Based on this you will need to assess what parts need to come from external resources. This could include sourcing, where you will do the marketing and sales; acquisition, where a new company will be integrated in to take on this role; or, via licensing, where you can leverage the competencies and bandwidth of third parties to execute those parts that complement what your team is going to do.

By developing an overall plan of what your expanded brand looks like; and a strategy for how, where, and when that will roll out; and with what packets of investment, you have the opportunity to empower their team members to work together, to judge every opportunity on its merits, and to better connect opportunities within the context of achieving your overall goals for brand worth.

Your Turn

OK, by this point you know the drill. Time to assess how Scalable you need to be as a brand and how far consumers will allow your brand to go. Please think about your answers to the six questions above and score your brand on how you intend to take your brand forward and what that will mean for your availability on the chart below. As always, there are no right or wrong answers. Some brands will feel that there are still plenty of room for them to grow; others will see that a more focused approach will enable them to gather the best returns. Choose the number that best describes how your brand expands geographically. We'll come back and get this number soon (see next page).

Does a particular Scalable score represent your brand well? Once you have settled on the right number, you are ready to contemplate the final LASSO element, that of your brands degree of Own-ability. Up to now you've run a steady race, contemplating how Lateral, Addictive, Storied, and Scalable your brand is today. If you're feeling a little unsure of yourself, please trust the process and plow ahead. If you're feeling pretty good, then let's roll forward to Own-able, the final element of the LASSO Model. Ready? Then, let's get started.

Scalable Expandability Score Chart.

1	2	3	4	5
We have a very small number of brands that are growing strongly. We generate intense profit out of keeping things condensed. We're looking for constant and controlled growth.	Our brand portfolio achieves growth by expanding to meet changing market demand. We're looking to keep pace with the prevailing rates of change.	We dynamically manage our brand portfolio across a growing number of countries. We buy, sell, create, and discontinue brands to achieve our revenue goals. We judge our success by how much each brand in our portfolio exceeds metrics.	We look for opportunities to grow our presence through arrangements with others, such as licensing, joint ventures, and project partnerships. We're looking for agreed rates of return from these initiatives.	Our brand portfolio is global, and spread across multiple sectors via many different arrangements. We use this diversified approach to make the most of rapidly growing markets and to counter downward movements in others.

Chapter 7

Understand what you need to have control of; here are seven searching questions to judge whether you have a highly own-able brand:

1. What structure do you need to deliver your idea to its full potential? How much of that do you need to have a stake in to make your goal a reality?

2. What do you need to own to succeed?

3. What do you expect to own in the next five years, what do you expect to lose or share, and what do you expect to be copied or to become industry standard?

4. Will your ownership model change over the next five years, and how will that affect what's own-able? What's not and what could be own-able?

5. Where are the revenue streams going? For what will you be remunerated, and for what else will customers be willing to pay going forward?

6. How important is your IP to you? How have you valued that IP? What weaknesses exist in your IP? How and when can competitors copy you?

7. Which is more important in your sector, speed-to-market or ownership of market?

Your Turn

You've come to an exciting place. In the course of this book so far, I've asked you to rate your brand on its ability to extend or expand, its addictive potential, the nature of your story, and the scale at which you are most effective. Now let's do the same thing for Own-able. Please think about your answers to the seven questions above, and score your brand below.

Own-able Expandability Score Chart.

1	2	3	4	5
We only act within what we know and for what we're known. We're fiercely protective of our IP. We have full ownership of everything we do.	We continue to add new products and IP to our brand through merger and acquisition.	We are open to a limited number of partnerships, joint ventures, and other arrangements that extend our perceived ownership in the marketplace.	We share ownership with other major brands in the marketplace through co-branded projects. We use these projects to redefine how our customers perceive us.	We cultivate an open model where individuals and groups can work with our properties to take them to new and exciting places. Only minimal guidelines are in place.

Base your score on how much you retain control and how you intend to fascinate consumers. There are no right or wrong answers. Some brands will feel that ownership is central to ownability; others will see ways to co develop new arrangements. Choose the number that best describes how your brand puts its mark on everything you do. We'll come back and get this number after the next chapter. If you've stuck with me so far, give yourself a pat on the back! You're now grown by a leap year in terms of the knowledge you have of your brand. Next, we're going to put this all together.

Appendix

▶ B

LASSO
Methodology

LASSO: An Algorithm for Automated Brand Self-Evaluation

Overview

In order to allow users to decide whether their own brand could be further extended, an algorithm was developed to determine a brand's extension based on the LASSO scoring framework. This algorithm allows users to self-evaluate their brand according to the guidelines provided in this book, and receive recommendations as to how optimally the brand is being extended. Using state-of-the-art statistical techniques, the algorithm aims to simulate an expert assessment of brand extension in automated manner, allowing both consistent and objective brand evaluation.

To develop an algorithm that accurately characterizes complex phenomena, the most effective current methods rely on fitting a statistical model to a verified, known set of training examples in a process known as "supervised learning." For the purpose of developing such an algorithm to characterize brand extension, a "gold-standard" dataset of brand evaluations was generated by an expert panel of three brand specialists, and this was used to optimize, train, and evaluate the model. The resulting algorithm produced by this analysis performs both accurately and consistently, providing a robust solution with which users may evaluate their own brands.

Data Collection

The dataset generated by the expert panel consists of both the LASSO scores and a corresponding determination of brand extension for 56 brands, including brands as famous and large as Coca-Cola, Mickey Mouse, and the NFL and as different as Chupa Chupps, FIFA World Cup, Nerf, and *World of Warriors*. The brands that were evaluated and each expert's determination of brand extension (as either under-extended or optimally/over-extended) are listed in Table 8.1. Roughly half of the brands characterized in this dataset were under-extended and the other half were either optimally extended or over extended. Note that this group of brands was selected by the panel to include companies across a diverse range of industries. By including brands of companies both large and small across many industries in this training dataset, the algorithm is able to generalize effectively to characterize a wide spectrum of brands. Indeed, the inclusivity of this training dataset should enable this algorithm to accurately classify brand extension.

To further improve the accuracy and real-world relevance of the algorithm, a subset of 25 of the brands was independently rated by each of the three experts. This overlap allows the model to capture the intrinsic, yet entirely valid, variation in these metrics. In addition, the overlapping set of examples allows a direct comparison of the agreement between predictions made by the algorithm and those made by human experts. See below a process flow chart depicting the steps taken from Data Collection through Model Selection and Training (see next page).

Model Selection

The task of determining whether a brand is extended to an optimal degree or not is best suited to the group of statistical models that aim to classify examples into one category or another, a

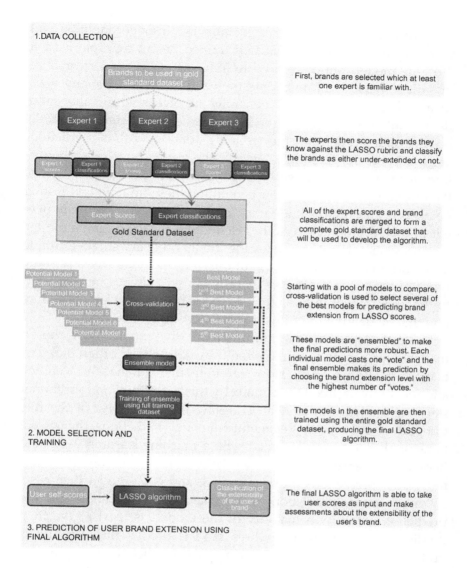

1. DATA COLLECTION

Brands to be used in gold standard dataset

First, brands are selected which at least one expert is familiar with.

Expert 1   Expert 2   Expert 3

The experts then score the brands they know against the LASSO rubric and classify the brands as either under-extended or not.

Expert 1 scores   Expert 1 classifications   Expert 2 scores   Expert 2 classifications   Expert 3 scores   Expert 3 classifications

Expert Scores   Expert classifications
Gold Standard Dataset

All of the expert scores and brand classifications are merged to form a complete gold standard dataset that will be used to develop the algorithm.

Potential Model 1
Potential Model 2
Potential Model 3
Potential Model 4
Potential Model 5
Potential Model 6
Potential Model 7

Cross-validation

Best Model
2nd Best Model
3rd Best Model
4th Best Model
5th Best Model

Starting with a pool of models to compare, cross-validation is used to select several of the best models for predicting brand extension from LASSO scores.

Ensemble model

These models are "ensembled" to make the final predictions more robust. Each individual model casts one "vote" and the final ensemble makes its prediction by choosing the brand extension level with the highest number of "votes."

Training of ensemble using full training dataset

The models in the ensemble are then trained using the entire gold standard dataset, producing the final LASSO algorithm.

2. MODEL SELECTION AND TRAINING

User self-scores   LASSO algorithm   Classification of the extensibility of the user's brand

The final LASSO algorithm is able to take user scores as input and make assessments about the extensibility of the user's brand.

3. PREDICTION OF USER BRAND EXTENSION USING FINAL ALGORITHM

process known as "binary classification." Many binary classification models exist, each with different strengths and weaknesses for various types of datasets and variables. To identify the best model for the problem of classifying brand extension, several of the most powerful model families from conventional statistics and modern machine learning were evaluated and compared.

According to the best practices in statistics, a model cannot be evaluated against the data that it was trained on; an example used to "fit" the model cannot be used to judge the model's performance, or serious biases will invalidate the results. There are many ways to avoid this bias, and all generally involve splitting the entire dataset into both "training" and "testing" subsets. Here, the model being evaluated is fit on the "training" data, and then predictions are made on the "testing" dataset. The accuracy of these predictions is then used to measure the performance of the model. One of the most effective methods for generating these training and testing datasets is a technique known as "cross validation." The main benefit of this technique, over other techniques for validating a model, lies in the fact that it evaluates the model on every single example in the original dataset. Because of this, a model that classifies some types of brands much better than others will always be penalized to the same extent, while other methods of model evaluation may rate this model higher or lower in a fairly random manner.

Using this cross-validation framework, five models were chosen that showed promise in predicting the expert classification of a particular brand's extension. However, to further enhance the accuracy and reliability of predictions made by this algorithm, one additional step was added. Rather than choosing the single best of the five top-performing models to generate the final predictions, the predictions of all five were combined with a machine learning technique known as "ensembling." Essentially, this technique generates individual predictions for each model, and each model then casts a "vote" for its prediction; these votes are then tallied and the prediction given by a majority of the models is used as the final prediction. For example, if three models predict that a brand is under-extended while the other two predict it is optimally extended, the final "ensembled" model will predict that the brand is under-extended. The power in this technique arises from the fact that the individual models, although performing fairly similar to each other, make mistakes that are not identical. Because the models do not make exactly the same predictions, the majority consensus will more often be right than any individual model. After applying ensembling to the five best-performing models identified with cross-validation, the algorithm's performance increased significantly to nearly the same level as human experts, as detailed below.

Agreement between Experts

The 25 common brands, for which the brand specialists independently scored on the LASSO rubric and assessed brand extension, provide an observation of the true, inherent variability in brand assessment. While the LASSO framework provides a powerful, quantitative approach to brand assessment, variability is present in all real-world datasets and this must be considered both when generating a model and when evaluating it. While training a model, including this inherent variability actually improves the performance of the resulting model. And, when evaluating the model, the agreement between human experts sets an upper limit on the predictive capabilities that can be expected of such an algorithm. To quantify this variability, the standard deviation between the expert scores for each of the LASSO metrics was determined for each brand in this set (Figure B1). These were then averaged for each brand, providing a look at the inherent ambiguity or complexity in rating each brand (gray bars in Figure B1), as well as for each metric, providing a comparison of the variability for each of the LASSO variables (rightmost set of bars in Figure B1).

Overall, the panel of brand experts showed a very high level of agreement in their LASSO scoring metrics. The overwhelming majority of scores deviated by at most 1 point in only one of the three experts' scores (on a scale of 1–5), suggesting that the LASSO rubric, when properly deployed, is capable of precisely and quantitatively characterizing brands. With regard to the classification of brands as under-extended or not, the expert panel produced a unanimous classification for 19 of the 25 brands, suggesting that it is straightforward to determine brand extensibility in roughly 80% of cases, while one out of every five cases may be more involved and require further consideration. As a matter of reference in Figure B1, 0.47 is the standard deviation for a score where one expert disagrees from the other two by exactly 1 (e.g., expert scores of 4, 4, and 5).

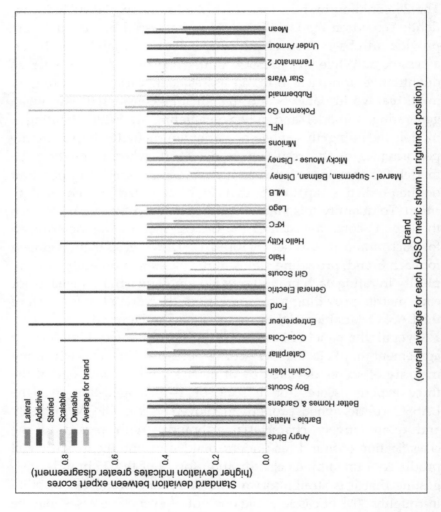

Figure B1. Agreement between Experts on LASSO Scores for Brands Scored by All Experts.

The standard deviation for MLB was 0.00 as indicated in the figure. Please note that the experts first rated brand extension on a more fine-grained five-point scale that was later down-sampled to a simpler "under or not-under extended" rubric. This was done due to limitations with the size of the dataset available, and may have resulted in the experts placing brands in the "slightly-under extended" category with differing frequency. Thus, a coarser rubric may have resulted in slightly higher unanimity between expert classifications.

Algorithm Evaluation

The final algorithm, using an ensemble of five well-performing models, was evaluated using two methods. As both methods involve cross-validation, which is difficult to apply to the scores for more than one expert at a time, only the scores and classifications for one expert (Expert 1) were used to generate the model and predictions for this step. For both methods of algorithm evaluation, cross-validation was used to first predict the extensibility of each brand in the dataset. The first method aims to assess the absolute capabilities of the algorithm to model this dataset, while the second compares the model's performance with that of the human expert brand specialists.

For the first evaluation, these predictions were compared to the "true" classifications chosen by Expert 1. In this test, the algorithm correctly predicted the brand extensibility for 39 of the 49 total brands (79.6%) assessed by Expert 1. Notably, three of the five best-performing individual models, all of which were used in the final ensemble, correctly predicted the classification of 36 of the 49 (73.6%) brands when evaluated by individually. Although this does not seem to be drastically different from the success rate for the complete ensembled algorithm, the fact that all three top-performing models are able to predict exactly the same number of brand assessments correctly suggests that this may be an upper limit to accuracy of individual models with these data, and ensembling or other such techniques may be required.

The second method of evaluation used the set of brands scored by all three experts to determine how the algorithm's predictions compare to a human's predictions. By comparing the number of times that all three experts agreed on a classification of a brand's extension to the number of times the algorithm correctly predicted the classifications of Expert 1, it is possible to characterize how well the algorithm performs with both ambiguous cases and for brands with more well-defined brand extension. When expert judgment could not consistently determine a brand's extension, the model performed poorly, correctly predicting only 3 of 6 (50%) of the classifications of Expert 1, a result no better than random. When all three experts agree on the brand's extension, however, the algorithm correctly classifies 15 of 19 brands (78.9%), indicating that the algorithm is truly capturing the intricacies of the LASSO scores that impact a brand's extensibility. Last, with this evaluation we are able to directly compare how well Experts 2 and 3 agreed with, or "predicted", Expert 1's classification of these brands with how well the algorithm predicted these classifications. In total, the two other experts predict Expert 1's classification for 19 of these 25 example brands (76%), while the model predicts Expert 1's choices on 18 of 25 examples (72%).

Again, with such a relatively small set of data it is difficult to make detailed inferences from these results, but the results do suggest that the algorithm performs respectably, even when compared to expert brand specialists. This is expected, as the algorithm is trained on data generated by these very experts. Also, since we believe that it is capturing the information relating to brand extension contained in the LASSO metrics, it follows that a larger volume of expert training data in the future will allow the model to better represent this information and become increasingly robust. Additional enhancements such as including industry information in the model and the previously mentioned fine-grained categories for brand extension are likely to further boost the model's accuracy and precision. In summary the algorithm, as it currently exists, provides a repeatable, widely deployable, and inherently objective method for both expert and amateur owners to evaluate their brands.

Appendix ▶ C

LASSO
Methodology Q&A

Below are some detailed responses put together by our team of Brand Licensing Experts for some frequently asked questions.

1. *How have you determined what is "gold-standard?" How many inputs were used in your dataset? How many companies? How did you qualify those companies and products?*

   Specifically, each of the experts scored between 28 and 50 brands, totaling 127 brand evaluations of 56 unique brands that served as the "gold-standard" dataset on which the algorithm was trained. These brands belonged to companies in 22 different industries, and included products, services, and media.

2. *The LASSO Model seems highly based on interpretation. Is that right? If so, how do you maintain consistency across scorers, or across your expert panel? Can the LASSO Model be run with true comparative value with any old person scoring the brand?*

   It is true that self-scoring based on the LASSO rubric will be subject to personal interpretations of the metric descriptions published in the book and that the scores will be affected by biases common in self-reported surveys. These pitfalls are to some extent unavoidable in this type of self-evaluation, but these drawbacks may be counterbalanced by the ability of the LASSO scoring assessment to reach a much wider audience and user pool by not requiring a user to retain a brand expert in each case. Regardless, there are mechanisms by which the impact of these response biases and individual interpretations has been blunted.

While it is impossible to phrase any survey question or evaluation description in a perfectly objective manner, guidelines that are specifically defined and neutrally worded will minimize these effects by reducing ambiguity and unintended, unconscious bias. The self-reported LASSO scoring model is unique to many surveys and self-evaluations, in that very detailed descriptions of not just the scoring methods but also the actual basis and background behind the metrics was provided in the chapters of the book. The users, when evaluating their brand, are provided with much more than a few lines describing the scoring guidelines. Rather, they are given a thorough delineation of the concepts that they are being asked to evaluate their brands on. This minimizes the ambiguity that arises when non-experts are required to perform these evaluations and maximizes the consistency in responses. Further, the questions have been phrased in a way that seeks to minimize the emotion involved in evaluating a user's own brand, reducing potential unintended biases on the user's part. Given that any user conducting self-evaluations, and especially non-experts, will always have both biases and individual interpretations regardless of the question's formulation, computational approaches must also be applied to reduce the effects of these confounding factors.[1] By expecting and accounting for these inevitable issues, the LASSO Model is able to predict and model out the effects of these confounding factors to a certain extent. For example, a user evaluating their own

---

1. Note, this part hasn't been done yet, as we have no data on non-expert user scores. However, this can be easily implemented once the algorithm has been publicly deployed and has over ~20 users.

brand on a quantitative metric for which lower responses indicate a deficiency in their brand or product is highly likely to inflate their score. By having our expert panel assess brands that were also evaluated by non-expert brand owners using the LASSO web application, it is possible to compare responses to the rubric between both the non-biased expert panel and the heavily invested and non-expert brand owners. With enough of these comparisons, a model is able to incorporate this information to predict this overestimation of user scores for self-reported users and subsequently make its final prediction of brand extension more robust to these effects.

3. *How did you make the numbers "relative" across the various sizes of companies and industries they were in? Does this matter here?*

It is certainly important, when training the model, to have a set of brands that represents the diversity of the companies which the users will be trying to evaluate with this algorithm. For example, if only one industry were surveyed, the model would not learn how to use the LASSO metrics to determine a brand's optimal extension, but rather it would learn how to predict this extension based on arbitrary features of companies in that industry. This would lead to the model performing very poorly in other industries, since these industry-specific features would not be present or useful with these new industries. Note that the training data do not need to contain *every* industry that a user might want to evaluate with the algorithm, but just a diverse enough set so that information from any industry-specific features becomes "drowned-out" relative to the information from the LASSO variables.

Here, brands were selected that the members of the expert panel were familiar with and felt comfortable ranking. The panel members did choose a set of brands that they felt to be representative across companies and industries. Although not perfectly stratified across these domains, over 20 industries were sampled, and no one industry represented more than a half of the surveyed brands. While there are several industries that were more highly represented than others, most significant being the entertainment industry under which nearly half of the surveyed brands fall, the overall diversity of the training set makes this a reliable dataset to train the algorithm on.

Company size was not specifically controlled for in the training set, and it is a fact that almost all of the brands in this set arise from large companies. This is a consequence of requiring the expert panel members to only consider brands with which they were familiar, in order to ensure that the expert scores were robust and repeatable. This does lead to a potential for the model to perform better on larger companies than smaller companies. Still, given the wide and disparate kinds of companies sampled, across very different industries and product types, the algorithm should be using the information from the LASSO variables to generalize well to companies that it has not seen before. While it is currently trained using brands from these large companies, the model's better predictive ability for larger companies will diminish as the LASSO web application is used more often and the model is able to incorporate information from additional companies across industry, sector, and size.

Industry	Brands (in the Training Set)	Industry	Brands (in the Training Set)
Entertainment	24	Magazine (Home Economics, Interior Design)	1
Consumer Products	10	Electrical	1
Gaming	10	Movies	1
Toys	5	Entertainment (Character)	1

Industry	Brands (in the Training Set)	Industry	Brands (in the Training Set)
Sports	4	Beverage	1
Machinery	3	Sporting Goods	1
Automotive	3	Electronic Manufacturing	1
Nonprofit	2	Fitness	1
Apparel & Fashion	2	Media	1
Restaurant	2	Consumer Electronics	1
Food	2	Food Production	1

Note that brands could be counted twice if they fell within multiple industries.

4. *"...the inclusivity of this training dataset should enable this algorithm to classify accurately brand extension even for industries not present in this dataset."* — *This seems like a big claim* — *almost implausible.*

We understand why this seems to be a grandiose or overconfident statement, but it is rooted in a more formal idea of the ability for a robust model to "generalize" to examples that it hasn't been trained on yet, even if they are unlike the examples it has been trained on. We kind of touched on this above when talking about how a training dataset does not need to include all industries to generalize well to industries that it hasn't seen. We'll try to expand on this a bit here to make this clearer.

Having an inclusive training dataset is important for multiple reasons. The most immediate obvious reason to have as inclusive of a training dataset as possible is that if an industry is in your training dataset, the model will be trained on it, and the next time the model sees a company or brand from that industry it may be able to apply specific "knowledge" from having been trained on companies in that industry to improve its prediction. However, a less obvious benefit from having an inclusive and representative dataset is that information in the data which is more generally relevant has more of an impact in the model's training, and the model captures these more widely applicable "ideas" better. If, for example, the model was only trained using brands in the gaming industry, where addictiveness may be overwhelmingly predictive of high brand extensibility regardless of other factors, the model might perform very poorly when faced with brands in the non profit industry where other factors such being Own-able and Storied are also important. However, if the model were trained using examples from both industries, its use of all three metrics in informing its prediction would improve its performance on sports brands, where again all three metrics are highly useful.

A more generic illustration of how using a diverse and inclusive training dataset allows a prediction engine to "generalize" better by considering more relevant features comes from how a young child might learn the definition of a pet. A toddler brought up in a household with only dogs and cats may identify pets as being any animal with four legs, fur, and a tail. A child raised with dogs, cats, and fish, however, would not consider the legs, fur, or tail, but more accurately understand pets to be any animal which the family actively tends to and keeps. Finally, a child who grows up on a farm would correctly learn that pets are animals which the family cares for and takes into their own home, as opposed to animals which are tended to but kept as livestock. In all cases, the "knowledge" learned is not inaccurate, but with more diverse examples the child learns to use features that define the true underlying concept better. When provided with animals that none of the children had seen, the first child may not identify a caged bird as a pet, while the second child might incorrectly assume that a goat was a pet. Although not guaranteed, the third child would be most likely to categorize both of these examples correctly, despite not having seen them before, due to their learning with more inclusive and diverse "training data."

5. *"To further improve the accuracy and real-world relevance of the algorithm, a subset of 25 of the brands was independently rated by each of the three experts. This overlap allows the model to capture the intrinsic, yet entirely valid, variation in these metrics. In addition, the overlapping set of examples allows a direct comparison of the agreement between predictions made by the algorithm and those made by human experts."* — Did a statistician help you create your model?

One of our team members has a significant amount of formal training in statistics at the graduate level, and although he has mostly applied statistics to biological data (he's a data scientist specializing in genomics), he has a good understanding of the necessary assumptions and best practices behind using these techniques for general data analysis. Regarding the statement here about incorporating information from overlapping training examples from all the experts, it is important to note that for this dataset, we used techniques more commonly classified as machine learning, as opposed to traditional statistics. Although there is considerable overlap between the two fields and a lot of ambiguity over what constitutes their differences, the general difference between the two lies in who selects the features (variables) that are used in the model. In statistics modeling, the data analyst performs this feature selection and manually sets up the model, which is then automatically fitted (trained) using the data. In machine learning, however, both the feature selection and the model training is performed automatically by the computer, with minimal input into the feature selection by the analyst. Both methods have benefits. Because statistical models are designed by the analyst, it is possible to interpret the model; statistical modeling lets you *explain* the relationship between the variables in the model. However, partly because of their reliance on human curation as well as certain computational limits, they are limited to relatively simple models. Machine learning, on the other hand, strives foremost to *predict* the dependent variable with the best accuracy possible, and because the feature selection and model choice is performed computationally, it is able to generate very complex models that predict complicated phenomena with state-of-the-art results. A consequence of this model complexity, however, is that models generated by advanced machine learning methods usually cannot be interpreted by humans.

We began this analysis trying to use only traditional statistical methods such as logistic regression, because we felt it would be helpful to be able to interpret the effects of the LASSO values on brand extension. However, we quickly found that machine-learning methods performed a lot better for generating predictions in this dataset, as they often do with highly intricate, nonlinear relationships between the variables such as exists here. As an aside, note that we do use our original logistic regression model in the final predictive algorithm, but it is only one "vote" among several other models. We bring all this up because it helps to explain why having this overlap in scores from the expert panel "allows the model to capture the intrinsic, yet entirely valid, variation in these metrics." If using traditional statistical models, the formal way to add this intrinsic variation in metric scoring between users would be to include an additional random effect feature representing user-judgment in the model. Machine learning, again, does not require or often allow the user to perform this kind of manual feature selection, and simply learns its own features if they improve the final predictions. This is why including these common examples from all three brand experts lets the final model incorporate this additional variation.

6. *"One out of every five cases may be more involved and require further consideration" — How does the LASSO Model help the layperson distill whether they fall in the 80% camp or the 20% exception camp?*

This is a valid concern, and one that is more difficult to address. Given the vast complexity of determining brand extension and the many intangible factors that affect this phenomenon, it is a challenging problem to objectively quantify and predict. At this point, 80% seems to be the best that can be expected from either human or algorithmic predictors. As more validated training data are collected, the power of big data machine-learning techniques may make it possible to model this phenomenon better and possibly more objectively than even expert humans can; techniques such as artificial neural networks have shown this kind of revolutionary success when given very large, high-quality datasets in many fields, such as business analytics and advertising. In the short term, however, we have a few more techniques to try which may be able to determine if a prediction is correct, even with these fairly small amount of curated data we currently have from this expert panel. Still, there will always be an upper limit to how complex this algorithm can get when trained on small datasets.

7. *"In all, however, the algorithm as it currently exists provides a repeatable, widely-deployable, and inherently objective method for both expert and amateur owners to evaluate their brand." — How can this be true?*

As discussed above, biases and misinterpretations of the scoring rubric are inevitable in this kind of application, but through both education of the user from the book, well-worded and clear guidelines, and algorithmic correction for biases once data begins to be collected, the effects of these challenges can be minimized. At the end of the day, the availability of this algorithm and online self-evaluation tool will allow much wider adoption of the LASSO Model than would be possible solely through expert consultation, and the benefits created by this higher accessibility must be weighed against the inaccuracies that go along with it. By observing the mistakes that are common and surveying amateur users of the application, over time it will be possible to incrementally improve the phrasing and user understanding of these metrics alongside the improvements to the algorithm.

Index

Original equipment
manufacturer (OEM),
85

Oscar, 223

Over Optimized scale, 145, 154

Own-ability, xxxiii—xxxv, 115,
132, 137, 139—140, 141,
167, 235
avalanche in areas of
consumer and retail
brands, 124
big not-for-profit programs,
134
brand additions, 138
brand potential, 132
brand protection, brand
valuation, and brand
strategy, 167
brands, 115, 139, 142
characteristics of successful
license, 171
co-branding types, 126—127
company to protecting
brands, 116
CrossFit, 140
current valuation models,
167
element, 217
Girl Scouts of USA's,
134—135
Graco lacked manufacturing
and sourcing
capabilities, 167
intellectual property lawyers,
128—129

licenses for Graco-branded
decorative bedding
and nursery décor, 169
maximization, 141
maximizing own-ability, 167
multi-dimensioned, 166
organizational structures
types, 119—120
own-ability maximization,
141
ownership models and
implications for brand
expansion, 120
Pinewood Derby program,
135
products make brands,
170—171
quality, 138
scarcity in brand modeling,
123
"seal of approval" program,
134
in several states, 115—116
Smithsonian, 135—136
tussle for IP rights, 130
U. S. Army licensing
program, 136—137
use of freelancers and
contractors, 117
Own-able. *See* Own-ability
Ownership, 117, 120, 129
models and implications for
brand expansion, 120

P&G. *See* Proctor & Gamble
(P&G)
P&L, 171